INSIDE THE
FINANCIAL
FUTURES MARKETS

Inside the
Financial
Futures Markets
Second Edition

MARK POWERS

DAVID VOGEL

JOHN WILEY & SONS
New York • Chichester • Brisbane • Toronto • Singapore

This publication is designed to provide accurate and
authoritative information in regard to the subject
matter covered. It is sold with the understanding that
the publisher is not engaged in rendering legal, accounting,
or other professional service. If legal advice or other
expert assistance is required, the services of a competent
professional person should be sought. *From a Declaration
of Principles jointly adopted by a Committee of the
American Bar Association and a Committee of Publishers.*

Library of Congress Cataloging in Publication Data:

Powers, Mark J.
  Inside the financial futures markets.

  Includes index.
  1. Hedging (Finance) 2. Forward exchange.
3. Commodity exchanges. I. Vogel, David, 1944–
II. Title.

HG6024.A3P68 1984   332.64′4   83-21802
ISBN 0-471-89071-5

Printed in the United States of America

10 9 8 7 6 5 4

Acknowledgments

A number of people have contributed to the ideas expressed in this book. It's not possible to enumerate all of those individuals but thanks go to those who at one time or another participated in discussions on financial futures and, wittingly or not, touched off a new avenue of exploration.

Special mention, however, goes to the International Monetary Market in Chicago and Arthur Andersen for permitting us to utilize the special report prepared by Arthur Andersen & Company, "Interest Rate Futures Contracts—Federal Income Tax Implications." It is the best and most complete treatment in existence today on the subject of taxes and accounting for interest rate futures. Chapters 19, 20, and 21 are extracted from that publication.

Special thanks also go to Richard Weissman, who so helpfully developed a number of examples for this edition and the earlier edition; Richard Wrightson, who provided some of the material and tables in Chapter 7; and Todd Lofton, who did the unwelcome job of editing the final manuscript.

Futures Magazine and Investor Publications, 219 Parkade, Cedar Falls, Iowa, also kindly granted permission for the use of material that had previously appeared in articles written for *Commodities Magazine* and that appeared in the book *Getting Started in Commodity Futures Trading* by Mark J. Powers.

Last but not least special thanks goes to Louise Milevois, who so tirelessly gave of her own time to type the manuscript, all the while maintaining good cheer.

MARK J. POWERS

New York, New York
January 1984

Contents

INSIDE THE
FINANCIAL
FUTURES MARKETS

PART ONE
Introduction to Futures Trading

CHAPTER ONE
Introduction

This book is about the most exciting new financial product to be developed in several decades—futures contracts on financial instruments. These new futures contracts include contracts on mortgage certificates, Treasury bills, Treasury bonds, Treasury notes, Eurodollars, CDs, commercial paper, and foreign currencies.

It's fair to say that very few new financial products have been as quickly accepted. During the 1980s they have the potential to completely reshape the way we conduct our capital markets. By 1990 most chief executive officers of major corporations will be intimately familiar with the concepts of hedging interest rates. Every major borrower, every major lender, every major underwriter, and every major portfolio manager who wants to remain competitive will find it necessary to have morning reports detailing how the firm's hedged positions have changed from the previous day.

PURPOSE OF THIS BOOK

The purpose of this book is to introduce, explain, and illustrate the basic concepts of trading interest rate futures contracts, the economic purpose of the trading, and its operational characteristics. The book focuses on the concepts of hedging, leading the reader step-by-step through the basics of developing a corporate hedging plan.

This is not a book designed to make the reader wealthy overnight through successful speculation. It does cover, however, some of the basic aspects of speculative trading.

3

ORGANIZATION OF THE BOOK

The book is divided into five parts. Part I introduces the reader to the economics and social purposes of futures trading and the basic concepts of futures trading. It explains the elemental aspects of getting started in trading, including the selection of a broker and the entering of orders to buy and sell.

Part II is a brief description of the two basic approaches to price analysis and forecasting—technical and fundamental. The technical analysis portion covers chart building and interpretation as well as statistical analysis of price movement. Fundamental analysis refers to the study of some of the basic economic data reflecting the supply and demand for funds in the capital markets.

Part III begins with a description of the role of money in our economy and then moves on to a discussion and comparison of the cash and futures markets for the various debt instruments traded on the futures exchanges. It ends with an explanation of yield curves: what they are, why they take on the shape they do, and what they reveal.

Part IV is devoted entirely to hedging. All of the concepts discussed in earlier chapters are pooled together into illustrations of hedging in rising rate markets and declining rate markets. The important concepts of basis estimation, cross-hedging, dollar equivalency, undervalue and overvalue, cost-of-carry, as well as a number of other important elements are discussed and illustrated. Two chapters are devoted to discussion of the special problems and opportunities of hedging by banks, insurance companies, savings and loans, mortgage bankers, and industrial corporations. This section also contains a chapter on arbitrage. It ends with three chapters on accounting and taxes and internal recording systems for corporate hedging programs.

Part V covers foreign exchange futures. It explains the relationship between interest rates and foreign exchange values and also discusses the economic factors affecting foreign exchange rates. Several illustrations of foreign exchange hedging are also provided. In addition, Part V includes chapters on options, stocks index futures, and foreign exchange futures.

CHAPTER TWO

The Role of Futures Markets

THE SOCIAL AND ECONOMIC PURPOSES OF FUTURES TRADING

The major difference between an economy that is guided by the market mechanism and one that is directed centrally is that the former is controlled primarily by two influences—consumer demands and relative costs of production. When markets operate with few imperfections, such as monopolistic pressures, the forces of competition tend to lead the economy to serve consumer demands effectively and efficiently. For this reason it is generally considered desirable to take steps that will reduce those market imperfections that limit competition and to encourage those activities that foster competition. Interest rate futures contribute on both scores.

An Aid to General Competition

Supreme Court Justice Louis D. Brandeis made the point best in the early part of this century, when he noted that the organization of an exchange is a society's attempt to capture the economists' concept of perfect competition. He said that the purposes to be accomplished by trading through such institutions are good in that they tend toward (a) greater equality of opportunity, (b) greater efficiency in physical markets and, (c) improvement in the flows of information. All of these are part and parcel of effective competition.

An Aid to Capital Formation

Financial futures not only add to the general competitiveness of the economy by reducing barriers to competition, but they also aid in capital formation by helping to improve our savings and investment flows. The long-run significance of this should not be underestimated. The lack of sufficient savings and investment has been a major contributor to a rampant increase in inflation, the decline in productivity, and the decrease in international competitiveness. Personal savings rates in the U.S. rank among the lowest of industrialized countries.

Financial futures help improve our savings and investment flows by providing strong and more stable commercial banking, investment banking, and brokerage industries. In today's uncertain times that is not an insignificant benefit. The maintenance of an efficient savings and investment process is dependent on investment banking and brokerage firms who can take the risk of carrying inventory of securities for periods of time while awaiting the resale and distribution of these securities to long-term investors.

No longer do the fortunes of a firm that is "making a market" in money instruments depend solely on a trader's ability to outguess the market. Now the risk of owning, building, and disposing of an inventory of bonds or commercial paper can be kept at a tolerable level while the market-making activities can continue apace.

During the 1980s any brokerage firm or dealer in credit instruments that does not learn how to use the financial futures markets will find itself at a competitive disadvantage. Those brokerage firms that are likely to survive the 1980s are those that learn how to use these markets as an integral part of serving their customers and in their market-making activity.

An Aid to New Product Development

Financial futures will aid in the mobilization of savings by spawning a wide array of new savings products offered by local banks, Savings and

Loans (S&Ls), and so on. These new products could not come into being without the financial futures markets. In the long run, the experience should not be too unlike that in other areas where futures are an integral part of the pricing process. In those industries a rich variety of risk repackaging services are now available. Indeed, many of the forward contracting devices used throughout the agribusiness, metals, and food industries could not exist today were it not for futures markets.[1]

During the 1980s we will see innovative new savings products being offered that will guarantee savers a rate on money they will deposit at some future date. For example, suppose Mr. Jones, a local businessman, has a certificate of deposit (CD) due six months from now. The bank where he has the CD knows that Mr. Jones is thinking of taking his money to a competitor when the CD comes due. The Bank could, through the use of a futures hedge, assure Mr. Jones today of the rate they will give him on a new CD six months hence if he will agree today to keep the money there. In other situations, both sides may use futures, maintaining the flexibility of entering the futures market at the time deemed most propitious by them for establishing the rate. Without the use of futures for transferring these risks, this wider variety of savings products would not be made available.

In short, the existence of financial futures should stimulate the growth of financial intermediation services, with a resultant increase in the flow of funds between savers and investors.

ECONOMIC FUNCTION OF FINANCIAL FUTURES

The basic economic functions performed by financial futures markets are competitive price discovery, hedging of price risks, financing of inventory, and the allocation of resources.

---

[1]Certainly meat packers, who are faced with very sharply veed short-run cost curves for operating their slaughter plants, would not be able to offer farmers forward contracts with open pricing dates if the futures for hogs and cattle did not exist. Metals firms would likewise find it difficult to attract capital to carry inventories if the futures did not facilitate cash-and-carry business.

Price Discovery

The prices of money generated by the interest rate futures markets reflect the combined views of a large number of buyers and sellers as to the current supply/demand situation and the relationship of prices 12 to 18 months hence. This does not mean that a futures price is a prediction that will hold true for all times. Instead, it is an expression of opinions concerning *today's* expectations about the level of interest rates and the shape of the yield curve at some point in the future. As conditions change, opinions change and, of course, so will rates. These changes do not make the markets' pricing function less useful. On the contrary, keeping the supply/demand equation current makes the system more useful than a one-time prediction. By coalescing all the diverse and scattered opinions into one readily discernible number, interest rate futures prices provide a consensus of knowledgeable thinking on the price of money in coming weeks or months.

Risk Shifting

The second major function of interest rate futures is risk shifting. A futures market allows the separation of the risk of price change from risk arising from other normal business functions similar to the separation of theft or fire risk from other business risks. Separating these risks allows them to be "packaged" in special ways and transferred from those who have them but may not want them (hedgers) to those who do want them (speculators).

The risk of price change is ever present and represents costs that must be borne by someone. In a competitive atmosphere those costs are passed on to consumers. If the mortgage banker has to assume the risk he will offset it by paying less for the securities, charging more for them when he sells them, or a combination of the two. If on the other hand, he can transfer the risk to someone else through a hedge he can lower his cost of doing business.

Hedging Function

Hedging refers to action taken to neutralize price risk, and is traditionally considered the *raison d'être* of futures markets. In this regard it's obvious that means other than the futures market can be used to hedge. This book, however, focuses on hedging as a futures trading technique. As such it flows from the natural pricing functions performed by the futures exchanges.

The best way to visualize a hedge is to think of it as a temporary substitute for a transaction one will make at a later time in another market. The concept is easiest understood through an example. Assume you are a corporation. It is December 1st, and you know that as a regular part of your seasonal cash flow you will have approximately $1 million in excess cash available for short-term investment next June. Further, assume that you expect interest rates to decline between now and June. You can on December 1 establish, within a small margin of error, the rate you will receive on the funds you will invest in June by buying a futures contract for June Treasury bills. When June arrives you simply purchase the T-bills through your normal channels and offset your futures contract by selling the contract you previously bought. The futures contract served as the temporary substitute during the December to June period. If interest rates have indeed fallen since December and if that fall was also reflected in futures prices, the gain on the futures contract will help make up for the lower rate of return on the T-bills. If interest rates have risen in the interim, the "loss" on your futures position is similarly offset by the greater return on the T-bills you buy.

The converse example may be a situation where you know on December 1 that you will need to borrow funds during June to finance inventories for 90 days. If you expect rates to be higher in June than rates currently reflected in the futures market you can protect against paying the higher rate by selling a 90-day T-bill contract. If rates do go up the gain on the futures contract will help offset the increased cost of borrowing. In the meantime the futures contract acts as a temporary substitute for the actual borrowing transaction you made in June.

The foregoing example demonstrates the very simplest concepts of hedging. More sophisticated considerations come into play in actual practice. Such concepts as basis pricing, exchange of futures for physicals, and dollar equivalency are all refinements in hedging that will be explored in later chapters.

Suffice it to say for now that the great benefit one gets out of hedging is the flexibility in timing his purchases, sales, and anonymity.

It's important to note also that there are many other ways of hedging interest rate costs. Using the futures market is only one of those ways.

Generally a manager will find it is the cheapest, easiest, and most efficient method available and that it fits nicely into a mix of strategies.

Market Efficiency—Reduced Monopoly Power

A futures market acts as a focal point where buyers and seller can meet readily. This improves overall market efficiency by reducing search costs. Buyers automatically know where the sellers are and vice versa. They do not need to search each other out. Accessibility is maximized.

A futures market in interest rates reduces segmentation in the market. It fosters competition by unifying diverse and scattered local markets. Local monopolists have a difficult time maintaining control when national markets easily accessible to all people offer their customers other alternatives. Integrated national markets mean that prices in all local markets tend to move more closely in unison with the national markets. Price relationships for a larger number of locations and a larger number of related products become more stable. This makes for more efficient and effective hedging of a wider number of risks.

Informational Benefits

The futures market has become an economical and efficient mechanism for improving the flows of information in the marketplace. It is those flows of information relative to prices, volume, and market expectations of participants that allow the futures market to make an overall contribution to competition. The futures market reflects more fully the scope of market information available and embeds this information in a way spot markets are unable to do. Some of this advantage flows from the fact that participation in futures markets is usually larger than in the spot markets. Given the same capital the futures trader can control about three times more government securities than his cash market counterpart who faces higher money requirements. Also, a futures trader can sell short in futures markets without the need first to borrow the securities and pay a fee.

Dr. Jacob Grossman, an economist at the Federal Reserve Bank of New York, has gathered preliminary evidence suggesting that the implied yield curves in futures markets anticipate the shape of the futures spot yield curve far better than the spot yield curve does for the six-month forecast. His evidence suggests that futures increase the efficiency of the cash Treasury bills market because it helps strengthen the relationships between the short-term rates and the long-term rates.

How much is the service of the futures markets worth to the consumer? That is hard to say. Some studies of the use of futures markets have shown that those who use futures for hedging purposes over several seasons have a more stable income pattern than those who do not. They do not always get the peak prices, but they don't often get the bottom prices either. The futures market provides them with the opportunity to stabilize their incomes and allows them to lower their operating margins to obtain a competitive advantage. In a competitive industry, these benefits ultimately get passed on to customers.

Of course, a futures market cannot do all things for all people, but if it functions properly it should foster an improved competition throughout the marketplace, thus encouraging more efficient use of resources.

HISTORY OF FINANCIAL FUTURES

The history of financial futures is closely intertwined with the growth of inflation in the United States and the relaxation of interest rate regulations.

Many of the interest rate restrictions and regulations that had been put in place during and immediately after the Second World War remained in existence into the early 1960s. But starting with the early and mid-1960s, as inflation rates began to creep up, interest rate regulations were relaxed. State usury laws came into question. The 4.25% coupon ceiling on Treasury bonds was removed. Regulation Q on large commercial accounts was relaxed. The prohibitions against interest paid on demand deposits were relaxed. And more recently automatic savings/checking account transfers have become usual. This relaxation of interest rate restrictions culminated in the action on October 6, 1979 when the Federal Reserve essentially switched their monetary policy to one of controlling the monetary aggregates from one of controlling interest rate levels directly.

The lessening of interest rate restrictions was born of necessity, principally the necessity of maintaining a strong housing sector in the face of higher interest rates, which in turn were caused by higher rates of inflation. The surge of inflation experienced in the U.S. in the late 1960s and early 1970s had its roots in the monetary and fiscal policies followed by the Johnson administration, when it decided to fight the Vietnam war by pumping up the money supply instead of raising taxes.

This underlying trend toward higher interest rates and increased volatility in rates was obvious in 1970 but not generally viewed as a permanent phenomenon. The sector of society that felt the undercurrents more directly than any other group was probably the commodity traders. Underlying commodity prices were becoming more volatile but, most important, price relationships between different time periods began to reflect interest rate volatility.

Contributing to the volatility of interest rates in 1971 was President Nixon's decision to devalue the dollar and withdraw the United States from the Bretton Woods agreement, an international agreement designed to maintain fixed exchange rates for the major currencies of the Western World. The impact of President Nixon's action was reflected immediately in higher and more volatile rates as countries adjusted interest rates to protect the value of their currencies.

The turmoil in the international monetary system and in interest rates, as noted earlier, was most obvious to the commodity people because the demand for hedge services in commodities began to grow rapidly. It was suddenly also obvious that a whole new market for hedge services was emerging. The risks that banks, borrowers, and lenders had were precisely the same sorts of risks that a grain exporter or a lumber wholesaler had. One was pricing credit instruments, the other pricing bushels of grain or board feet of wood.

So it was that in 1972 the first futures exchange in the world designed exclusively to trade financial futures contracts came into being—the International Monetary Market. At the announcement of the organization of the exchange, it was noted that the intent was to make the exchange a center for trading a wide variety of financial instruments, including government debt securities. The first contracts listed for trading were futures in foreign exchange. They caught on quickly.

Also, during the early 1970s the Government National Mortgage Association's (GNMA) cash market in mortgage certificates began to grow rapidly. The GNMA market had been established by the government in order to facilitiate the flow of funds into the housing industry. Rising interest rates and inflation had created the fear that the demand for housing would decrease and the housing market, a very important segment of the economy, would collapse causing a severe recession and unemployment. As these markets in GNMA certificates began to grow there emerged a forward contract market in the certificates. These forward contracts became the precursor to the formalized futures contracts in GNMAs that emerged a few years later.

By 1975 the economy had been through severe shocks from the Russian wheat deals and the increase in oil prices and was just coming out of the 1974 recession. In October of 1975 the Chicago Board of Trade offered the first interest rate futures contract, the Government National Mortgage Association pass-through certificate futures contract. It caught on immediately and during the first three months of its existence traded 20,000 contracts.

A few weeks after the GNMA contract began trading the International Monetary Market began trading in the Treasury bill futures. And 10 years after the first financial futures were offered, Kansas City began the trading in stock index futures.

Today we have a whole array of financial futures contracts offered for trading. In foreign exchange they include contracts in the Swiss franc, the deutsche mark, the Mexican peso, the French franc, the Italian lira, the Canadian dollar, the pound sterling, and the Japanese yen. On the interest rate side there are contracts in commercial paper, 90-day Treasury bills, Eurodollars, Treasury notes, GNMA certificates, certificates of deposit, and long-term Government bonds. In stock indexes there are the Value Line Index, S & P 500, S & P 100, CBOE 100, NYSE, and a range of others.

In summary, the financial futures markets emerged out of economic necessity. As the underlying volatility and the risk associated with the holding of inventories or the borrowing or lending of money increased the capitalistic system reponded with the development of the financial futures contracts for hedging. To date, the growth in volume of trading has been phenomenal, but it is only a small percentage of the volume that will exist 10 years from now.

CHAPTER THREE

The Major Concepts of Futures Trading

Futures trading is not a new endeavor. It's roots go back to the Medieval fairs and beyond. But in all its history, few more exciting growth periods have existed than the last decade.

This section is designed to provide the reader with a quick overview of the futures industry, its institutions, and its participants. These include exchanges, clearing houses, brokers, government regulatory bodies, and trading participants. Each will be explained briefly.

THE EXCHANGES

In a legal/economic sense, exchanges are an attempt to capture the economists' concept of perfect competition. Justice Brandeis in the early part of this century noted that the exchanges are a set of rules that assure open access to many sizes and kinds of buyers and sellers; exchanges provide equal opportunity for participation, foster information flows, and in general restrict certain liberties in the marketplace in order to expand certain larger liberties that maximize the overall contribution of the marketplace to society.

From a practical standpoint exchanges are defined as meeting places. They actually serve as communication centers and can be likened to a giant funnel. The sides of the funnel are composed of the communication lines that go out all around the world and collect orders from buyers and sellers located in various places and collect and disseminate information relevant to the supply/demand factors affecting price. Inside the funnel is the exchange floor where the trading takes place in the hubbub of an auctionlike atmosphere. And out the neck of the funnel come the prices one after another as the trades are consummated.

Basic Functions

The basic functions of an exchange are:

1. To furnish the facilities for the buyers and sellers to meet and conduct their business.
2. To set and enforce the rules under which this trading will be conducted.
3. To collect and disseminate information relative to the market and to the factors affecting prices.
4. To provide an institutional framework for arbitrating disputes and settling differences that may arise in the conduct of the trading.

Locations

Commodity exchanges offering financial futures are located around the world. (See Table 3.1.) The first exchange to open its doors to financial instruments trading was the International Monetary Market (IMM) established in 1972. Trading began in foreign currencies on May 16, 1972. Although the first contracts dealt only with foreign currency, the IMM initiated trading in Treasury bill futures in January 1976.

The first interest rate futures contract was developed on the Chicago Board of Trade (CBT) in October of 1975 when the contract calling for delivery of Government National Mortgage Association Certificates was listed for trading.

In 1978 the American Stock Exchange established a subsidiary called the American Commodities Exchange (ACE). It was the first exchange located in New York devoted exclusively to the trading of financial instruments. Shortly thereafter, the New York Stock Exchange an-

Table 3.1

Commodity	Exchange	Options
90-day T-bills	IMM	No
90 Day Certificates of Deposit		No
90 Day Eurodollar Time Deposit		No
GNMA CDR	CBT	*
T-Bonds		Yes
T-Notes		No*
Stock Indexes		
Value Line	KCBT	Yes
S&P	IMM	Yes
NYSE	NYFE	Yes
Currencies		
Swiss Franc (See current table)		
Japanese Yen		
British Pound		
German Mark		
Canadian Dollar		

Foreign Exchanges	Exchange	Options
United Kingdom		
90 Day Eurodollars	London	No
20 Year Gilts		No
Australia		
Currencies	Sydney	No
T-Bills (Australian)		No
Canada		
T-Bills(Canadian)	Toronto/Montreal	No

Note: The above listing reflects only the most active financial futures contracts traded in 1982. A number of the above listed contracts as well as a number of other financial futures contracts are listed on exchanges, but were inactive in 1982.

*Options on the futures are not listed, but options on the underlying instrument are listed on securities exchange.

nounced its intentions to open the New York Futures Exchange (NYFE) as a subsidiary, also devoted solely to trading financial futures contracts. NYFE opened its doors in August, 1980 and in September absorbed the struggling ACE.

Several foreign countries have established such exchanges in their parts of the world. The most notable of the recent start-ups have been in London, U.K.; Toronto, Canada; and Sydney, Australia; Singapore; and Hong Kong.

Internal Organization

Commodity exchanges are membership organizations. Membership is usually, though not always, limited to individuals, who may assign their membership privileges to a corporation. Only members of the exchange are allowed to conduct the actual trading in the futures contract. Members are also allowed to participate in the management of the exchange through their voting privileges.

Obtaining a Membership

Changes in membership occur only as privately held exchange seats become available for purchase on a bid and offer basis. Exchange memberships are bought and sold just like any other asset. Recent prices of memberships range from $6,000 to $165,000. (See Table 3.2.) Memberships are broadly held both occupationally and geographically. Bankers, investment bankers, mortgage bankers, money market dealers, commercial manufacturing firms, brokers, futures commission merchants, and individuals such as lawyers, dentists, farmers, and shopkeepers own memberships. Memberships may be held by U.S. or non-U.S. citizens.

There are generally two reasons for owning a membership. First is to obtain physical access to the floor where one can participate directly in the trading. The second is to reduce the cost of trading, but this reason is less important now that commission rates are no longer fixed by the exchange and are instead negotiated. The former reason is particularly important if one wants to establish a brokerage business. Probably the reason most professional speculators desire physical access to the floor, however, is because it gives them immediate communication ability to the market. They have no time lag between making a decision to buy or sell and entering the order into the pit.

Although memberships are held by individuals, many memberships are controlled by corporations. Many members are employees of firms whose business involves futures trading. The companies sponsor the applicant, loan him the money to purchase the membership, and get agreements for surrender of the membership if the employee leaves the company. The member in turn assigns his privileges to the company. Memberships may also be leased.

Table 3.2 Exchange Membership Prices—High and
Low, 1983

	Price	
Exchange	High	Low
IMM	246,000	165,000
CBT		
Financial instruments only	145,000	62,000
Full membership	255,000	161,000
NYFE	38,000	5,000

Source: Exchange Records.

The principal requirements for membership are that the applicants be of good character and financially responsible. Obtaining a membership is not complicated or difficult. The exchanges are relatively open. A net worth of slightly more than the price of the membership and the absence of a bad reputation appear to be all that is required for exchange membership. Of course, exchange membership alone does not qualify one to execute trades on the trading floor. One must also obtain a personal financial guarantee. That aspect is discussed below in the section on clearinghouses.

Exchange Management

The exchange is governed by a board of directors elected or appointed from a slate of nominees selected from the membership and, on most exchanges, from several nonmember candidates who represent the public at large or the various commodity interests affected by the contracts traded on the exchange. The board is responsible for establishing major operating policy and for making and amending the exchange's rules. In addition, it may act in a judicial capacity in conducting hearings involving member misconduct.

Daily administration of the exchange is in the hands of an appointed and salaried president employed with the approval of the exchange board. The president as chief executive officer of the exchange is assisted by such other officers and staff as he deems necessary. The staff functions include (a) auditing and investigating the activity of member firms, (b) reviewing the conduct of the member firms in their daily trading, (c) collecting and disseminating information about the markets and the trading, (d) conducting feasibility studies into new areas of business the exchange might develop, and (e) providing educational materials and services to the various segments of the public concerned with or interested in the function and operation of the market.

Usually the exchange members play an important role in the governing of the exchange by serving on committees. Certain committees are common to almost all exchanges. These include arbitration committees, membership committees, rules committees, business conduct committees, public relations and marketing committees, floor practice committees, floor broker qualifications committees and contract specifications committees. Their titles explain their functions and responsibilities.

The Trading Floor

The most visible and exciting part of an exchange is the trading floor. The central points of the trading floor are the trading pits or rings—specified areas in which the floor brokers and floor traders do their buying and selling. All bids and offers are made by open outcry and by hand signals in the trading pit.

To the casual observers standing in the visitors' balcony of the Chicago Mercantile Exchange or Chicago Board of Trade on any given day there is a mystery about the markets. The trading floor looks to be the size of a football field. As one views it from above one can see several thousand people. A few are sitting or standing at small cubicles with telephones. Others are on their feet and there is a constant motion of coming and going, some walking casually and others with great intensity. Where the action is frantic there are concentrations of people, with men and women shouting and waving their arms and signaling with their fingers simultaneously. They are trading. To the first-time visitor it seems chaotic. But history has shown it to be an efficient means of arriving at competitive prices for the purchase and sale of futures contracts.

As bids and offers are made and trades are consummated, prices are reported by an observing reporter (an employee of the exchange) and posted on the quotation board which may be a huge electronic score-

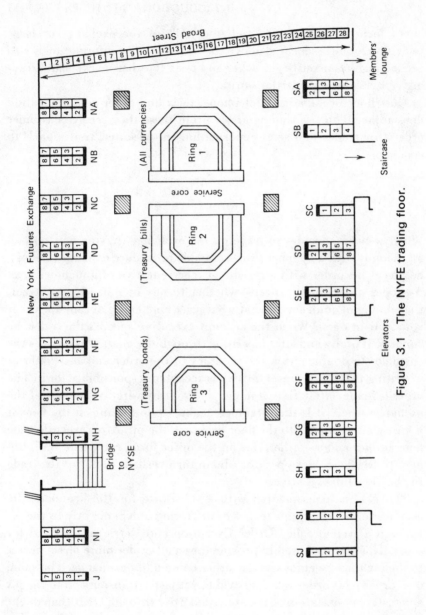

Figure 3.1 The NYFE trading floor.

board located on the ends and side walls of the exchange or large television monitors located above the pit. This price information is also carried instantaneously via ticker and telex to other markets and trading centers throughout the world.

Most floor brokers have telephone, telex and other communication lines adjacent to the trading areas. From these they receive customer orders for trades and send confirmations of executed trades back to customers.

Execution of Trades

When someone decides to trade on the exchange (having first opened an account with a member firm—a simple procedure explained below), he places his order with a registered representative of a member firm. A proper order should specify whether to buy or sell, what contract, the number of contracts, and at what price and length of time the order is to remain open. When the account executive accepts the order, he confirms it orally and later in writing through the mail. This enables the customer to double check the accuracy of the order and also confirms in writing that the representative has accepted responsibility for it. The order is immediately time stamped and sent by wire to the floor of the exchange where it is time stamped again. Upon receipt on the floor it is sent via a "runner" to the floor broker in the pit. After execution the floor broker endorses the price on the order form, returns it via "runner" to the floor telex operator who in turn verbally confirms the trade to the account executive.

The NYFE experimented with a substitute for the "runners" by establishing an electronic means of delivering orders directly to the pit through a system called Order Execution and Retrieval, or OER for short. This was supposed to provide the small trader more direct access to the pit than he enjoys at any other commodity exchange. The small one- or two- lot order was expected to get faster transmission to the pit and faster confirmation of the execution price through OER than might be the case where a "runner" is used. The system was discontinued due to lack of use.

According to federal regulation all exchanges and registered persons eligible to accept orders from the public must maintain a record-keeping system requiring each handler (except the pit broker) of an order to record the time at which he receives the order. Such a time record makes it easier for the exchange, the federal government, or any customer (who believes a broker has taken advantage of his order by trading ahead of it or by some other abusive practice) to reconstruct the life history of that order and to determine with a high degree of certainty whether the complaint is valid. Such a time-stamping system protects the brokers as much as the customers.

At the end of each trading day the member firm reports all transactions to the clearing house which reconciles (or matches) the trades and assumes the opposite side of the trade for both the original buyer and seller. This assumption of responsibility by the clearinghouse as the second party to each contract greatly simplifies the settlement and delivery process and facilitates the offsetting of futures positions by traders.

THE CLEARINGHOUSE

When bank robber Willy Sutton was asked why he robbed only banks, he replied, "Because that's where they keep the money." Precisely for that reason anyone who desires to become familiar with commodity trading should spend a good deal of time becoming familiar with the clearinghouse, because that's where they keep the money. Most of us are familiar with the clearinghouse operations our nation's banking system uses to expedite the flow and transfer of funds from one bank to another within the system. In the case of a futures exchange the clearing operation exists to perform a similar function. It facilitates the flow and transfer of funds resulting from its member firms' execution of trades. As is true in the case of the bank depositor, the individual commodity trader has no direct contract with the clearing organization. This organization serves simply as a central point for depositing and dispensing funds to be credited or debited to the accounts of member firms.

In addition, the exchange clearinghouse acts as the guarantor of contract performance. The fulfillment of contract obligations of a clearing member is guaranteed through the collective financial resources of the clearinghouse, regardless of what happens to the original individual member parties of the contract.

Furthermore, the exchange clearinghouse performs the important function of assigning and overseeing the deliveries of futures contracts when they mature.

Membership in the clearinghouse is normally confined to exchange members. Those exchange members who are not clearinghouse members must have their trades cleared (verified and guaranteed) by another member who is part of the clearinghouse. Put another way, each exchange member who executes trades must either be a member of the clearinghouse or affiliated with a clearing member.

The Clearinghouse Guarantee

As noted, the clearinghouse becomes the guarantor of the contract to both the buyer and the seller. After the transaction is completed in the trading pit the two parties cease to deal with each other and instead deal with the clearinghouse. Hence, to the person trading on the exchange a most important element in the financial integrity of his transaction is the financial soundness of the clearinghouse.

Although there are individual differences among clearinghouses, there are three major elements that help assure financial security of the transactions. These are:

1. The collection of a security deposit from both the buyer and the seller.
2. Daily settlement in cash by both buyers and sellers of all changes in contract value.
3. The capital resources of the clearinghouse corporation and of its shareholders or members, if they are assessable.

The first two of these elements are explained in detail below. The assessability aspect of the third element refers to any assessments that might be made against clearing members as a result of a financial failure by one of the members. For example, at the IMM a class A clearing member could be assessed up to $500,000 based upon the proportion of the open interest the clearing member held prior to the occurrence of the financial difficulty. Any remaining loss after the initial assessment of $500,000 per clearing member would be further assessed against the clearing members based upon their proportion of the total number of contracts cleared during the period six months prior to the day the financial difficulty was declared by the clearing house. Since the capital requirements to be a clearing member are quite large at most exchanges, it is evident that in the case of an assessable clearinghouse the total financial resources to back the integrity of the futures contracts are quite large.

The Clearinghouse Function

The function of the clearinghouse begins after the trade is executed. Clearinghouse members submit trade confirmation cards for each trade executed. These cards are then matched or verified by the clearinghouse. Once that process is completed the member brokers cease to deal with one another directly. Now, they each deal exclusively with the clearinghouse. In effect, they are now long or short to the clearinghouse, since it has assumed the position of second party to each member's transaction. The liquidation of the contracts is facilitated through this system, because a trader can now offset his contract without the necessity of obtaining the agreement of the original second party to it. The clearinghouse merely notes that the original obligation is canceled through a countervailing position. The clearing member, not the individual customer, is ultimately responsible for fulfillment of a contract with the clearinghouse. The customer's responsibility lies solely with his clearing member. The brokerage firm, after executing the trade, then deals exclusively with its clearing member, who deals with the clearinghouse.

Margin or Security Deposit

Whenever a transaction is made in the market, both parties to the trade are asked to post a "good faith bond" in the form of cash, T-bills, listed securities or letters of credit. This "good faith" money is referred to as "margin." It is really a security deposit, a term which much more accurately describes it and distinguishes it from margin in the securities market.

The clearinghouse establishes and maintains strict control over these minimum security deposits (margins) both for initiating and for maintaining positions. Member firms are required to collect these minimum amounts from customers. Brokers may and frequently do charge customers more than the minimum but they may not collect less. Clearing member firms must in turn deposit and maintain a specified level of funds in the clearinghouse to back up either their aggregate or their net market positions.[1]

The purpose of requiring these funds is to ensure performance under the terms of the futures contract. It is a safeguard or surety bond to both buyer and seller (and to the carrying broker) that there will be funds available to make proper settlement when the contract is terminated. When the contracts are offset or delivered upon, this money is returned to the trader along with his profit on the transaction, or it is applied toward his debts if he has lost money.

A trader who has a paper profit on his transaction may usually withdraw his gain over and above the minimum security deposit required at any time before he offsets his position. On the other hand, if his transaction shows a paper loss, his account will be debited accordingly. If the loss causes the equity in the account to fall below 75% of its original margin, he may be asked to deposit additional funds in order to maintain the value of his account at the required minimum amount. These additional deposits are called "variation margin deposits."

Daily Settlement

The clearinghouse requires daily settlement in cash for all price variations in every contract traded. This means that each day the clearinghouse credits the accounts of the clearing members showing a net gain due to favorable price movements during that day's trading, and requires immediate payment from those members showing a net loss on their positions. Since there is a buyer for every seller, the monies paid out must equal the monies collected and the clearinghouse must show neither a gain nor a loss. It must balance before a new trading day begins. Brokers use the cash payments received from the clearinghouse to pay out trading profits to customers. Conversely they have to pay additional money to the clearinghouse to cover losses sustained by customers.

[1]Some clearinghouses margin positions on a net basis (100 long and 100 short in the same month is net zero) and others require margin on a gross basis (100 long and 100 short in the same month is 200 contracts).

As noted above, margin in the commodities markets is a different concept from margin in the securities market. When an investor buys a stock on margin, the margin represents an equity interest in the security and the investor owes the unpaid balance as debt. In futures the trader is not buying or selling the commodity but only agreeing to buy or sell it at a later date. In one sense you could look at the purchase or sale of a futures contract as a purchase or sale of the right to participate in the price change. The margin payment is considered a "sign of good faith" or "earnest" money such as might be used in acquiring a piece of property. The purchaser and the seller promise to fulfill their contracts during the delivery month.

Margins on securities are set by the Federal Reserve Board and their purpose as stated in the Securities and Exchange Act is to prevent the excessive use of credit for the purchase or carrying of securities. New purchases of stock on margin generate credit in a way that adds to the national money supply. When stock is bought the entire purchase price is paid to the seller a few days after the transaction. If the purchaser is buying the stock on margin the balance of the purchase price must be borrowed in order to make his full payments. Ordinarily this balance is borrowed from the broker or from a bank and in either case the effect is to expand the national total of bank credit leading to an expansion of the national money supply by at least the amount borrowed. This points up a major distinction between margin in commodities and margin in the stock market. Margin in commodities does not in and of itself involve the borrowing of money nor does it affect the money supply.

Margins and Leverage

One of the great myths about commodity trading is that commodity prices fluctuate much more than stock prices. This is simply not true. Take a look at the stock tables in your daily newspaper. It is not hard to find a stock that fluctuates more than 50% in value within the same year. Compare that to the commodity prices and you will find that very few commodity prices fluctuate from the high to the low by more than 50% in any single year.

The point to be made here is that the volatility of commodity prices is not the reason for the great risk associated with commodity trading. That risk arises from the use of leverage. Leverage is defined as the amount of money needed to control a given amount of resources. Leverage is high in futures markets because margins are low. In the stock market margins are currently at 50%. In futures markets the margins are usually less than 10% and in some instances less than 1% of the market value of the futures contract. Because of the low futures margins, one can control large amounts of resources with small amounts of capital. Hence, a slight change in the value of the total contract results in a substantial change in the amount of money in your account. For example, a 1% change in $10,000 invested in the stock market via a nonmargined account will equal a 1% change in equity, or $100. A 1% change in a futures contract valued at $10,000 is equal to a $100 change in account equity also. But in order to control that $10,000 futures contract you probably needed to put only $750 down as your initial margin, and a $100 change in that $750 is equal to a 13% change in your equity. It is this leverage factor that causes commodity futures to be considered a high-risk investment. Of course there is nothing that says you must use all that leverage. You can arbitrarily set your personal margin higher, say at 30%. This would reduce your leverage and render your trading more conservative.

MARKET PARTICIPANTS

Participants in the market can be divided into four groups: commission houses or futures commission merchants, floor traders and floor brokers, speculators, and hedgers.

Futures Commission Merchants

A futures commission merchant (FCM) is precisely what the name implies. It is a business that acts as an intermediary and stands between the brokers in the pit and their customers who are the real principals to the trade. In a legal sense an FCM obtains its license to do business from the Commodity Futures Trading Commission, which monitors and oversees the activity of the FCM.

Most FCMs own their own exchange memberships or have working relationships with members of all of the active commodity exchanges. Some are integral parts of large brokerage or investment-banking houses. And some are affiliates with or subsidiaries of firms that conduct most of their business in the cash market.

The services provided by an FCM include a communications system for transmittal of orders, research, trading strategy suggestions, trade execution, and record-keeping services. In selecting an FCM the following areas should be examined.

Communications Systems. One of the most important services an FCM, acting as agent for its customers, provides is a fast and efficient communication system that links the customer as quickly as possible with the auction system on the floor of the exchange. Usually this link is accomplished by telex or direct telephone, the latter being faster.

Research. One will find a good deal of variation in the quality and extent of the research available from various FCMs. Some FCMs concentrate on price forecasting and provide intraday, weekly, and long-term price forecasts. Others concentrate their efforts on market interpretations, such as analyses of who is buying and who is selling in the market. Almost all FCMs provide news and "rumor" analysis. Probably the greatest amount of market research concentrates on technical analysis of the market. Technical analysis, as explained elsewhere in this book, refers to the study of market activity itself; for example, quantitative research relating to changes in trading volume, open interest, and price activity. The last is usually accomplished through the observation and study of various chart patterns.

Trading Strategy Suggestions. In addition to providing the types of market research suggested above, FCMs generally provide their customers with recommendations on trading strategies. These strategies may relate to spreads and straddles, or may identify overvalued contracts and undervalued contracts. Some recommendations concentrate on arbitrage strategies designed to take advantage of temporary differences between the cash yield curve and the futures prices.

Trade Executions and Record Keeping. Of all the services, this is probably the most important an FCM provides its customer. Most FCMs maintain offices scattered throughout the country and sometimes overseas. Most of them maintain large staffs on the floors of the exchanges and in the "back office." The sole function of these floor personnel is to facilitate and expedite the customer's order, and see that it gets executed at the best possible price and that accurate paper work recording the transaction is accomplished quickly. One will find great diversity among FCMs with regard to their ability to perform in this area. Some are better organized than others.

Floor Traders/Floor Brokers

Trading on the floor of the exchange is conducted as a continuous auction where every person in the pit is his own auctioneer. Orders can be executed only by open outcry. The people who specialize in executing orders for others are called "floor brokers." They get a small fee—usually a couple of dollars—for each transaction they execute. Each floor broker is a member of the exchange, and, if he is not himself a clearing member, he is affiliated with a clearing member.

Also participating in the trading in the ring are "floor traders." Floor traders are speculators who, as members of the exchange, trade for themselves. Some of them can be classified as "scalpers." A scalper is a person who stands ready either to buy at a price slightly below the last price or to sell at a price slightly above the last price. He attempts to predict the very short-run direction of price changes and to profit from them. A scalper is usually not worried about major moves. If the scalper is an astute trader, he can make a lot of money on very small changes in price. From an economic standpoint the scalper provides good trade-to-trade liquidity in the market. Indirect evidence suggests that the scalper is well compensated for the liquidity he provides.

Some floor traders are "position traders." These persons tend to carry the positions for longer periods of time. They may attempt to take advantage of the spread between prices for different delivery months for the same commodity, or the price spread between different commodities with the same delivery date when such price differences cannot be explained. They add to the liquidity of the market just as scalpers do and help to lower the cost of hedging.

Speculators

Speculators deal with changes in the expected price levels over time. They usually do not own or use the cash commodity in which they deal.

Profit on their futures position is their only motive. Speculators help assume price risk. They also help produce information about future events that may be important in affecting the price of the commodity. Speculators also act as arbitrageurs. Arbitrage refers to the simultaneous purchase and sale of the same instrument in different markets to profit from unequal prices. The arbitrageurs ensure that cash and futures prices converge at delivery. When the futures price differs from the spot price by more than the cost of arbitrage, the opportunity for risk-free profit occurs, and arbitrageurs will act to buy in the low market and sell in the high market, thus forcing the prices toward their proper equilibrium. The arbitrageur also keeps a close watch on the differences between near and distant futures for a given commodity. If the spread moves beyond the "cost-of-carry," again an opportunity for risk-free profit is created. Actual response to these price discrepancies must be quick, since there are others also paying attention to the profit possibilities. Thus, the prices are forced back into line with carrying costs in a relatively short time.

SELECTING A BROKER

There is probably no decision, related to getting started in trading, that puzzles people more than selecting a broker. In truth it is difficult to know in advance, without a good deal of independent research, what kind of service one will get from an individual broker and the broker's firm. To minimize this risk consider the following guidelines.

First, visit the prospective broker in his office. A face-to-face meeting with him at his place of business, where you can observe the surroundings and the people associated with him, can provide you with valuable information about the character of the individual and firm with whom you are dealing.

Second, find out if he's registered with the Commodity Futures Trading Commission in Washington, D.C. According to federal law both he and the firm must be registered with the Commission. If the individual or the firm have any outstanding charges against them as a result of allegations relating to fraud or misfeasance, a check with the Commission will reveal that information.

Third, one must look beyond the man to the firm. Does the brokerage firm provide good communications facilities for keeping posted on up-to-the-minute prices? Do the facilities provide for direct relay of your orders to the floor of the exchange? What sort of research facilities does the firm have and how good are they? How good is the firm's back office? Can they provide fast and accurate record keeping? There are no precise answers to these questions. They are value judgments you must make on your own. You can probably best judge a firm by comparing it with other firms and by talking to customers who deal with the firm you are considering.

It goes without saying that a broker cannot be all things to you. He can't promise you profits and spend all his time pondering your account or discussing it with you on the phone, and he can't be right all the time. Further, some brokers take a very short-run view of things and are more interested in getting the immediate order than in giving proper thought to whether or not that particular transaction is appropriate for the strategy the customer wishes to follow. The encouraging aspect of this situation however, is that those people gradually are eliminated by the natural market forces.

If misunderstandings should arise or mistakes should be made by one party or another, the first place to go to complain about a broker is to his immediate superior. Most complaints are settled there. If you are right, a settlement of the dispute will be made to compensate you. If further action is necessary, both the exchange on which the transaction was made and the Commodity Futures Trading Commission have departments to receive and investigate complaints about broker activities. They need evidence, however, to do the job and the burden of proof is on the customer.

In summary, finding a good broker is not difficult if you know what you are looking for. A true professional interested in providing quality service and who has a strong brokerage organization behind him can strongly enhance the profitability of your trading.

CHAPTER FOUR
The Order

One of the most elementary, yet most important, aspects of commodity futures trading is developing an understanding of the different types of orders that may be given to brokers and how, why, and under what conditions such orders should be used.

An "order" is by definition an instruction given to your broker directing him to take certain action for your account. There are seven basic parts of the commodity order, and each part is a specific instruction. These instructions are:

1. To buy or to sell.
2. The quantity involved, for example, one contract or ten contracts.
3. The month involved, for example, March or June.
4. The commodity involved, for example, GNMAs or Treasury bonds.
5. The exchange on which the order should be executed, for example, Chicago Board of Trade or NYFE.
6. The price, for example, a market order or a limit order.
7. The time limit in which the order is in effect, for example, one day or "Good till Canceled."

Although these elements are part of every order, the fact that each element can vary independently gives the trader a wide latitude in the types of orders he can enter. It will be readily apparent from the examples given below that a fairly substantial number of order types can be used, with each designated to cover a special situation.

Here are some caveats and reminders before we review the individual orders. First, some futures contracts are traded for more than one year ahead. When you give an order, it is important that you indicate the year in which the contract matures as well as the trading month. Second, in the absence of any specified time limit entered as a part of the order, all commodity orders entered are considered day orders. That is, they are effective only during the specific trading session in which, or immediately prior to which, they are entered. Third, all orders in which a price is not specified are considered market orders and are to be executed immediately at the best price possible. Finally, it is illegal for a broker or a customer to enter opposing orders to buy and sell the same futures contract for the same customer simultaneously. Such a transaction would be considered fictitious and is known as a "wash sale."

When placing orders with your broker, be sure that your instructions concerning each of the seven elements are clear and complete. It is surprising how many misunderstandings result from failure to ensure that the broker knows exactly what his customer wants done.

SOME ILLUSTRATIONS OF COMMODITY ORDERS

One can categorize orders into four basic groupings. These groupings are not mutually exclusive, but for illustrative purposes they help one understand the versatility and flexibility of entering orders. The groupings used in what follows include time orders, price orders, combination orders, and stop orders. The examples listed under each group attempt to illustrate a major characteristic of the order type.

1. Time Orders

1a.   Time Order:
       "At 11:30 A.M. Chicago time
       BUY 4 June 1984 IMM T-bills MKT"
       "BUY 3 June 1984 CBOT 10-year T-notes 84.12 GTC"
       "SELL 3 June 1984 CBOT T-bonds 78.00 GTW" (or "GTM")
       "BUY 2 Sept 1984 IMM T-bills 92.20 GT Mar 10, 1984"

We have already noted that, in the absence of specific instructions to the contrary, all commodity futures orders entered expire at the close of the trading session following or during which they are entered. Futures orders, however, can also be entered good at or good through (GT) specified time periods. For example, a specific time order, as in the first illustration above, must be entered by the floor broker as close to the exact time specified as possible. The symbol "GTC" used at the end of an order directs that the order be kept open until it is canceled. A "GTW" order expires at the close of the trading *week* following or during which it is entered. A "GTM" (Good Through *Month*) order expires at the close of the trading session on the last trading day of the current month. Time orders, such as GTC, GTW, GTM, and GT orders, that continue in effect for a specified time beyond the trading session during which they are entered are also known as "open orders."

1b.   Market-on-Close Order:
      "SELL 10 Dec 1984 NYFE Composite Index MKT on Close"

The market-on-close order must be executed only during the official closing of the market on the day it was entered and the execution price must fall within the range of closing prices for that specified contract month.

1c.   Fill or Kill (FOK) Order (also called a "Quick Order"):
      "SELL 3 Dec 1984 CBT T-bonds 85.63 FOK"

An FOK order instructs a floor broker to execute the order immediately at the price stated or, if such an execution is not possible, to cancel or "kill" the order. An FOK order can be filled either in whole or in part. Any part remaining unfilled is immediately canceled. A report on the part executed must come back immediately.

1d.   Opening (OPG) Only Order:
      "BUY 20 June 1984 IMM T-bills 89.40 OPG Only"

Such an order is to be executed only during the official opening of trading on the day for which the order is placed. If the floor broker is unable to execute it during that time period, the order is immediately canceled. If the order happened to be a market order for execution on the opening only, the actual execution need not be the exact opening sale as long as the execution falls within the range of prices that took place during the official opening of the exchange for the delivery month involved.

2. Price

2a.   Market (MKT) Order:
"BUY 1 Oct 1984 CBT GNMA MKT"

Such an order is executed at the best possible price immediately following the time it is received by a floor broker on the trading floor.

2b.   Limit Order:
"BUY 1 June 1984 IMM T-bill 89.00"
"SELL 1 Sept 1984 IMM T-bill 89.50"

A limit order is used when the customer wishes to buy or sell at a specified limit price or better. On a BUY order, a limit order may be filled at the price specified or at a price below it. On a SELL order, a limit order may be filled at the limit price or at a price above it. A limit order never becomes a market order.

2c.   Market If Touched (MIT) Order:
"SELL 10 Dec 1984 IMM T-bills 89.40 MIT

The use of the acronym MIT gives that particular order some priority that enables it to be executed when the price limit is reached by the market even though only one contract may have traded at the limit price. It should be understood, however, that when the market reaches the specified limit price, an MIT order becomes a market order for immediate execution. As a result, the actual execution may or may not be at the limit price. The advantage obtained from using MIT orders is that the trader is usually assured of getting an execution somewhere near his limit price. An MIT sell order is placed at a price above the existing market. An MIT buy order is placed at a price below the existing market. This is in contrast with the buy-stop (sell-stop) order placed at a price above (below) the existing market.

2d.   Not Held (NH) Order:
"SELL 3 June 1984 CBOT T-bonds 86.63 NH"

Such an order gives the floor broker some discretion in execution. If, for example, the market is trading close to 86.63 but looks strong, the floor broker can elect to try for a better price than 86.63 if he wishes. In the event that he does so and misses, however, he cannot then be held to an execution at 86.63.

2e.   Scale Order:
"BUY 5 Dec 1984 CBOT 10-year T-notes MKT and 5 each 20 points lower, total 30 GTC"
"SELL 5 Dec 1984 IMM T-bills 89.60 and 5 each 20 points Up, Total 30, GTC"

Both illustrations represent a form of contingent order. The floor broker is instructed to buy or sell additional contracts on a scale, provided he is able to execute the first part of the order. Scale orders to BUY or SELL may also be entered, with the contingent part(s) of the order to be executed only on stop orders, for example "SELL 1 June 1984 IMM T-bill 89.60 and STOP-SELL 1 Each 20 points down, total 4." Note that the first order in the examples above could just as well have been entered with a limit price, 89.60 for example, for the first part of the order instead of "MKT," and could have been a day order instead of a Good till Canceled order.

2f.   Discretionary Order:
"BUY 1 March 1984 IMM T-bill 89.00 with 4 pts. Disc."

Such an order may be executed by a floor broker as high as 89.04, or at any price lower than 89.04. In the case of a Discretionary BUY order, the amount of discretion given is used at a price "above" the limit price, while in the case of a SELL order, the discretion given is used at a price "lower" than the limit price.

3. Stop Orders

If there is an art to commodity trading it is probably knowing where to place stop orders. Just as in the stock market, you can use stop orders to automatically get out of losing positions or automatically get into desired positions if the price moves to the level you specify. A stop order does not guarantee you will get the price you stipulate, but it does ensure that the broker will do the best he can to get it when the market moves to the appropriate level. This order does help limit risk. Stop orders are a must if you can't be in constant contact with the market.

3a. Stop Order:
   "SELL 3 June 1984 CBT T-bonds 79.10 Stop" "Buy 2 Sept 1984
   NYFE Composite Index 80.10 Stop"

A sell-stop order becomes effective only when the contract trades at or
below, or is offered in the trading ring at or below, the stop price. A
buy-stop order becomes effective only when the contract trades at or
above, or is bid at or above, the stop price. If either of these things
happens, then an existing stop order becomes a market order in the
hands of a floor broker and is filled immediately thereafter at the best
possible price which may or may not be the trigger price. A sell-stop
order is used to limit losses or protect a profit on long futures positions.
A buy-stop order is used to limit losses or protect a profit on open short
futures positions. Stop-orders are also used by some traders to initiate
or liquidate positions when the market penetrates key support or resistance points. Stop orders may be entered as day orders, as Good till
Canceled (GTC) orders, or as orders good for a limited time span.

3b. Stop-Limit Order:
   "BUY 1 June 1984 IMM T-Bill 89.10 Stop Limit"
   "SELL 25 Sept 1984 IMM T-Bills 89.40 Stop Limit 89.15"

A stop-limit order is used in much the same way as a regular stop order
except that its execution is restricted to the limit price specified or a
better price. In the first example, if June 1984 IMM T-bill contracts
trade at or above 89.10, or are bid at or above 89.10, the stop-limit
order becomes effective. The floor broker with such an order in hand
must try to buy one contract of June 1984 T-bills at 89.10 or less. He
may not pay more. In the second example, when and if September 1984
T-bills trade or are offered at or below 89.40 the sell stop-limit order
becomes effective. The floor broker must sell 25 September 1984 T-bill
futures at the market, provided he can do so at a price not lower than
89.15, the limit price. Note that because the execution price is limited
with a stop-limit order, there is a risk that in a very fast-moving market
the broker may not be able to execute it. Thus, the trader who wishes
to protect his position against the possibility of a disastrous loss may
want to consider using regular stop orders rather than stop-limit orders
for protection against loss.

3c. Enter Open Stop (EOS) Order:
   "SELL 2 Dec 1984 IMM T-Bills MKT Enter Open Stop 61.50"

Most brokers accept EOS orders only on a "not held" basis; that is, the broker cannot be held for failure to enter or execute the "stop" part of the order. Just as with a regular stop order an EOS BUY order has a limit price above the prevailing market. An EOS SELL order has a limit price below the prevailing market.

4. Combination Orders

4a.   Contingent Order:
    "If March 1984 CBT GNMA's sell 77.20 or higher, BUY 20 December 1984 CBT T-bonds MKT"

Contingent orders are entered with the understanding that the execution of one order is dependent upon another element. Brokers who accept such orders usually assume no responsibility for simultaneous or exact price execution, since it is physically impossible for them to be in two places at the same time.

4b.   Cancel Former (CFO) Order:
    "SELL 1 March 1984 CBT T-bond 69.10 GTC, CFO SELL 1 June 1984 CBT T-bond 70.10 GTC entered (date)"
    "BUY 10 Sept 1984 IMM T-bills 89.10, CFO BUY 10 Sept 1984 IMM T-bills 89.00 entered today"

The identification of former orders to be canceled may also be made by referring to the brokerage firm's original internal entering number of the order as well as the date on which it was entered. When entering a CFO order, it is important to make sure that the new order includes a complete identification of the former order that is to be canceled.

4c.   Give-Up (GU) Order:
    "BUY 10 Dec 1984 IMM T-Bills MKT, give up XYZ & Co. J. Doe (account number)"

In the example above, J. Doe, a customer of XYZ & Co., may have been traveling, and presumably was in a city where XYZ & Co. did not have an office. To accomplish his desire to BUY 10 Dec 1984 IMM T-bills, he utilized the office of one of the competitor firms. He asked an account executive at that firm to buy 10 Dec 1984 IMM T-bills for his account at XYZ & Co. The account executive would likely ask J. Doe for identification, or check with XYZ to be sure that Mr. Doe has an account with the firm. Assuming that all is well, the order would then be executed and the trade turned over to an XYZ & Co. representative on the exchange floor for clearance by that firm. In return for the service performed, the out-of-town broker would bill XYZ & Co. a "wire toll charge" for the use of its wires in entering the transaction.

4d.   Intermarket Order (Same Commodity):
      "BUY 20 March 1984 IMM S&P Index SELL 20 March 1984 NYFE Composite Index, N.Y. 2 point premium"

This order represents a spread order executed between the Stock Index futures contracts traded on the NYFE and on the IMM. Both sides of such an order are usually communicated to a floor broker on one of the two exchanges involved. It is then his job, through interexchange communication by phone or wire with a floor broker on the other exchange, to arrange for the execution of both ends of the spread as nearly simultaneously as possible, but in any event at a difference not less favorable than that specified by the customer. Only a few brokerage firms accept these orders regularly except from very large customers.

4e.   Limit or Market on Close Order:
      "BUY 5 Dec 1984 IMM T-bills 89.40 or Market on close"

This order directs the floor broker to buy December 1984 IMM T-bills at 89.40. If, however, the broker is unable to fill the order at 89.40 or lower during the trading day, he is instructed in any event to buy five December 1984 IMM T-bills at the market during the official closing period of trading for December T-bills that day.

4f.   One Cancels the Other (OCO) Order:
      "SELL 1 Sept 1984 IMM T-bill 89.10 or 88.60 Stop, OCO"

This type of order provides the customer with two or more alternatives. In the OCO order above, the floor broker is directed to sell 1 contract of Sept 1984 IMM T-bills at 89.10 or at 88.60 stop, whichever comes first. If he has not yet sold at 89.10 and the market drops so that the September contract either trades at or is offered at or below 88.60, then the broker is instructed to sell the contract "at the market" and cancel the other half of the order. The price received may, in fact, be less than 88.60.

4g. Spread or Straddle Orders

"Spread   Sell 50 Dec 1983 CBT GNMA's
Buy 50 March 1984 CBT GNMA's Dec 20 points or less premium"

"Straddle BUY 8 March 1984 IMM T-bills
SELL 8 Dec 1983 IMM T-bills even"

"Straddle BUY 3 Dec 1984 IMM T-bills
SELL 3 June 1984 IMM T-bills, June 50 pts or more premium"

"Spread   BUY 1 June 1984 IMM T-bills
SELL 1 June 1984 CBT T-bonds market"

"Straddle BUY 1 March 1984 CBT cert. deposit
SELL 1 March 1984 IMM cert. deposit Market"

The first three examples illustrate the most popular type of spread order; that is, where both sides are in the same commodity and exchange. (Note that straddle or spread orders may be placed at specified limit differences as well as "at the market.") The fourth illustration portrays an intercommodity spread order; the fifth one illustrates an intermarket straddle order.

4h. Switch Order:

"Switch BUY 2 June 1984 IMM T-bills SELL 2 Dec 1984 IMM T-bills, June 100 pts premium or less"

A switch order is used to move an existing long or short commodity futures position from one delivery month to another or from one market to another. In appearance and in handling on the floor such an order closely resembles a straddle order but the effect is different. Some brokers give reduced commissions on switch orders.

4i. Exchange For Physicals (EFP) Order or an Against Actuals (AA) Order:

"SELL 5 June 1984 IMM T-bills 90.00 EFP to XYZ Co. vs. cash"

An EFP or AA order represents one of the two types of orders that can legally be communicated to an exchange trading floor and does not require competitive pricing. Such an order would be used, for example, by a dealer who has just made a sale of T-bills in the spot market to the XYZ Co. Presumably the XYZ Co., prior to the spot market transaction, had an open long hedge in June 1980 futures. By using an

EFP order the dealer eliminates the short hedge he had in June 1980 T-bill futures and transfers the June futures sale to the XYZ Co. which, when received, offsets the XYZ Co.'s long hedge in June futures. Obviously the use of an EFP order requires some advance negotiations between the two principals to the related spot market transaction. Note that any transaction completed ex-pit—that is, outside the trading ring —must be reported to and be approved by the proper exchange officials.

PART TWO
Price Analysis

CHAPTER FIVE

Price Forecasting Through Technical Analysis

In 1912 a Jesuit library in Verona, Italy sold an ancient volume to Wilfred Voynich, a dealer in antiquities. The book, reputed to have been written in the 13th century by Roger Bacon, a Franciscan Monk with a fascination for cryptography, contains page after page of what appears to be Arabic handwriting.

For the past 70 years or so cryptographers have attempted to decipher the text. Even the legendary William F. Friedman, captain of the team that broke the purple Japanese diplomatic code just before Pearl Harbor and considered by most to be the greatest cryptographer who ever lived, has tried. None has succeeded. Today the Voynich manuscript lies in a museum vault, a silent challenge to cryptanalysts the world over seeking to uncover the secret of its message.

Technical analysts approach commodity price analysis in much the same manner that cryptographers attempt to decipher a code. They have no less expectation that written in those squiggly lines is a message containing the ultimate secret to forecasting commodity prices—if only the code could be broken.

Technical analysis refers to the study of market activity itself—

prices, trading volume, open interest, and other numerical data that can be derived from those three statistics. Technical analysts prefer to study the market itself rather than the supply/demand factors that affect the price for a given commodity. They believe that even if one knew where to find all the fundamental information about the supply and demand for a particular product, one still wouldn't be able to predict market response to that information. Technical analysts believe that the only place where all the factual supply and demand data—plus the mass moods, hopes, fears, estimates, and guesses of everyone in the market—are cyrstalized is in a commodity's price, volume, and open interest.

They believe that by studying *how* prices have acted you can obtain more insight about future price movement than you can by studying *why* prices have acted a certain way. The basic assumption underlying the technical approach to the market is that by studying statistics generated by the market it is possible to come to meaningful conclusions about future prices. In short, they believe that the way the market behaved yesterday may indicate how prices will behave tomorrow.

Technical analysts do not believe futures prices represent a purely random walk. They point to the futility of trying to know and understand all the factors that affect supply and demand, and argue that there are so many fundamental elements in play at any one time that it is easy for an important one to be overlooked or improperly weighted.

But the most likely reasons that technical analysis is so popular is that it is easy, efficient, and esoteric. Only three series of data are required—price, volume, and open interest. These data are easy to get and to store in computer models. The models used to massage the data are relatively simple and straightforward. Thus, decision-making is efficient and easy.

Technical analysts usually approach their market analysis task by using one or a combination of the following basic approaches:

1. Analysis of patterns on price charts.
2. Moving average and statistical analysis.
3. Analysis of market composition.

We will describe briefly each of these approaches.

PATTERNS ON PRICE CHARTS

Probably the oldest method of technical market analysis known is the interpretation of patterns of movements on price charts. There are two basic types of price charts used in technical analysis: bar charts and point and figure charts. Both kinds of charts are easily constructed. All you need is the price information, volume, open interest, some graph paper, and a pencil.

If you don't want to be bothered or don't have the time to build and maintain your own charts there are numerous chart services available to provide ready-made charts for a fee. Some of these services provide only one type of chart while others provide a combination of various types of charts and also offer interpretations of the price patterns.

The first step in constructing any chart is to decide on the frequency of the prices to be plotted; that is, daily, weekly, or monthly. Normally, commodity charts are kept on a daily basis, but many analysts also keep weekly and monthly price charts in order to get a longer term perspective.

Bar Chart

Figure 5.1 is a typical bar chart. In standard procedure, each day's price activity is represented by one vertical bar (line) in the open area on the graph. The top of the line marks the point of the day's highest price. The bottom of the line marks the day's lowest price. The closing price is shown by a short horizontal "tick" mark extending to the right.

Across the bottom of the chart is a daily calendar with the weekends left out. Each square contains only a five-trading-day week. This prevents the two-day weekend "gap" in the chart between two sets of weekly data.

The numbers running up the right side of the chart are the prices. Each day is plotted to the right of all preceding days.

Below each price plot on the chart another vertical bar is frequently drawn from the bottom up to indicate volume of trading for that day. And a dot is usually placed to indicate the total open interest on that day.

A number of variations are possible in this standard procedure. Some

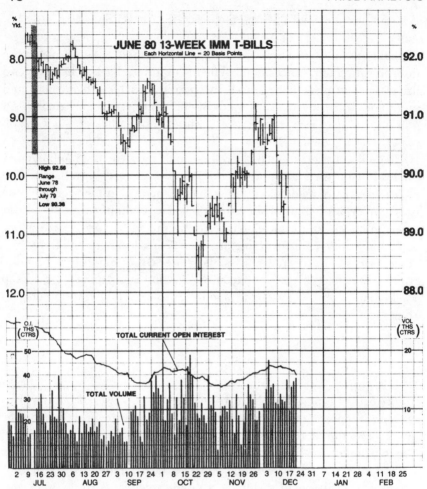

Figure 5.1   June 80 13-week IMM T-bills.

technicians chart only the closing prices. Others enter a midrange that consists of the high plus the low divided in half. The opening price is sometimes shown as well. All these procedures have advantages and disadvantages and each technician must decide which he considers most useful.

As the data is recorded, the analyst will begin to observe price formations or patterns that, according to traditional chart lore, are recurring and have forecasting significance. This chapter will not attempt to detail all of the different patterns that various technicians have discovered during the years, but Figure 5.2 contains the most publicized patterns. For those interested in a more definitive source of information on chart patterns and their analysis, *Technical Analysis of Stock Trends,* by Robert D. Edwards and John Magee (Springfield, Mass.: John Magee Inc., 1948), is recommended.

Point and Figure Charts

Point and figure charting of futures prices have their roots in securities analysis, just as bar chart analysis does. The construction of a point and

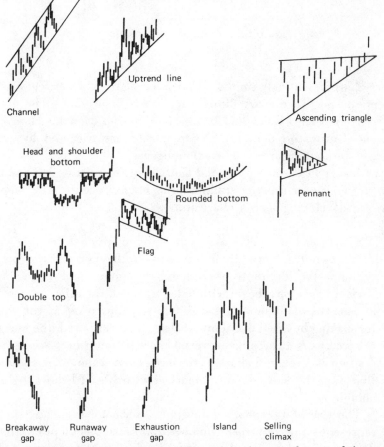

Figure 5.2   Typical chart patterns. The mirror image of most of these patterns has an opposite implication.

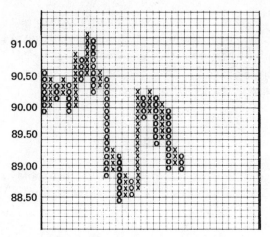

Figure 5.3   Point and figure chart.

figure chart is relatively simple. As with bar charts the vertical axis of
the point and figure chart shows prices. (See Figure 5.3.) The major
difference is that a point and figure chart has no calendar along the
bottom. Entries on point and figure charts are triggered by price
changes without regard to when they occur.

Entries are made on a point and figure chart by putting X's and O's
in boxes whenever a predetermined price change occurs. The general
rules for developing such a chart are:

1.   X's represent price increases; O's represent price decreases.
2.   The range of the day (difference between the high and the low) is
     the important datum to use in making the point and figure chart.
3.   To start the chart, begin with a day in which the range represents
     at least the minimum number of boxes you are using as your basis
     for making buy/sell decisions. If three boxes are used, the chart is
     referred to as a three-box reversal chart. If four boxes are used, it
     is a four-box reversal chart. If the day's close is above the midpoint
     that day, the first column is marked with X's; if below, the first
     column is O's.

     The size of the box is important. Normally each box should
     represent some convenient number that reflects small price moves.
     This may be the equivalent of one "point" in the contract value
     or it may be more. Most good chart services optimize their charts

by periodically reviewing the effectiveness of various box sizes and reversal criteria. As the volatility of a market changes, the appropriate size of a box and reversal distance also change. Optimizing helps keep the charts reflective of current market conditions.

4. If the most recent entry is an X (O), review the daily high (low) first. If the high (low) is at least one box higher (lower) than the last entry, add the appropriate number of X's (O's).

5. If you are currently plotting X's and the daily high does not require drawing more X's, then consider the low. If the day's low is lower than the highest X by the agreed upon number of boxes to constitute a reversal, begin a column of O's one box below and one box to the right of the highest X. Otherwise, no additional entry is made for that day.

6. If you are currently plotting O's and the daily low does not require drawing more O's, then consider the high. If today's high is higher than the lowest O by the reversal criterion or more, begin a column of X's one box above and one box to the right of the highest O. Otherwise, no additional entry is made that day.

7. A simple buy signal occurs when the current column of X's rises one box higher than the top box in the immediately prior column of X's.

8. A simple sell signal occurs when the current column of O's falls one box lower than the lowest O in the immediately prior column of O's.

Point and figure charts can be used to follow intraday price moves or long-term trends. As in bar charts, one will find various chart patterns revealed in point and figure charts.

(See Figure 5.4 for a sampling of some of the typical patterns identified in financial instrument futures.)

SETTING PRICE OBJECTIVES

Bar Charts

It is one thing to be able to identify price direction; it is another to be able to identify the price objective. A well-disciplined trader has a price objective in mind at the time he enters the trade. This objective may

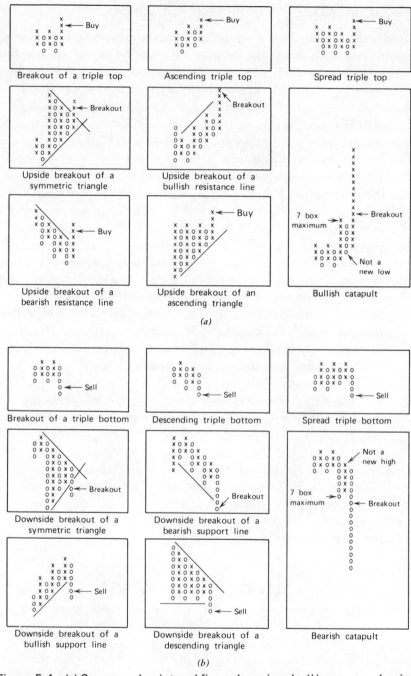

Figure 5.4 (*a*) Compound point and figure buy signals; (*b*) compound point and figure sell signals. (Courtesy P.J. Kaufman)

be stated as a percentage of return on margin desired or it may be obtained from an analysis of the price activity. The most logical price objective for a trade is the major support or resistance level established from previous market activity. For example, in attempting to set a price objective when entering a long position, one should look at the most well-defined resistance level above the purchase point. If the market tests that level by a price move, there is a possibility you will see one of the top formations described earlier and shown in Figure 5.2. A conservative trader would locate his price objective a reasonable distance below the prior major resistance level and use intermediate resistance levels as a means of adding to his positions on technical setbacks. A more aggressive trader might wait to see how prices deal with the major resistance level, in the hope of a breakthrough to new highs.

If one were entering a short position, one would set the downside objective in precisely the same manner, except one would be considering major support levels.

It is important to keep in mind that there are no rigid rules to be applied in setting price objectives. Support and resistance, trendlines, price formations, mathematical rules of thumb—all can be utilized to help estimate the distance a price move will travel before it is exhausted.

Point and Figure Charts

Generally, point and figure chartists set their price objectives by horizontal and vertical counts of the boxes comprising a particular chart formation. The theory behind this technique is that the amount of price activity at a particular level is important in determining the extent of the following price move. The logic is similar to the "support and resistance" logic used in bar charting. Previous contract highs or lows should always be used as a substitute objective if another technical method indicating potential strength or weakness causes a test of the highs or lows.

As tempting as it is to rely on such techniques as the counting of boxes or the width of a rectangular consolidation pattern on a bar chart as a means of setting price objectives, one needs to be warned of the dangers inherent in relying too heavily on such rote methods. Keep in mind that there are many ways of determining an objective of a trade and that there are no precise rules that are completely reliable.

For the reader desiring a more complete and sophisticated discussion of the methods of technical analysis, chart building, interpretation and price objective analysis, Perry Kaufman's book *Commodity Trading Systems and Methods* (New York: Wiley, 1979) is highly recommended.

CHAPTER SIX
Statistical Analysis Approach

Prices can do only one of three things. They can go up, they can go down, or they can go sideways. What they are doing at any one time is identified as the "trend." There are a wide variety of ways to determine a trend in a series of prices. One can do it by simply drawing two lines connecting the successive major lows and successive major highs on a chart to get a price "channel," or one can do it statistically through a variety of econometric techniques, such as regression analysis.

In any event, free market prices do not normally move in a straight line from one point to another. Instead there is usually a good deal of backing and filling in price movement. This backing and filling reflects the diversity of influences on prices, such as government programs, political events, short term changes in supply and demand, emotions, hopes and fears, and just plain trading activity. This is referred to by statisticians as "noise."

In order to make the most efficient use of the data, the technical price analyst needs to be able to smooth out some of that "noise" occurring around the trend. By eliminating as much of it as possible without distorting the underlying trend information embodied in the price movement, an analyst can improve the probability of developing an effective and profitable trading system.

55

Probably the simplest and best known technique for eliminating "noise" and smoothing a price series is the moving average.

MOVING AVERAGES

The moving average is best explained by an example. A three-day moving average of closing prices is calculated by summing three successive days of prices. To calculate the average for the fourth day, one drops the closing price for day one from the calculation and adds the closing price for day four. To calculate the moving average for the fifth day, one drops the closing price for day two from the calculation and adds the closing price for day five, and so on. The same procedure holds for calculating moving averages of other spans, such as 10 days or 20 days, and for other prices, such as daily highs or lows.

Daily closing prices	3-day moving average
89.00	
89.10	
89.50	89.20
88.20	88.93
88.00	88.57

One could also calculate the averages in a slightly modified way by adding each new day's price to the prior average and subtracting the last *moving average* value. The convenience of this technique is that the user no longer has to keep the individual components of the average, only the prior moving average value and the new price.

The choice of whether one should use a three-day, five-day, ten-day, or whatever length moving average is related to several elements. The first is the sensitivity desired. The more days one uses in a moving average the more smoothing will occur and the less effect short-term fluctuations will have on the average price. (See Figures 6.1 and 6.2.) The more sensitive one wants his average to be in reflecting turning points in the trend, the shorter the averaging period should be.

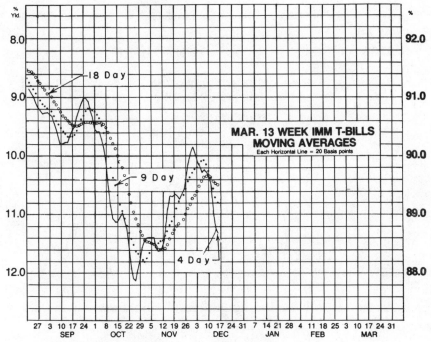

Figure 6.1   March 13-week IMM T-bills moving averages.

Second, in selecting the average one needs to keep in mind the uses to which it will be put. The financial executive who is making weekly decisions on a portfolio would want to wait as long as possible while prices continue to trend before he makes his buy or sell decision. In such a situation a three-day moving average won't aid his decision making very much, but a 20-day moving average may.

What Prices to Use

In calculating the moving average one obvious question is, "Should one use opening prices, closing prices, an average for the day, the high price, or the low price for the day?" The answer is that one can use any of these but each of them may serve a different purpose. Most people use the closing price. Some calculate separate averages for the high and the low independently, thus obtaining a "band" representing the daily trading range or volatility.

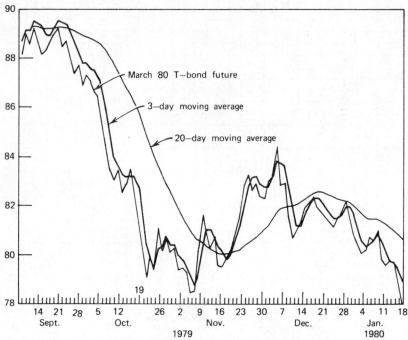

Figure 6.2 T-bonds March 80 versus 3-day moving average and 20-day moving average.

Other Types of Moving Averages

Perry Kaufman, in his book *Commodity Trading Systems and Methods,* reviews a wide variety of other types of moving averages. The accumulative moving average, weighted moving averages, and exponentially smoothed moving averages are discussed as additional ways of obtaining a smoothing of price series. Exponential smoothing has a lot of intellectual and theoretical appeal, but the user needs to have a thorough understanding of statistics to make the fullest use of it as a trading tool. An important feature of exponentially smoothed averages is that all previously used prices are part of the new result, but with decreasing importance as they go back in time. There is a dilution effect based on time elapsed and on the smoothing constant. Hence, such averages react slower than most linear moving averages.

Leads and Lags in Plotting

Moving averages can also be plotted in different ways, with each having a major impact on their interpretation. Most analysts plot them the conventional way by placing the moving average value for that day on the same vertical line on the chart as the price for that day. If prices have been trending higher over the period of calculation, this will cause the moving average value to lag behind or below the actual prices. And when prices are declining, the moving average will be above the actual prices. One can adjust for this by plotting the moving average with a lead or lag of several days. In this way the turning point in the moving average and in the actual price series can be put in phase and will coincide more closely on the chart.

RULES FOR USING MOVING AVERAGES

As is obvious from the preceding discussion, there are so many possible combinations of moving average techniques that the rules for applying these techniques can be extremely challenging. Our goal here is to cover only some of the very basic rules.

Regardless of which of the moving averages one uses, the value of an unadjusted moving average will lag behind the actual market price. As pointed out above, this lag will cause the moving average to be below the market price when prices are rising, and it will cause the moving average to be above the market price when prices are falling. When prices change direction the moving average and the actual commodity prices will cross. When this crossing occurs a basic trading signal is generated. If the rising price line crosses the moving average, it is considered a buy signal. If the declining price crosses the moving average, it is a sell signal. (See Figure 6.3.)

Of course, if one has built his moving average based on closing prices, the buy signal refers to the rising price closing above the moving average and a sell signal is generated when the declining price closes below the moving average. If the moving average is based on the average daily high and low then signals occur when the new daily average is above or below the previous day's moving average.

The timing of the entry and exit points may be adjusted according to the wishes of the decision maker. One can adjust the decision-making rules to delay an entry or exit for a day or two after the buy or sell signal is generated in an attempt to reduce the potential for being whipsawed and to allow a longer time for a newly developed trend to confirm its existence or for the signal to reveal itself as false.

Some traders, in order to avoid whipsaw, utilize a technique called a price "band." A band is an area above and below the price track that acts as a buffer zone for the trader in making his decisions. For example, a trader may decide to close out his long position when a moving average is penetrated from the upside by a price but not to enter the short position until price exits the lower boundary of the band. Most traders create bands by developing a percentage of the current price or of the current trend line value. Others use an absolute point value, for example, 30 points. (See Figure 6.4.)

MULTIPLE MOVING AVERAGES

By combining various moving averages into a system, one can develop a means of timing trading decisions. For example, a three-day moving average combined with a 20-day moving average allows one to use a three-day moving average as a timing technique while retaining the 20-day moving average for defining the long-term trend. This way a trader can be more comfortable entering the market when he sees a recent short-term surge of prices in the direction in which he intends to establish his new positions.

Two different rules which can be followed in applying multiple moving averages are:

1. Buy when the shorter moving average crosses the longer moving average going up, or sell when the shorter moving average crosses the longer moving average going down, as shown in Figure 6.4. This rule keeps one always in the market, going from long to short and back again as the long-term trend is violated by the short-term trend.

2. Buy when the current price crosses above both moving averages and close out your long position when he price crosses below either moving average, or sell when the current price crosses below both moving averages and close out the short position when the price crosses above either moving average. For example, one would have

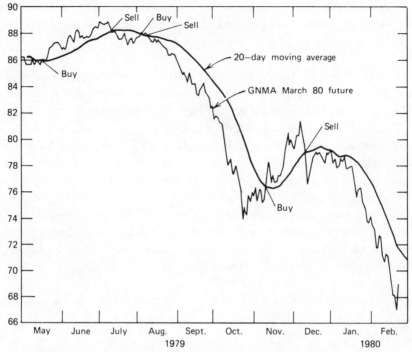

Figure 6.3 GNMA March 80 versus 20-day moving average.

gone short at point A in Figure 6.5 and remained short until point B, at which level one would take a neutral position. The short position would have been reinstated at point C. Following this rule allows one to remain neutral when closing out a current position

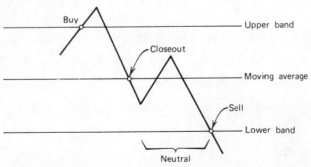

Figure 6.4 Trend line value. (Courtesy P.J. Kaufman)

even if the long term trend has not been penetrated. One does, however, suffer the potential for possible whipsaw as a result of being too close to the current price.

Kaufman demonstrates a number of these multiple moving average systems and tests several of them. His book is well worth reading by anyone seriously interested in technical trading systems.

The five- and 20-day multiple moving average system of trading is quite popular. One of the best known of these systems is the Donchian method, which uses volatility-penetration criteria relative to a 20-day moving average. Donchian personalizes the system by adding judgmental factors relating to the extent to which the 20-day moving average must be penetrated and the day of the week the signals occurred.

As you can see, the combination of different factors and criteria one can put into a moving average trading system are multifold and dependent very much upon choice and experience.

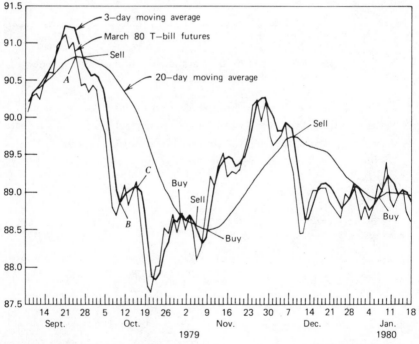

Figure 6.5   T-Bills March 80 versus 3-day moving average and 20-day moving average.

OSCILLATORS AND THE MEASUREMENT OF MOMENTUM

For many commodity analysts, merely being able to discern a trend in market prices is not sufficient refinement or understanding of the price activity to give them confidence in making decisions. Consequently, they want to know not only what the trend is but also to obtain a measurement of the *rate* of change in price. Or, to put it another way, they want to know the slope of the trend line.

Momentum is usually calculated by taking the difference between prices for fixed time intervals. For example, today's three-day momentum value wold be the average difference between today's price and the price three days ago. If the price of T-bills has changed 60 points during the past three trading days the momentum measurement would be 20 (60/3 = 20).

Another popular method of measuring momentum is to calculate the difference between a three-day and a ten-day moving average, or some other set of short- and longer-term moving averages. The rationale behind this procedure is to take advantage of the smoothing effect of moving averages; if the analyst uses the same moving averages for generating buy/sell signals, he has some of his calculations already completed.

One will note as momentum calculations are plotted that a trend may continue up, but in smaller and smaller increments. As the increment of increase lessens, it suggests a decrease in momentum and an approaching turning point in the trend—or at the very least a flattening out of the trend line.

At that point the momentum index achieves its greatest value in determining whether a market is "overbought" or "oversold." When the momentum index is high and begins to slow its ascent or turns down, the market is considered oversold and a downward price reaction is expected. Conversely, when the momentum index is low and starts to slow its decline or turns up, the market is considered oversold and ready for an upward move. (See Figure 6.6a and b.)

There are some significant risks in developing trading rules around momentum indicators. For example, to use a rule that considers crossing of the "zero" line by the momentum index as a change in price trend, requiring you to buy when the momentum index crosses the zero line going up and sell when it crosses the zero line going down, creates risk of being whipsawed. See Figure 6.6 for examples of whipsaw action

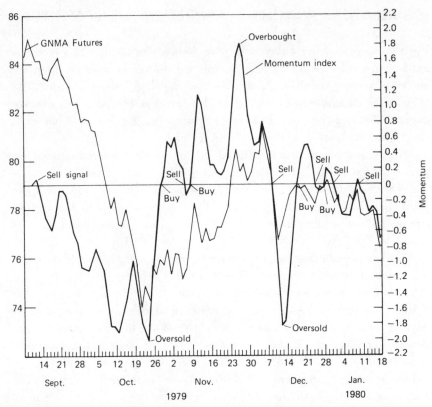

Figure 6.6a   GNMA March 80 versus (3-day–10-day)momentum.

where the zero line (rate of change in price is zero) is used for determining trend changes. You could easily find yourself selling into an upward market at the time the market is strong; and, if you don't get an immediate reversal of the price trend, you might need substantial margin reserves to hold your position. The important thing is that you must realize you are essentially trading against the trend and making an informed guess that you will be able to identify very closely the turning point in the trend.

The terms "oscillator" and "momentum index" are frequently used interchangeably. Although they are calculated differently, for all practical purposes they measure the same thing. Perhaps the most popular type of oscillator is one that compares the daily highs and lows to the previous day's close. It is calculated by subtracting the previous day's close from today's high and dividing that number by the absolute difference between the high and the low for today. The extreme values will be $+1$ and -1, with the former indicating an overbought condition and the latter an oversold condition. The middle of the scale, zero, would imply a sideways price trend. For example, if yesterday's close for March T-bills was 89.00 and today's high and low were 89.40 and 89.90 respectively, the oscillator value would be $+0.80$ (89.40 $-$ 89.00 $= 0.40$; $0.40 \div 0.50 = 0.80$)

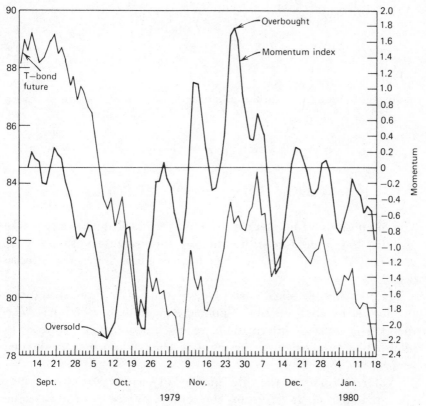

Figure 6.6b T-bonds March 80 versus (3-day–10-day) momentum.

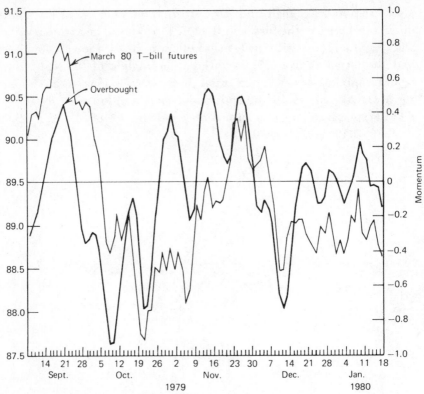

Figure 6.6c   T-bills March80 versus (3-day–10-day) momentum.

MARKET COMPOSITION APPROACH

The composition-of-market approach is a technical approach to market analysis and price forecasting that is supplementary to other approaches. Alone it does not provide much of a basis for refined forecasting.

Traditionally technical analysts have studied the basic structure of the market by analyzing its volume and open interest activity. When these two pieces of information are combined with other available information they heighten the sense of what's happening in the markets.

"Volume" refers to the total number of contracts traded during a given time period. It represents the total of purchases or of sales, not of purchases and sales combined. So each time a transaction is completed (whether it involves the establishment of a new position or the offset of an old position), the volume is increased by one.

"Open interest" refers to the futures contracts that have been entered into and not yet liquidated. It is the total purchase or sale commitments or the number of contracts outstanding. As with volume, the open interest figure is for one side of the market only—not for the long and short sides combined. However, unlike volume, the effect of a transaction upon open interest depends on whether new positions are being established or old ones closed out.

Open interest increases only when new purchases are matched with new sales. Decreases in open interest occur only when old longs close out their positions by selling to old shorts, who are buying to cover. Open interest also decreases when a short makes a delivery of actuals on a futures contract. There is no change in open interest when a new purchase is matched with an offsetting transaction (sale of a previous purchase, or if a new sale is matched with an offsetting transaction (purchase of a previous sale).

All open contracts must ultimately be closed out in one of two ways —by an offsetting futures transaction or through delivery of the physical commodity. Table 6.1 summarizes the effect of a particular transaction on open interest.

To illustrate the concept of open interest and the impact of a transaction on the open interest, consider the following. Assume that you now have no position in the market but decide today to buy one futures contract of GNMAs. If the seller on the other end of your transaction was closing out a previous long position in GNMAs, the open interest would not change. You would have in effect "replaced" him in the market. He was long. Now he isn't and you are.

On the other hand, if your seller was initiating a new short position there would be a new long (you) and a new short (him) in the market and open interest in GNMAs would go up by one.

If sometime later you have a profit in your GNMA position and decide to sell and take those profits, you close out your long position. If the buyer on the other end was closing out a short position to stop his losses, your transaction would reduce the open interest by one, as the GNMA positions outstanding would be reduced by one long (you) and one short (him). On the other hand, if his was a new long position, he would "replace" you and the open interest in GNMAs would remain unchanged.

Table 6.1   Effect of Transaction on Open
Interest

Transaction	Effect on open interest
Purchases by old sellers from old buyers	Reduced
Purchases by old sellers from new sellers	Unchanged
Purchases by new buyers from old buyers	Unchanged
Purchases by new buyers from new sellers	Increased
Sales by old buyers to new buyers	Unchanged
Sales by old buyers to old sellers	Reduced
Sales by new sellers to old sellers	Unchanged
Sales by new sellers to new buyers	Increased

Statistics on open interest and volume of trading are easily available from the exchanges, your local broker, and many major metropolitan newspapers. In addition, the Commodity Futures Trading Commission (CFTC) publishes monthly statistics on open interest and volume of trading for all of the commodities. The commission also provides information about the nature and size of traders who hold the open contracts and whether they are generally classified as large and small speculators or hedgers. (See Table 6.1) Some traders follow this information on the belief that it provides a good indication of the relative buying or selling strength of the people in the market.

INTERPRETING CHANGES IN VOLUME
AND OPEN INTEREST

Most technical analysts believe the changes in open interest and volume of trading have forecasting value only when considered in connection with price changes. Almost any book on technical analysis provides a summary of rules of thumb for relating changes in open interest in

volume to price action. Generally these rules of thumb and their rationale are stated as follows:

1. If the open interest is up and prices are also up, this indicates new
    buying and a technically strong market. The increase in open
    interest means new contracts are being created, and since prices are
    advancing buyers must be more aggressive than sellers.
2. If open interest is going up while prices are going down, short
    selling or hedging is taking place and the market is technically
    weak. Again, the increase in open interest means that new con-
    tracts are being established. However, since prices are decreasing,
    sellers must be more aggressive than buyers.
3. If the open interest is going down and prices are also declining, this
    comprises liquidation by longs rather than new selling pressure, and
    implies a technically strong market.
4. If the open interest is going down and prices are going up, this
    suggests short covering rather than new buying, and a technically
    weak market.
5. If the volume of trading follows the price—that is if volume ex-
    pands on price strength and declines on price weakness—the mar-
    ket is in a technically strong position and should go higher. By the
    same token but to a lesser extent, if the volume of trading expands
    on price weakness and declines on price strength, the market is
    considered to be in a technically weak position and ready to go
    lower.

Like all rules of thumb however, there are many pitfalls in their
rote application. Further, there's very little statistical evidence
indicating that these rules of thumb are actually successful in
generating trading profits.

CHAPTER SEVEN

Fundamental Price Analysis

Fundamental price analysis is the process of forecasting the supply of and demand for credit and the resultant prices of fixed-income securities. It involves the simultaneous evaluation of economic information, political forces, and investor attitudes as they interact with each other.

This chapter presents a review and enumeration of the economic factors that affect the economy and interest rates. The chapter does not attempt an in-depth evaluation of credit availability or flow of funds in the economy, nor does it attempt subjective evaluation of investor attitudes and political forces.

The chapter does provide the reader with a checklist of economic information and gives a preliminary sense of the importance of each piece. The list is not exhaustive or all-inclusive. Whole books have been devoted to this subject and it is impossible in the short space provided here to do justice to the topic. The hope, though, is that the reader will get sufficient flavor from what is written here to appreciate the scope and complexity of the topic and will thus be motivated to delve further on his own.

ECONOMIC INFORMATION

A market analyst is constantly bombarded with information relating to the state of the economy, changes in prices, indicators of future economic activity, and facts and figures relating to monetary growth. His success as an analyst will depend on his ability to sort out the relevant from the irrelevant and give proper weight to the relevant.

Table 7.1 shows a schedule of various economic reports released by the federal government during the month of June 1980. These reports provide an excellent source of information on the factors that affect the performance of the economy and thus determine the supply and demand for credit. The elements that make up these reports can be categorized into leading, concurrent, and lagging indicator groups.

Leading Indicators

Leading indicators provide advance signals about the health of the economy during the coming months. They reflect coming changes in the business cycle and consequently provide the interest rate analyst with an early warning system for identifying changes in interest rate trends.

Certain pieces of economic information relating to various sectors of the economy act as leading indicators in measuring the underlying health of the economy and the strength of business. The federal government has combined a number of these statistical series into a single index called the Leading Indicator Index. These leading indicators, while helping to predict some of the other variables, are themselves sometimes difficult to predict. One reason for this is that they are, in general, highly sensitive to disturbances of all kinds and are particularly volatile. Many of them are tied to expectations that change rather rapidly.

The components of the Leading Indicator Index are:

1. Average work week of production and manufacturing workers.
2. Manufacturing layoff rate.
3. New orders for consumer goods and materials.
4. Vendor performance-percent of companys reporting slower deliveries.
5. Net business formation.
6. Contracts and orders for plants and equipment.
7. New building permits for private housing units.
8. Net change in inventories on hand and on order.
9. Changes in sensitive prices.

Table 7.1 Announcement Dates of Economic Indicators—June, 1980 (Source: Courtesy R.H. Wrightson & Associates, Inc.)

M	T	W	TH	F
26 Holiday	**27** Machine tool orders February $501.0 MM March 528.7 April 415.0	**28** U.S. trade balance February — $5570 MM March — 3160 April — 1870	**29**	**30** Leading indicators February — 0.4% March — 2.1 April — 4.8 Agricultural prices released
2 New factory orders February — 0.1% March — 1.6 April — 5.5 Manufacture inventories February + $2850 MM March + 3250 April + 4100	**3** Construction spending February $243.1 B March 229.9 April 221.7 (released yesterday)	**4** March April May Domestic car sales 667M or 7.6MM(saar) 538 or 6.0 497 or 5.3	**5** Consumer credit February + $2300 MM March + 1430 April — 1990	**6** Unemployment rate March 6.2% April 7.0 May 7.8 Producer Price Index March + 1.4% April + 0.5 May + 0.3
9	**10** Retail sales March — 2.3% April — 1.2 May — 1.0*	**11** Business inventories February + $3550 MM March + 2550 April + 4800*	**12**	**13** Industrial production March — 0.7% April — 1.9 May — 2.0* 10-day car sales
16	**17** Personal income March + $14.0 B April 0.5 May + 2.2* Housing starts March 1.041 MM April 1.019 May 0.980*	**18** GNP, real (%) 1979.IV +2.0 1980.I(Prel.) +1.1 1980.I(Rev.) +0.6 1980.I(Rev.) +0.4*	**19**	**20** Durable goods orders March — 4.3% April — 6.6 May — 4.4*
23	**24** Consumer price index March + 1.4% April + 0.9 May + 1.1* 10 = day car sales	**25**	**26**	**27** U.S. trade balance March — $3160 MM April — 1870 May — 2500*

*Projected.

10. Changes in total liquid assets.
11. Stock prices of 500 common stock.
12. Money supply—M2.

These elements reflect changes in the early stages of the production and investment processes in our economy. For example, increased output calling for additional labor input is likely to be met first by manufacturers lengthening the work week and only later by manufacturers hiring new workers. Similarly, reductions in hours worked will precede layoffs in times of falling demand. Thus, cyclical changes in average hours worked precede those of changes in employment, particularly in manufacturing. The components of the Leading Indicator Index are selected by the federal government on the basis of their economic significance, their statistical adequacy, and their usefulness in identifying turning points in the business cycle.

As these indicators are released throughout the month, traders tend to give immediate reactions to the numbers. This frequently results in some short-term volatility in prices. If the indicator shows signs of a weakening economy, lower rates are likely to follow as the market begins to discount the expectation of a weaker economy ahead.

Concurrent and Lagging Indicators

Concurrent and lagging indicators show the general direction of the economy and confirm or deny a trend or change in the trend implied by the leading indicators. These indicators show the degree of change that has and is taking place in the economy. Often the release of a report on one of these indicators causes the market to adjust rapidly as investors are made aware that the declining or advancing activity has confirmed earlier signals of the leading indicators. Thus, concurrent and lagging indicators are often used to forecast the slope and the direction of business cycles.

Some of the key indicators in these groups are:

• **Unemployment.** Released at the beginning of the month, this report reflects the change in employment for the immediately preceding month and shows current economic activity.

- **Trade Balances.** Released monthly, these figures are very important to the strength of the dollar. The dollar's health is often followed very closely by the market as an indicator of potential foreign buying of securities. A strong dollar draws private foreign buying, but often causes selling by foreign central banks.

- **Domestic Car Sales.** This monthly figure shows the seasonally adjusted and annualized number of cars sold during the past month. It is a good indicator of consumer confidence and overall economic activity, since the auto industry is such a big part of our economy. Statistics on ten-day car sales are released during the month.

- **Consumer Credit.** Released monthly, this report provides a clue to the attitude of consumers toward spending. It is an indicator of the demand for credit from a large and important sector of the economy.

- **Retail Sales.** Released monthly, this report reflects the total of past retail activity and credit purchases, as well as cash. It is another good indicator of consumer confidence and overall economic activity.

- **Producer Price Index.** Released at the beginning of the month, this report covers the immediate past month. This replaces the old Wholesale Price Index. It reflects the cost of resources needed to produce manufactured goods, and is a good indicator of future consumer price increases as it shows the rate of inflation for raw materials.

- **Business Inventories.** This is an important key indicator, as it reflects the demand for short-term credit by businesses. As inventories build, they are usually financed through bank loans or commercial paper. Increases or decreases usually signal changes in the demand for credit. Inventory levels are generally good indicators of the duration and intensity of a business slowdown or speedup. If inventories are high when a slowdown begins, the recession is usually expected to be longer and more severe because factories will run at reduced levels until inventories are sold off. High inventories may also act as a short-term support for interest. Demand for credit to finance inventories could keep interest rates higher longer than they normally would be if inventories were low and if the economy were still in a business slowdown.

  Low levels of inventories going into an upturn in the business cycle may result in a short inflation spurt and a quick acceleration of business activity. The process of rebuilding inventories creates jobs and ultimately causes consumer demand to increase. This consumer demand often cannot be met by existing inventories, so prices climb, economic activity increases, and factories open to meet the new demands.

- **Housing Starts.** This report is released monthly. The levels of economic activity in the whole economy are greatly affected by the level of home construction. Housing starts are a good indicator of the demand for long-term mortgage money and short-term construction loans. They also give indicators of the number of GNMAs and other types of mortgage-backed securities that will need to be supplied in the near future.

- **Industrial Production.** This indicator concerns the level of factory output in the previous month. It is a good lagging indicator that shows the depths of recessions and the highs of booms.

- **Personal Income.** This indicator reflects consumers' buying power. It measures potential demand for goods and services, and reflects general levels of economic activity.

- **GNP.** This figure is usually regarded as past history. It confirms direction and amplitude of economic change. It is not a useful item for making trading decisions.

- **Consumer Price Index.** This is the measure of inflation. It is a key factor in bond prices, as investors usually demand a real rate of return of at least 2% for government bonds over the long term. The CPI is usually released during the third week of the month. Market participants watch these numbers very closely as indicators of future changes in long-term bond rates and money market rates.

WHERE TO FIND THIS INFORMATION

All of this economic information is reported in daily newspapers as it is released to the public during the month. Because market experts make forecasts of the data prior to their actual release, the market frequently begins to "discount" or react to the news before it is actually announced. A schedule of release dates and forecasts similar to those in Table 7.1 is usually available from your brokerage firm. It should not only give the dates of release but also a synopsis of recent numbers and an estimate of the new numbers. This type of information is vital for making short-term trading decisions and timing long-term investments.

Which Piece of Economic Data Is the Most Important?

No single economic indicator will permanently dominate the market. As times change, indicators replace each other as the "most important" factor in the market. Sometimes the market will concentrate on one or two elements and pretty much ignore all others for a short while. It is the job of the trader to identify which factor is of most concern at present and key off that factor for short-term trading. For example, during most of 1982 most market analysts watched the money supply and ignored other indicators. The feeling was that the Federal Reserve was going to dominate the market and that the Fed was making policy decisions based on money growth and inflation rates. Later in the year and early in 1983 the money supply and inflation began to be down-played as other eonomic indicators showed the economy was in a general downward slide and the Fed indicated it was going to pay less attention to the money supply in policy making. Money numbers hardly caused a ripple in this environment.

In summary, watch all the economic factors but try to identify what the market perceives to be the most important at that time. What is most important can be ascertained by reading traders' comments as quoted in the various news media, by consulting your broker, and by watching the market's reaction to indicators as they are released.

The Calendar of New Debt Offerings

All markets move up or down on expectations but eventually the new supply of securities will bring investors and traders down to earth and force the market to a level justified by the fundamental factors. Newly marketed issues are the acid test. Market prices may deviate from equilibrium on a short-term basis but new supply sets the longer term levels. Therefore, new supply is a check point through which a market must move to be accepted by investors as a true indicator of value and price trend. A new issue of bonds that cannot be successfully underwritten at current price levels often will cause a general market decline. This happens because market participants come to realize that they may have miscalculated investor demand.

New and abundant supply by itself is not always an indicator of a forthcoming market decline. A new supply of corporate, municipal, or government bonds sometimes brings investors into an underpriced market. This demand often causes all market participants at both ends of the yield curve to reassess value and the whole market to move higher in price.

There are also times even in bull markets when the supply will temporarily overwhelm the economic fundamentals reflecting the state of the economy. In these situations the market will seek a level at which bonds can be sold to the public and temporarily ignore the longer run economic conditions. Eventually the new supply will be underwritten and the market will once again react to the economic fundamentals.

In analyzing the supply side of the equation there are two key questions to keep in mind. First, what is the future supply? Second, which new issues coming to market are the "bellwether" issues that will reflect the general near term price action?

Future Supply

The future supply of new issues can be found every Monday in *The New York Times* and the *Wall Street Journal*. Both of them review the issues scheduled to be brought to market during the coming week and the "street comment" about their likely prices and rates. In addition, both of those papers publish weekly the "visible 30-day supply" of corporate and municipal bonds. (See Table 7.2.)

The regular financing of the U.S. Treasury can be anticipated by watching the newspaper and learning the financing cycles explained in Chapter 11. The amount to be issued is usually estimated by professional market analysts and economists. Their estimates can be found in the daily market news releases. Indication of things to come can be found in the monthly Treasury deficits, as budget deficits play an important role in determining future Treasury supply.

The Federal Reserve of New York publishes data on the amount of commercial paper, bankers acceptances, and certificates of deposit outstanding each week. This information is available as part of the Friday money figures report.

Table 7.2 Forward Visible Supply: 30 Days as of Friday, May 16, 1980 (Source: Courtesy R.H. Wrightson & Associates, Inc.)

Sector	Week ending 5-24	Week ending 5-31	Week ending 6-7	Week ending 6-14	Total
Governments					
Coupons					
Gross issues	—	4000 2-year note	3000 5-year note	—	7000
Maturities	—	(2820)	—	—	(2820)
New money	—	1180	3000	—	4180
Treasury bills	12-month TBs	CMB (6/17)			
Gross issues	7000 + 4000 + 7000	7000	7000	7000	39000
Maturities	(6370) + (2762) + (6564)	—	(6565)	(6592)	(28853)
New money	630 + 1238 + 436	7000	435	408	10147
Agencies	FFCBs		FNMA		
Gross issues	3647	—	1500	—	5147
Maturities	(3047)	—	(1000)	—	(4047)
New money	600	—	500	—	1100
Corporates					
Bonds	125 Mapco 100 Manufacturers Hanover 400 GMAC	300 New England Telephone	100 Wisconsin Tel. 100 Cincinnati G&E 100 Houston P&L	100 Alabama P&L	
	1197	651	340	235	2423
Preferred stock	70	40	—	—	110
Total issues	1267	691	340	235	2533
Municipals					
Negotiated	98 Columbus, Ohio 193 Battery Park 65 Greensboro 100 Silver Bay, MN		79 Lowndes Co. 150 Okla. Hsg.	124 Minn. Hsg.	
	517	13	229	124	883
Competitive	76 Massachusetts 50 Mo. Hsg.	120 California 122 Maryland	300 Oregon 50 Mont. Co., Md.	75 Hawaii 50 Ariz. Dept. Trans.	
	404	370	415	175	1364
Total issues	921	383	644	299	2247
Tax-exempt notes					
Gross issues	41	—	—	—	41
Maturities	(50)	—	—	—	(50)
New money	(9)	—	—	—	(9)

79

Bellwether Issues

Which issue keys the market's near term direction? Often a large utility bond issue or a municipal bond underwriting will set the tone of the market. Sometimes an issue that follows a significant price change will be the crucial test of a market. In short, there are no hard and fast rules for identifying bellwether issues. One needs simply to remain alert to market needs.

In summary, one needs to be aware of the importance of supply in making short-term trading decisions. But be aware also that supply alone usually will not set the long-term market direction. The real overall direction will be determined by a combination of fundamental economic factors affecting demand and supply.

Federal Reserve Information

The Federal Reserve system provides information that is very helpful in analyzing the economy and predicting Federal Reserve activity.

Weekly reports are issued every Friday at 4:15 P.M. EST. These reports contain information on:

- The money supply growth on a one-week lagged basis. It is often instructive to plot the money growth against the Federal Reserve's monthly growth targets. See Figure 7.1 for a sample chart of money supply superimposed on the Federal Reserve's targets. When the growth rate for money violates the target ranges, the Fed frequently takes corrective action and increases or decreases the money supply. This indicator is a fairly reliable predictor of future Federal Reserve policy changes.
- Loan demand, both nationwide and in major money market banks.
- The average rates for Fed funds.
- Dealer positions in Treasury issues.
- The conditions of the Federal Reserve Bank of New York's account.

On Friday afternoons, after 4:15 P.M., the Federal Reserve announces its weekly statistics relating to the money supply and credit. These statistics are carefully watched by all traders because they give indica-

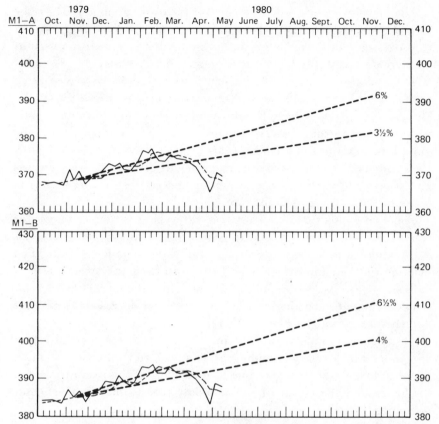

Figure 7.1 Monetary aggregates and the Federal Reserve's long-term growth targets (seasonally adjusted, in billions of dollars).

tions of changes in federal policy and of potential activities the Federal Reserve may need to undertake in order to accomplish its public policy objectives.

Generally, the Fed announces changes in M-1, which measures checking accounts, cash, and other deposits that are readily available for spending, and M-2 and M-3, which measure other deposits and accounts which are less readily available for spending. These weekly money supply figures are annualized to give an indication of whether the Fed is meeting its money supply growth target rates each year.

The Fed also reports on the velocity of turn-over of money. The same level of monetary aggregates in the economy, but a faster rate of turn-over can have similar impact as a constant rate of turn-over but an increase in the total amount of money outstanding.

The Fed also reports level of reserves which the banks are required to maintain at the central bank. Net borrowed reserves result when the banks as an aggregate have to borrow more than they have on deposit with the Fed to meet reserve requirements. Net free reserves is the opposite situation, when banks as an aggregate have more on deposit then they need to meet reserve requirements. These net free reserves give clues as to the Fed's need to enter into securities transactions in order to affect the Fed funds rate.

The Fed funds rate is an interest rate charged among banks for reserves they borrow and lend to each other. It is watched closely as a good indicator of short-term Federal Reserve policy. If the Fed believes the Fed funds rate is getting away from the level it feels is consistent with its reserve policies, it may enter the market and buy or sell government securities in order to increase or decrease the reserves and thereby affect the Fed fund's rate.

The Fed also reports weekly on the total of commercial paper and industrial loans outstanding at financial and nonfinancial institutions. These statistics give one a good idea of the overall demand for credit and the sector of the economy from which that demands is coming.

One of the best sources of fundamental information is the minutes of the Federal Reserve's Open Market Committee monthly meetings. These can be obtained by contacting the Federal Reserve Bank of New York. A most rewarding exercise is to review these minutes by making note of the economic factors the Open Market Committee discussed in their deliberations. After doing this several times you will quickly note how their attention shifts from a certain economic factor one month as a key element in establishing their policy to another factor the next month. With experience the successful market analyst will come to anticipate those factors that are most important to the Fed at any given time.

In summary, the information needed to do good fundamental analysis is vast and complex. It is often advisable to subscribe to a service that presents the information in a timely and orderly fashion.

Treasury Financings and Interest Rates

The Treasury competes in the marketplace for money just like everybody else. The timing of Treasury borrowings, the amount and the maturity of it all have an impact on the demand for money and on the resulting interest rates. Sometimes this impact can be substantial—at other times it may be insignificant. For example, in the fourth quarter of 1982, the Treasury had record borrowings (an annual rate in three months of $230.1 billion, up from $186.8 billion in the previous quarter), yet interest rates fell. A sharp contraction in corporate borrowing as a result of a sharp contraction in economic activity allowed the Treasury to fill its needs without overwhelming the market. Further, investors who had liquid cash bid aggressively in the early auctions for Treasury debt. Evidently, they expected rates to fall and wanted to get the higher rates while they could. That investor activity built on itself and allowed rates to continue falling even as the Treasury auctioned more debt.

The large government deficits are the major reason for large government borrowings. Since the deficits are not expected to decline soon, there is fear that as economic activity begins to build again interest rates will be bid back up as the Treasury competes with business borrowers for the savers' dollars.

The Fed's Credit Guidelines

For anyone interested in understanding interest rate movements, it is a good idea to study the sources and uses of funds in the economy. The Federal Reserve provides a large volume of quarterly information showing the flow of funds in the economy. Generally, the data is adjusted for seasonal variation.

In late 1982 and early 1983, the Federal Reserve moved away from its previous heavy emphasis on the money supply and toward targeting the growth of total credit. The credit guideline is based on the total outstanding debt of all American businesses, individuals, federal, state, and local governments.

This move toward less reliance on the money supply numbers was made necessary by the introduction of new money market accounts,

Super-Now accounts, and other innovations in the financial system. Discrepancies between the growth of the monetary aggregates and the performance of the economy were appearing. The Fed needed another measure of the impact its actions were having, or were likely to have, on the economy. The growth of total credit is closely related to the growth of U.S. economic activity and the relationship has been relatively stable for a couple of decades. Total credit outstanding has hovered near $1.45 for every $1.00 of the economy's GNP. Furthermore, statistical comparisons have shown that both prices and output are as closely related to credit as they are to the supply of money. Lastly, total credit measurements do not get as easily distorted by the introduction of new financial products. New regulations or financial innovations that merely cause borrowers to substitute one form of debt for another leave total credit unaffected.

Despite this, one shouldn't believe that the Fed's new reliance on total credit will necessarily result in a quantum leap in the ability of the Fed to manage monetary affairs. Common sense and recent history caution against relying too heavily on any strict guideline whether it is total credit or the total money supply. Nevertheless, it is useful to have specific policy tools and to have specific objectives related to them, and the available evidence indicates that current movements of total credit do contain information about future business activity.

All of this suggests then that one of the regular statistics an analyst should watch is Federal Reserve credit creation. That can be monitored through the Federal Reserve's balance sheet. That balance sheet is the record of Fed policy. If the Fed is creating credit, its assets expand. If the policy is stand pat or restrictive, its assets hold steady or decline. Weekly Federal Reserve reports net out the activity for the week and show the end result.

In this regard it is also useful to look at how credit flows have generally acted at various stages of the business cycle. A study by Salomon Brothers, a major investment banking house, found that the volume of transactions in various financial markets did indeed respond to the more general expansion and contraction of the trade cycle. They did not, however, march lockstep—up, then down—with the overall cycle.

PART THREE
Cash and Futures Markets for Debt Instruments

CHAPTER EIGHT
Money in the Economy

Money is the grease that makes an economy run smoothly. Imagine the economy of a country as one big machine. This machine represents all the mills, factories, farms, offices, and shops that turn out the goods and services consumed in the society. Everyone with a job works on this big machine. Some are repairmen, some are operators, but all of them are producing goods and services the people use.

Naturally, all of the workers are paid and these workers use their money to buy things produced by the machine. Thus, a nice smooth circle is completed of people working on the machine, being paid by the machine, and buying their goods and services from the machine.

If the people buy all that is produced, then everything is in balance and the economy for this country is healthy and stable. Sometimes, however, imbalances appear and interrupt the smooth flows of labor, money, and goods and services. When this happens, prices change and we get increases or decreases in economic activity.

These imbalances may arise because of leakages in flows of spending by the machine or by the people. For example, people may decide not to spend all of their money on goods and services but may decide instead to *save* some of their income. Thus, they do not buy as many cars and television sets. Since the flow of money back to the machine is reduced, the machine slows down its production. Fewer people are needed to run the machine, and total income and total buying power are reduced. Economists refer to this set of affairs as a recession.

Usually, however, these savings find their way back to the machine through the hands of businessmen who borrow the funds from the people and reinject the money back into the spending flow by increasing the size of the machine, i.e., building plants, buying new equipment and inventory. Depending upon how much of the savings businessmen want from people, they raise or lower the price (interest rate) they are willing to pay people for the use of their money. These activities, which are analogous to modernizing and expanding the machine, create new jobs and increase total income, thus bringing the flows of spending back toward a balance.

A second imbalance, or drain on the flows, can be caused by taxes collected by the government. Taxes are paid to local, state, and national governments and have the same slowdown effect that savings have. However, just as with savings, the tax money finds its way back into the system because the government hires people and buys goods and services.

Just as increases in savings and taxes can create imbalances in the system through withdrawals, imbalances can also be created by people refusing to save and simply demanding more goods and services from the government. The government can either refuse the demands or pay for them by raising taxes or by printing money which is then given to the machine in payment for the goods and services. Refusing the demands and raising taxes are not always popular with the people; hence, governments frequently opt to print more money. Frequently, this is more money than is necessary to keep the machine running smoothly. In order to meet this output, the machine foregoes repairs and hires untrained workers. All the income is used to produce goods to meet current demand and none is used for expanding, rebuilding and updating the machine. This results in reduced efficiency. Ultimately, costs increase and the machine reaches the limits that it can produce. To alleviate this, consumers need to be convinced to postpone their purchases. This is best done by raising prices. This is referred to as inflation. Hence, when too much money gets into the system, the result is inflation.

MONEY, THE MACHINE, AND THE BANKING SYSTEM

It should be obvious from the above that if the flows of money spending match the flows of goods and services, prices will remain stable and the machine will run smoothly. If imbalances in flows of money occur, the machine slows down or works at such a furious pace it generates more momentum than it can handle. Thus, the amount of money and the smoothness with which it flows from individuals back to the machine through the land, labor and capital become most important in determining the health of an economy.

In order to make this all flow smoothly in an economy, every country has a banking system through which they facilitate the flow of funds and adjust the supply of money. Banks serve as depositories for people's savings. They act as intermediaries by making these savings available to businessmen for investment expenditures and the vital function of furnishing business and government with credit. Through their lending function, banks are able to adjust the money supply to make the flow of spending match the flows of goods and services, land, labor, and capital.

Naturally, most governments do not allow banks to operate willy-nilly in this system. Instead, the governments establish a Central Bank which acts to regulate the actions of commercial banks and to manipulate the expansion and contraction of the money supply. Thus, the ultimate control of the money supply rests with the government.

In the U.S., the Federal Reserve Board, through its network of regional federal reserve banks, acts as the Central Bank. Its methods of operation differ only in degree from Central Banks of other countries. The Fed operates to control the money supply by controlling the amount of excess reserves in the banking system. Long ago banks found it prudent to maintain reserves against their deposits in order to meet the normal cash withdrawals of their customers. Current federal law requires them to maintain certain minimum reserves. The amounts over and above the minimums needed are called "excess" and are funds available for lending. The Fed controls excess reserves by:

1. Adjusting the required ratio of reserves to deposits. By lowering the required reserve ratio, the Federal Reserve decreases the amount of reserves that member banks are required to maintain in their accounts and makes additional reserves available to the member banks. Thus, a reduction in the required reserve ratio from 12% to 10% would increase the amount of excess reserves and thereby increase the amount of money available for lending. By raising the required ratio, the opposite would occur.

2. The purchase or sale of government securities, T-bills, bonds, and

so on. When the government buys the securities, it pays money to the banks which increases member bank reserves, and vice versa when the government sells.

3. Lending reserves to member banks.

A commercial bank may be short on reserves relative to its demand for loans and may then borrow from the Federal Reserve. The bank will pay a rate of interest known as the discount rate. The Fed can set the discount rate at whatever level it wants. By raising this rate of interest, borrowing is made more expensive and commercial banks will be less inclined to borrow reserves. They will have to raise the rate of interest to customers, and as the price of credit to customers goes up, usually the demand for such credit will go down. Conversely, by reducing the discount rate, borrowing is made less expensive and banks will be more inclined to borrow reserves and make loans to their customers.

Thus, the Central Bank of the government acts to regulate the actions of the commercial banks and thereby to regulate the supply of money to accomplish specific objectives related to levels of employment, personal income, and price stability.

The extent to which the Central Bank accomplishes these objectives has a great influence on interest rates.

REPOS

"The Fed is doing Repos." Traders hear or read these words daily or at least weekly.

Anybody who trades interest rate futures needs to become familiar with the Federal Reserve's daily activities to affect interest rates. One of these activities is buying and selling securities and doing it through "Repos."

A "repo" is short for a "repurchase agreement." A repurchase agreement is a transaction that involves the sale of a security, usually U.S. Governments, with the simultaneous commitment by the seller that, after a stated period of time, he will repurchase the security from the original buyer for the purchase price plus an agreed rate of return on the original value. It is a short-term loan.

The repo provides the temporary seller of securities with a source of borrowed funds that can be used to finance an inventory or cover a deficit cash position. An exception to this is the Fed. When the Fed is said to be doing repos (RPs), it is lending money, that is, increasing bank reserves.

The opposite of a repo is a reverse repo which is a purchase-resell agreement. It consists of the purchase of a security, usually a U.S. Government security, with the simultaneous commitment by the buyer that, after a stated period of time, he will resell the security to the original seller for the original price plus an agreed rate of return. Reverses are used by dealers to borrow securities they have shorted. Again an exception is the Fed. When it is said to be "doing reverses," it is borrowing money; that is, absorbing or decreasing reserves.

In short, a repo is executed by a temporary seller of securities or the borrower of funds while a reverse repo is executed by the temporary buyer of the securities or the lender of funds.

Federal Reserve's Role

One of the ways the Fed controls excess reserves is by the purchase or sale of government securities (T-bills, bonds, and so on). When the government buys securities, it puts more money in the member bank reserves. When it sells securities, it collects money from the bank, thus reducing member bank reserves and the supply of money available for lending.

If the money market is temporarily tight (demand for loans high relative to the supply of loanable funds) and the Fed needs to supply reserves to the banking system, the Federal Reserve Bank of New York may agree to enter into repurchase contracts with non-bank government securities dealers. These agreements, which are usually made at the discount rate and only at the initiative of the Federal Reserve, are an important complement to regular purchases and sales of government securities in the open market. They are particularly useful when reserves are needed only for a few days.

In such a case, the Federal Reserve may make repurchase agreements scheduled to mature when reserves will probably be more readily available. This procedure makes it unnecessary to buy outright a large block of securities one day and sell them the next or in the very near future. Normally, the "bewitching hours" for the Fed activity is late morning or early afternoon (EST).

Influence on Rates

Repos also have been used by the Federal Reserve when it is making an effort to keep short-term rates up for balance of payments reasons. Their use avoids the direct downward pressure exerted on bill rates when the system buys short-term government securities outright. When repos are used, dealers know that the reserve injection is not permanent and will be reversed shortly.

In the mid-1960s, the Federal Reserve system initiated the practice of using reverse repos to withdraw reserves on a temporary basis. Analogous to the case of the repo, the reverse repo is thought to exert less upward pressure on interest rates than an outright sale, primarily because the technique provides dealers and other market participants with the knowledge that the reserve absorption is only temporary.

The Federal Reserve usually sets a target for the interest rate it calls the Federal funds rate. That's the rate banks charge each other for the overnight loan of reserves. Sometimes the Fed funds rate fluctuates widely within a single trading day. For example, some days the Fed funds rate has fluctuated by as much as 100%. This sort of volatility frequently occurs on Wednesdays. Wednesday is an important day of the week for Fed watchers because it's the last day for banks to meet their reserve requirements for the latest statement week. Hence there are sometimes last minute scrambles for funds. Traders usually ignore the funds rate on Wednesdays.

The volatility may also be due to technical factors. For example, a few years ago during a particularly volatile period, the Fed had been buying securities to add reserves and keep the funds rate close to its target. When the market became volatile, the Fed announced that it planned to add reserves by buying government securities temporarily through four-day and seven-day "repurchase agreements." This had the desired effect on the market of stabilizing the Fed funds rate by providing the needed reserves for the banks. Traders knew, however, that by the following week those securities would be sold back and reserves would be reduced again. Thus, upward pressure was being maintained on interest rates.

The Federal Reserve did not invent repos. Indeed, it was a reaction by the banks to Federal Reserve regulations that resulted in banks developing the repurchase agreements. Repo agreements involving U.S. Treasury and federal agency securities have become the fastest growing source of discretionary funds to commercial banks. The repo interest rate is to a large extent the marginal cost of funds for a bank.

Today many commercial banks regard repos as one of a number of alternative sources of funds that may be used to finance their securities portfolios or their lending activities. The rate paid by commercial banks generally ranges from 10–15 basis points below the Federal funds rate but may vary depending upon the availability of securities.

Corporate Users

The government and banks are not the only ones involved in repos.

A repo can be used by a corporation to temporarily provide cash in lieu of issuing commercial paper, liquidating investments in adverse markets, or borrowing from banks.

One of the reasons for the growing volume of repos done by business corporations has been the recent development of sophisticated cash management techniques. Corporate cash management involves procedures designed to speed the receipt of income and delay disbursement of payments, and reduce the uncertainty about daily cash flow patterns, thus permitting businesses to hold only a minimum amount of funds without explicit interest return.

These procedures have resulted in a more efficient use of corporate funds and have served greatly to increase the availability of funds for investment in money market assets. Corporate treasurers have increasingly used repos as an attractive alternative to maintaining surplus funds in noninterest earning demand deposits.

Repos may be tailored to any short-term maturity and are relatively free of risk. In addition, like money market assets in general, repos may be used not only to invest temporary excess cash but also to earn interst on funds being accumulated for tax or dividend payments and on the proceeds of long-term financing temporarily awaiting disbursement.

In summary, Federal Reserve activity in the cash market is very important to anyone trading interest rate futures. One of the ways the Fed affects interest rates on a daily or even intraday basis is through the purchase or sale of repos.

Fed activity in the market depends very much on how closely the market rate for Federal funds reflects the Fed's target rate for Fed funds and whether the Fed believes any deviation of the market rate from the target is of a temporary or longer run nature. If Fed officials believe it is temporary, they are more likely to use repos as their method of entering the market; if they do use repos, you know that their activity and impact will be reversed in a day or so.

INFLATION AND INTEREST RATES

Inflation rates become important in forecasting interest rate levels because the expectations about levels of inflation get built into the price for borrowing money. Look at it this way. Four years ago the dollar would buy a newspaper, a gallon of milk, and a package of gum. Inflation (rising prices) has caused the domestic purchasing power of the dollar to decline so that today it takes two dollars to buy the same amount and quality of goods. So, if you loaned someone a dollar ten years ago and if the average annual rate of inflation was 10%, when he pays it back today it is worth only about half as much as when you loaned it to him. If you had charged him 5% per year interest, you would have collected $.50 in interest and, counting that, would find your dollar worth only about three-fourths as much as ten years ago.

Had you anticipated the 10% average annual inflation rate, you would have asked for at least a 10% interest charge in order to maintain your purchasing power over the ten-year period. More likely you would have asked for 15% interest, reasoning that you expect money to provide a 5% real rate of return after accounting for the 10% expected inflation. It is this latter way that businessmen and bankers react. Thus, expected inflation rates get built into interest rates. That is what has happened in recent years.

The Inflationary Process

Monetary economists trace the inflationary process through as follows. First, a change in the rate of the growth in the money supply causes a change in people's incomes in the same direction about six to nine months later. This money "burns a hole in the pocket" and people rush out trying to spend their extra income. It usually takes about another six to nine months before this increased demand catches up with the available supply and prices start to rise. Thus, about a year to a year and a half after the money supply increases, one can expect to see a rise in prices. The CPI reflects the general prices of things people buy and thus it becomes the most handy means of measuring inflation. The extent to which the money supply is increased, of course, will affect the extent to which incomes increase, which in turn will affect the amount of money people have to spend and their ability to bid up prices. So a small change in the money supply beyond the amount necessary to maintain economic growth, employment, and stable prices will probably result in small amounts of inflation.

CHAPTER NINE
Yield Curves

Some months ago a young man fresh out of college walked into the office of an older gentleman who was revered for his knowledge of the government securities market. The young man nervously explained that he had become interested in the T-bill futures market and wanted to learn how to trade them. How, he asked the older gentleman, should he learn to identify opportunities?

The old gentleman sat and looked at the floor and said nothing. The young man began to feel embarrassed. Just as he was about to repeat his question, fearing the old fellow hadn't heard him or had forgotten it already, the old gentleman looked up and said, "Study yield curves!"

The young man rose, thanked him and left feeling disappointed. Nine months and $25,000 of profit later, the young man realized how valuable the old man's advice had been. For indeed, the yield curve reveals all.

LOOK AT RETURN

If you want to do an intelligent job trading the interest rate futures market, spend your time studying the yield curve.

In the financial instruments market, yield refers to the annual rate of return on an investment. It is determined by interrelating the interest rate, the price paid, and the remaining life of the investment.

For example, if you loan someone $100 for one year at 7% interest, the yield on that investment is 7%. If you paid $100 for a $100, 8%

97

bond that matured in one year, the yield would be 8%. But the picture in bonds, or any other debt instrument competitively bought or sold in the marketplace, is complicated by the fact that their prices change. If you bought the same $100, 8% bond for say, $95, the yield would be 13.26%, or the sum of the 8% coupon rate and 5.26% (5/95 = 0.0526). Yield adjusted in this way for market price and time to maturity is called "yield to maturity." This is the figure to be plotted on the yield curve.

Yields become important because they reflect interest rates in various money market investments. These interest rates reflect powerful linkages that connect the money market, the bond market, the stock market, the mortgage market, and the commodity markets. Money moves rapidly from one market to another, seeking its best return. That return is reflected in the yield.

A "yield curve" refers to the shape of a line you get when you plot yields of various Treasury securities or any other homogeneous group of securities against their various maturities. Normally, you plot maturity dates or time on the horizontal scale and yields on the vertical scale of the graph as in the accompanying illustrations.

When a number of issues are plotted on the graph, you will see that a sort of pattern emerges from the placement of the dots. Draw a line through the dots so that most of them fall on the line. Those that don't should be nearly evenly distributed on either side of the line. Now you have a yield curve picture.

To demonstrate, consider the data in Table 9.1, which reflects the yields for government bonds and notes of various maturities. Figure 9.1 is the yield curve plotted from that data.

THE STUDY OF YIELD CURVES

There are several major reasons that one should study yield curves. First, it causes one to focus attention on the cash market, something too few futures traders do. Cash market activity provides clues to price relationships in the futures market. Second, study of yield curves focuses attention on the concepts of value, undervalue, and overvalue. The yield curve becomes a general standard by which to measure individual value. As the reader can readily see in Figure 9.1, not all the dots fall on the "curve." Those that do not fall on it are candidates to be

Table 9.1 Yields for Government Bonds and Notes

Maturity Date	Yield
June 1983	8.57%
Sept. 1983	8.85%
Dec. 1983	9.08%
March 1984	9.16%
June 1984	9.33%
June 1985	9.86%
May 1985	7.33%
May 1986	10.13%
May 1987	10.46%
May 1988	10.13%
Jan. 1989	10.76%
May 1990	10.05%
May 1995	10.57%
May 2001	11.07%
May 2003	10.85%
May 2011	11.00%

investigated as possible buy/sell opportunities. Because of the inverse yield/price relationship in fixed-income securities, those represented by dots above the lines are relatively underpriced while those below the line are relatively overpriced. For example, the May 1988 note seems to be overpriced, offering a lower yield than adjacent issues. On the other hand, the May 1987 note seems to be slightly underpriced, providing a slightly higher yield than adjacent issues.

Why the Difference?

Variations of this kind can usually be explained by several factors:

1. Differences in coupon rates. For example, the May 1985 note carries a coupon of 3.25%, one of the lowest of any outstanding Treasury issue.
2. Difference in the supply of or demand for a particular issue. The May 1985 bond, for example, is in short supply. It is what is called

Figure 9.1   Yield curve.

a "flower bond," which merely means it is eligible to be used to settle estate taxes at full value. There are only a few such issues around, yet the demand for them remains high. Thus, their price gets bid up and the yield falls.
3. Differences in the marketability of issues. Trading in some issues is naturally more liquid than in others. Generally, short-term issues have much more liquidity than long-term issues.
4. Risks that the general level of interest rates will change in adverse direction.

The Changing Shape of the Yield Curve

It is not enough to know what yield curves are and how they are derived. One also needs to know why they take on the shapes they do.

As noted previously, the so-called "normal" yield curve is an upward sloping curve to the right, reflecting lenders' demands for higher rates of return to compensate them for tying up their money for longer periods, as in Figure 9.2a.

In the normal yield curve the near-term rates are thus lower than far-term rates. Money market economists refer to this as a "positive carry" market. One can borrow short-term and lend long-term at higher rates. Sometimes however, the curve takes on a flat look, as in Figure 9.2b, where rates are fairly even across the time spectrum.

Sometimes the world gets turned topsy-turvy and short-term yields are above long-term yields as in Figure 9.3a. This is referred to as a "negative carry" market.

And sometimes yield curves become humped, as in Figure 9.3b,

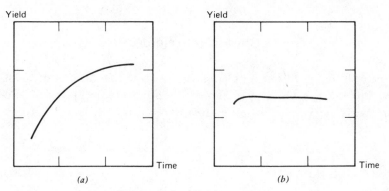

Figure 9.2   Yield curves.

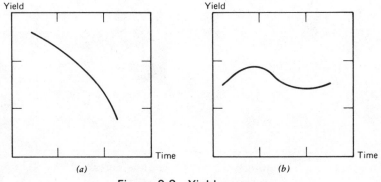

Figure 9.3   Yield curves.

where the short-term rates rise sharply at first, then fall sharply to a point where the curve for long-term rates becomes flat.

What does all this mean? Simply that knowing and understanding the yield curve, the shapes it takes on, and what those shapes mean can provide some trading ideas. For example, in the fall of 1979 the yield curve in the cash bond market was humped. It looked something like the curve depicted in Figure 9.4.

That information, and the belief that in the long run it will return to a normal curve, leads to a logical trading strategy, namely, a spread between long-term and short-term rates in which you buy the short-term instruments and sell the long-term instruments. If the yield curve does indeed return to normal, this strategy is almost sure to be profitable. However, the risk in such a strategy is that the yield curve will become more inverted. If such would be the case the losses could be great.

A Shift in the Yield Curve

Not only do yield curves change shape, but they also shift from one level to another. Curve A in Figure 9.5 shows a hypothetical yield curve for May. Curve B shows the same curve a month later, in June.

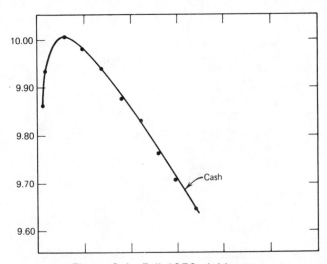

Figure 9.4   Fall 1979 yield curve.

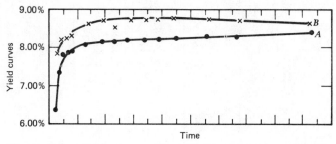

Figure 9.5   Yield curves: May 25 (*A*) versus June 30 (*B*).

At a glance, you can tell that two things occurred. First, the curve has shifted upward; second, it has flattened out somewhat.

The upward shift of the curve reflects higher yields across the board. Interest rates rose between May 25 and June 29.

The flattening out of the yield curve indicates that short-term rates rose more than long-term rates. Graphically, this is shown by the narrowing of the space between the curves for the distant maturities. Had all rates risen equally, the distance between the lines would be equal.

An easier way to see this is shown in Table 9.2. The data in column 5 represent the change in the rate between the dates. Notice that the differences get progressively smaller as the time to maturity gets longer.

Yield Curve Lessons

There are several very basic and very important lessons to be learned from this relative change in the yield curve.

First, if you were long the bonds in the sample porfolio shown in Table 9.2, you lost money. Their value or price went down as their yield went up. If the situation had been reversed and their yields had gone down, you would have made money.

Second, it is "normal" (if there is such a word any more) for short-term rates to be more volatile than long-term rates. Hence, the fact that long-term rates did not move up as much as the short-term rates is not unusual.

Third, although long-term rates are generally not as volatile as short-term rates, *prices* on long-term issues are more volatile than on short-

Table 9.2 The Impact of a Rate Rise on Sample Portfolio

	Coupon	1 Bid price	2 Yield (May)	3 Bid B	4 Yield (June)	5 Yield change	6 Loss
Bond A 5,000,000 (9-83)	6¼	99.18	7.33%	99.18	7.73%	+40	0
Bond B 5,000,000 (4-84)	6's	98.15	7.77%	98.12	8.13%	+36	$ 4,687.50
Bond C 5,000,000 (5-88)	7's	95.30	8.15%	95.40	8.43%	+28	$ 40,625.00
Bond D 1,000,000 (5-89)	3¼	76.12	7.48%	76.22	7.68%	+20	$ 6,250.00
Bond E 5,000,000 (5-90)	8¼	98.22	8.36%	97.80	8.57%	+21	$ 75,000.00
Bond F 5,000,000 (2-06)	7⅞	93.20	8.49%	92.10	8.65%	+16	$ 65,625.00
							$192,187.50

term issues. Long-term issues show greater swings in prices than short-term issues for the same change in rates.

Perhaps the best way to show the relationship is to consider a bond with one year to run paying a 6% coupon. par, it will be priced at $100. If you assume that the yield rises to 7%, the price of the $100 bond issue will drop to $99.05 (i.e., 99²⁄₃₂). If the yield falls to 5%, its price moves up to $100.95 (100.30+/32).

Thus, a swing of 1% either way in yield equals approximately one percentage point in price. The reason it doesn't equal exactly 1% is because of the effect of compounding (interest earned on interest) the coupon payment.

Now, if you assume the bond is a five-year issue instead of a one-year issue a 1% change in yield (i.e., moving from 6 to 7%) results in a price fall to $95.84 (99²⁷⁄₃₂). The change in price approaches but doesn't equal (again because of compounding effects) five percentage points, which would be expected by multiplying the one-year results by five years. In other words, a five-year bond will rise or fall in price almost five times as much as a one-year bond in response to the same change in yield.

The principle can also be shown with 90-day T-bills. Bills are traded on a discount basis and, unlike bonds, do not carry a coupon. A 1% change in price results in a 1% change in yield in the opposite direction for a T-bill with 360 days to maturity. Therefore, a $1,000,000 T-bill with 360 days to maturity changes in value by $100 for every 0.01% change in yield.

If a bill has only 90 days to run, it changes in value by only $25:

$$\left(\frac{90}{360} = \frac{1}{4} \quad \frac{\$100}{4} = \$25 \right)$$

On a six-month or 180–day bill, .01% change in yield equals $50 change in price:

$$\left(\frac{180}{360} = \frac{1}{2} \quad \frac{\$100}{2} = \$50 \right)$$

Although the rationale behind the above principle may be hard to grasp simply remember that interest rates and value (price) of the instrument move in opposite directions. Because that is true, the following rules of thumb should be followed in trading a portfolio:

1. If interest *rates* are *rising,* try to keep your cash portfolio position in *short*-term issues because the *price* fall will be less for each 1% change in yields than will be the case with long-term issues.
2. If interest *rates* are *falling,* try to keep your cash portfolio position in *longer*-term issues because the *price* rise will be greater for the long-term issues than for short-term issues.

Real-Time Use

From these fundamental rules for trading the cash portfolio, the natural question is: If I expect long-term rates to rise, how could I use the futures market to shorten the maturity of my portfolio.

The answer: Sell the futures to hedge the long-term issue bonds and reduce their exposure to price erosion. Thus, any reduction in the price of the portfolio bonds will be offset by a gain in the futures. Further, by keeping the long-term bonds in the portfolio, you will continue to get the coupons. Any new money coming in during the month could be put in short-term issues.

How would such a strategy work out?

Assume you have a small portfolio with the maturities shown in Table 9.3.

In short, if you had not hedged but simply held your portfolio, you would have lost $140,625 in value. By hedging, you cut that loss by $82,762. You accomplished the same results as if you had shortened your maturities, and you continued to collect the coupons on your portfolio. Most of all, you bought time to roll out of your longer-term issues at a more convenient moment.

Basis Factor

One further and very important point to note in this example is that the basis (difference between price of the cash bonds and price of the futures) declined by 16 points. The value of the cash portfolio fell by more than the value of the futures. Futures had anticipated the rate rise so cash prices had to catch up. Gains and losses between the futures position and the cash position would have been exactly equal, if they

Table 9.3 Hedging a Bond Portfolio

	Cash	Basis		Futures
May 25	Bid price of Bond E 8¼ = 98.22 to yield 8.36% Bid price of Bond F 7⅞ = 93.20 to yield 8.49%	2.23	May 25	Sold 100 T-bond contracts for December delivery at 93-14 to yield 8.698%
June 30	Bid price of Bond E 8¼ = 97.6 to yield 8.57% Bid price of Bond F 7⅞ = 92.10 to yield 8.65%	2.70	June 30	Bought 100 T-bond contracts for December delivery at 92-17 to yield 8.800% Gain 29 basis points $90,625

Loss May 1990s = 48 basis points
Loss February 2006s = 42 basis points
 Loss $140,625
Transaction costs: Basis loss 16 points = $50,000

Commissions 100 contracts at $70 each =	$7,000
Interest on margin $1,000/contract at 9.00% for 35 days =	863
Total	$7,863

Net reduction in portfolio loss from transaction = $82,762

had moved by the same amount. Note also that the weighting factor (see Chapter 11) used here was 1 to 1 because the coupons and maturities were about equal in both the cash and futures markets.

THE FUTURES YIELD CURVE

Just as you can develop a yield curve for the issues traded in the cash market, you can also develop a yield curve for the futures market. Indeed, as noted in Chapter 1, a major economic contribution made by the futures market is added information. This is most obviously evident in the futures yield curve. The process of constructing the futures yield curve is similar to that for constructing the cash market yield curve. The obvious major difference is that one uses data from the different futures contracts; that is, the 90-day T-bill contract, the 10-year T-note contract, the GNMA contract, and the T-bond contract. Just as in constructing the cash yield curve, one needs to put them all on a bond equivalent basis, and one needs to select issues of comparable quality and credit worthiness.

The futures yield curve shifts and changes shape just like the cash market curve. It will sometimes anticipate changes in the cash market. At other times, it follows or moves in loose concurrence with the cash market changes. It is important that one use the same contract months for each of the futures instruments, because each different futures month represents a different future time period and therefore a different expectance curve. If one mixed different delivery months (say, June and December) in the same yield curve, one would be mixing apples with oranges by comparing the expected structure of interest rates in June with the expected structure of interest rates in December.

The Strip Curve

As noted above, the existence of futures markets provides a whole new set of yield curves, reflecting *expected* rates. But it also allows the development of a third yield curve called the "strip curve." The strip curve provides another benchmark of value.

By definition, the "strip" is simply a series of successive T-bill futures contracts. For example, if you were to purchase the December, March, June, and September futures contracts, you would own a one-year strip.

In actuality, ownership of that strip is the same as owning a 12-month T-bill, because the series of futures provides the rights to purchase a 90-day T-bill every three months, and the four separate bills cover a total maturity span of 12 months.

To obtain that coverage, you simply take delivery of the December futures, thus receiving a bill in December that matures in March. Money from the maturing March bill is then used to take delivery of the March futures and receive another 90-day bill maturing in June, and so on.

The Strip as a Measure of Value

Knowing the value of the strip provides a benchmark against which to measure the value of a number of other alternative investments. To take another example, suppose the Treasury is auctioning one-year bills and you are considering entering the auction. You can compare the price you would need to pay in the auction with the price you can get by buying the nearby cash bill plus three consecutive futures, and select the better alternative.

To illustrate, assume on October 2, you could have purchased a two-year Treasury note and obtained a yield of 8.71%. Assume also that the values for the individual futures contracts were as shown below. On that same day a strip of futures contracts covering approximately two years would have yielded 8.97%, or 0.26% more.

Cash bill maturing December	7.95
December futures	8.52[1]
March futures	8.66
June futures	8.75
September futures	8.82
December futures	8.87
March futures	8.92
June futures	8.97

A major advantage of the strip over the two-year note, however, is that you are completely flexible on the front end of the strip. Since you are always carrying an actuals position at the front end of the strip, you can move from T-bills to CDs to bank acceptances to Fed funds or to whatever instrument will provide the best short-term yield while keeping the latter part of the strip intact with the "locked-in" yield. That flexibility provides the opportunity to increase the yield over the two-year period to more than 8.97%.

To put it another way, the yield floor with the strip is 8.97%. The ultimate yield could be much higher, depending on your ability to maximize the return on the "actuals" part of the strip.

Compounding Factor

The value of the strip is more than the average of each of the successive futures because of the effect of compounding the interest. Each time a T-bill matures, the interest earned during the life of that T-bill is

[1]This yield includes the yield of both the cash bill and the yield to maturity of the bill deliverable on that futures.

available for reinvestment during the next quarter. This "interest-on-interest" increases the total return of the T-bill strip. The yield curves for both cash bills and for futures are therefore best compared if converted to bond equivalents first.

There are, of course, some risks associated with this strategy. If rates change significantly, you could receive margin calls on the open futures positions. The opportunity cost of such calls needs to be considered.

Further, if you move from one cash instrument to another, transaction costs could get to be expensive. Last, if short-term rates on the cash instrument increase rapidly while the longer-term futures remain unchanged or go down, you could get caught rolling from an instrument with a higher rate to one of a lower rate.

To use this strategy, you need to monitor the markets continuously and be able to make calculations instantaneously. Such opportunities, although regularly available, are not available all the time. It is not unusual to find a strip more favorable than the actual for a two-year investment and, simultaneously, the reverse for a one-year investment.

The message here is quite simple: Learn to understand the yield curve for futures as well as the yield curve for the actuals. Once you learn that, you will have the beginnings of a standard of value. The standard of value then becomes the means of identifying profit opportunities.

The Economy and the Shape of the Yield Curve

The yield curve changes shape as monetary and fiscal policy change and as the economy moves through the business cycle. For example, in the spring of 1982 the yield curve was inverted (short-term rates were higher than longer term rates). But the widely advertised recession of 1982 had begun.

So for those of us interested in trading interest rate futures, the important issue is: What will the realization of the recession mean to interest rate levels and relationships? How will the yield curve change?

A slowdown in economic activity should result in a decrease in the demand for short-term loans to finance consumer purchases. Consumer expenditures account for two-thirds of the GNP. In a recession, particularly in an economy where high oil and and gasoline prices hurt new car sales, overall retail sales fall. Consumers find themselves in a tighter and tighter squeeze between income growth and the cost of living. As consumer spending falls businesses begin reducing inventories. Unemployment starts to climb, putting an even further squeeze on consumer income. Inflation and the burden of past debts cause most consumers to cut back even more and to be very cautious in making major purchases such as automobiles, homes, major appliances, and other durable goods. All of this will tend to reduce the demand for short-term loans. Consequently, in such a situation one should expect a fall in short-term interest rates. Inflation and expectations about continued inflation may keep intermediate and longer term interest rates from falling as much as short-term rates.

As an economic slowdown becomes apparent, one should expect to see two basic changes in the yield curve. First, the inversion of short-term rates above long-term rates should disappear. A normally shaped, upward-sloping yield curve should reappear. Second, the overall level of the yield curve structure should fall. In a time when the economy is on the upswing and at the beginning of a new business cycle one would expect the yield curve to be normally shaped. Money should be relatively easy. Short-term rates should be below long-term rates. Consumers income should be expanding and the proportion of consumers income needed to support consumer debt should be declining. Consumers should find they are able to increase their purchases through borrowed money, and businesses should expand their production to meet the new demand.

As the borrowing pressure builds and inflation begins to creep up, one should expect that short-term interest rates will rise and the yield curve will flatten out. Ultimately, as tighter money policies take effect and the business cycle matures, the yield curve will invert again.

Movement Along the Yield Curve Versus Different Yield Curve Level

The yield curve represents a snapshot at a single point in time of the yields on debt instruments ranging in maturity from a few days to many years. Thus, points along the yield curve represent the yields of different instruments. The yield curve for, say, 90-day T-bill futures does not represent movement along the yield curve but rather the same debt instrument at the same maturity point on a yield curve for different dates in the futures. Thus, the futures prices for different months

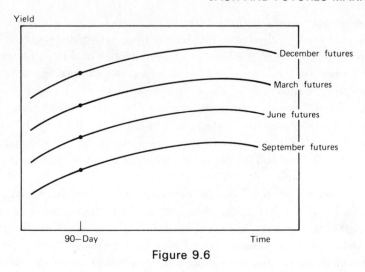

Figure 9.6

represent a moving picture of today's expected yield for a single issue
with a given maturity at some future time period. When one takes all
the different instruments (e.g., T-bills, T-bonds, T-notes, etc.) traded on
futures contracts and lines up the individual snapshots for any particular delivery month, one develops today's market expectations of the
yield curve.

The purchase of December T-bill futures versus the sale of March
Treasury bill futures represents a difference in the expected level of the
yield curve. Basically the December and the March futures contracts
represent precisely the same time point on two different expected yield
curves—December as opposed to March.

CHAPTER TEN

The U.S. Treasury and Debt Instruments

As noted in Chapter 8 the government may create imbalances in the economy through excessive spending. The government pays for the goods and services it obtains by raising taxes or by borrowing from the people through the sale of various debt securities. These debt instruments are created by the Treasury Department and various government agencies. Collectively, the U.S. government is the largest borrower of money in the economy and the Treasury is the single most important issuer of debt.

To finance the huge U.S. national debt the Treasury issues several types of securities. Those of most interest for this exposition are T-bills, T-notes, and T-bonds.

TREASURY BILLS

T-bills are U.S. debt securities with a maturity of one year or less. They are direct obligations of the U.S. Treasury and are sold to investors through the Federal Reserve System acting as agent for the U.S. Treasury. T-bills do not bear interest. Instead, they are sold at a discount to par and are redeemed at face value at maturity. The difference between the discounted selling price and the par or face value received at maturity comprises the yield or the interest earned. Thus, the amount of the discount and the length of time the bills have to maturity implies a specific annualized yield on the bill if held until maturity. For example, a 90-day bill sold for $977,250 would yield 9%.

T-bills are good indicators of money market conditions. They are widely held by many different types of investors. The economic factors that affect their prices also affect the prices of other money market instruments. Their price movements are closely correlated with commercial paper, bankers acceptances, certificates of deposit, discount notes of the Federal National Mortgage Association (FNMA), Federal Home Loan Bank (FHLB), and Federal Farm Credit (FFC), agencies, and, to a lesser extent, the prime rate.

T-bills are currently issued in three-month, six-month, and one-year maturities. The bills are issued by the U.S. Treasury Department and the discount is established through an auction held by the Federal Reserve each Monday afternoon, with the bills going to those bidders offering the highest price; that is, the lowest interest cost to the Treasury. This auction technique allows the Treasury to let the prevailing market conditions establish the yield with each new bill issue sold.

The Auction

As mentioned, the Federal Reserve banking system acts as the agent for the Treasury in the auction. All bids must be submitted to a Federal Reserve bank by 1:30 P.M. (New York time) on the day of the auction.

The U.S. Treasury accepts two types of bids in their bill auctions— competitive bids and noncompetitive bids. Competitive bids are submitted by money market banks, dealers, or other institutions who buy large quantities of bills. They express their bids as discounted prices on the basis of par (one hundred). For example, a dealer who wants to buy three-month bills may pay a price of 96.199, equivalent to a yield of 15.037% on a discount basis.

Large investors who submit competitive tenders usually wait until the last minute before submitting their bids. They survey the various primary dealers to get the latest "feel" for the market. Just before the deadline they phone in their final prices and quantities to an agent who is in close proximity to a Federal Reserve branch. That agent has the customer's forms already filled out and signed. The agent inserts the prices and amounts and runs the bid into the Federal Reserve bank at the very last moment. Only the agile stand at the front door of a Federal Reserve bank at 1:29 EST on a Monday.

Noncompetitive bids emanate from agencies of the U.S. government, the Federal Reserve banks, and small investors who are generally not prepared to make the precise calculations required by the competitive bids. The minimum denomination is $10,000 and the absolute maximum is $500,000. In the sequence of awarding bids, a sufficient amount of the issue is set aside at the start of the auction to fulfill the noncompetitive awards first. All noncompetitive awards are made at the average price of the auction. Governments and Federal Reserve banks who make noncompetitive bids are awarded their bids in full. Noncompetitive tenders by private investors are then accepted in multiples of $5,000 (above $10,000) up to the individual limit permitted. The remainder of the issue is then allocated among competitive bidders, beginning with those who bid the highest and ranging down in price until the total amount is issued. The lowest price accepted by the Treasury is called the "stop-out" price. If there are a number of bids that have been entered at the "stop-out" price, the Treasury may award each of the bidders a proportionate share of the amount requested.

After the auction is completed, the amount and price range of accepted bids are announced and the bidders are advised of the acceptance or rejection of their tenders. Competitive bidders pay their bid price while the noncompetitive bidders pay the weighted average price of the accepted competitive bids.

As noted above, at these weekly auctions the Treasury sells bills with 90- and 180-day maturities. Thus, not only is the Treasury selling new bills every week, but it also has bills maturing as a result of auctions held 90 and 180 days previously.

Three- and Six-Month Treasury Bill Cycles. T-bills originally sold with 180 days to maturity eventually become 90-day bills. Thus, the auctioning of new 90-day bills is in a sense a "reopening" of the old 180-day bill auction. The Treasury reopens that auction in order to adjust more closely its need for funds during the next 90 days. Knowing that the U.S. Treasury has a six-month cycle in its issuing of bills, with the opportunity for reopening that issue as time passes, is important in evaluating the potential deliverable supply of bills for a futures contract. Since the 180-day bills will ultimately become 90-day bills available for delivery on the futures contract, one can track the potentially deliverable supply of T-bills 90 days prior to settlement. The supply of 90-day bills available to satisfy futures contracts includes the newly issued bills as well as the old 180-day T-bills auctioned 90 days earlier.

The One-Year Bill Cycle.   The Treasury does not auction 360-day or one-year bills every week. Instead, the Treasury sells 360-day bills once every 28 days. Unlike the 180-day bills, this group of bills is not reopened before maturity. The 28-day cycle allows for 13 auctions each calendar year.

At one time the 360-day bill was reopened after 90 days and a "nine-month" bill was created. This practice was abandoned several years ago and has not been reinstated.

Cash Management Bills

Cash management bills are sold periodically by the Treasury to smooth out short-term cash flow problems. Generally, these bills are sold in the third and fourth quarter when cash receipts are low and disbursements high. The bills are then paid off in the second quarter when tax receipts are higher. The dates of the maturities for cash management bills usually coincide with three-month maturities and fall just after tax collection dates.

These bills are very similar to the Tax Anticipation Bills (TABs) that were once sold. When the Treasury ceased leaving the proceeds of T-bill sales in Treasury tax and loan accounts at commercial banks, they also stopped selling TABs and began to sell cash management bills.

The Federal Reserve in the Auction

The largest single holder of any maturing bill will almost always be the Federal Reserve Bank of New York and its customers. The Bank's customers are usually foreign monetary authorities. The Bank acts as their agent in making new purchases and in rolling over existing T-bill holdings that are maturing. It is not unusual for this group to control 50% of maturing T-bills.

The amount of bills owned by the Federal Reserve Bank of New York is an important consideration for anyone entering a competitive bid, because it can, through its priority status reduce the bills available to the public by 50%. Further, the Bank may not roll over or replace all the bills they own and are maturing. The Federal Reserve Bank cannot purchase more Bills in the auction than they have maturing.

Sometimes the Bank will use the auction to subtly drain reserves from the banking system by allowing bills to mature and refusing to purchase new bills to replace them; this difference between maturing bills and new purchases must then be bought by the public. When the public pays for the bills, money leaves the commercial banking system and goes into the Treasury's account at the Federal Reserve, where it is effectively withdrawn from circulation. Such activity frequently means that the price of the auctioned bill will be cheaper than would otherwise be the case. So, going into an auction, it is important to know if the Federal Reserve Bank of New York is in a reserve "adding" or "withdrawing" position before the auction.

Evaluating the Auction Results

The day following the auction the Federal Reserve system (Fed) publishes the auction results providing the high, low, and average price; the percent of the total awarded at the lowest price; the amount of the noncompetitive tenders; and the total amount tendered.

The auction results frequently provide clues in advance about the secondary market. Some of the things to watch for are:

1. The size of the noncompetitive tender. A large noncompetitive tender suggests that the investing public, and the Fed, have taken a large portion of the bills and "put them away"; that is, taken them out of the secondary market. A small noncompetitive tender means the dealers may hold a large percentage of the newly auctioned bills, and thus the floating supply is quite large.
2. The auction results compared to the general range of preauction "talk" or expectations. As mentioned previously, there is usually a guesstimate of what prices will be necessary to clear the market in the auction. If the actual results reflect those early estimates, this situation usually indicates a good underwriting from institution buyers. Prices lower than those anticipated prior to the auction usually reflect less institutional interest than ex-

pected. In these situations, dealers underwriting bids will win more bills than anticipated and will increase the supply in the secondary market.

3.   The auction "tail." The tail is the difference between the average price and the lowest price. The difference between the highest price and the average price is usually ignored because it is likely to reflect a misinformed bid. A long tail shows the issue was poorly underwritten and investor interest was not great.

When the difference between the average and lowest accepted bid is less than two basis points, this usually reflects a strong underwriting with aggressive bidding. A tail of more than two basis points suggests the underwriting was weak with no really strong demand. In this latter situation many of the underwriting bids of primary dealers will be hit or awarded, and one should expect that there will be an overabundance of supply when the bill opens for trading in the secondary market.

THE SECONDARY MARKET

Trading Characteristics of the Treasury Bill Market

The trading characteristics of the secondary market for T-bills can best be understood by breaking the market into three distinct sectors—each sector reflective of a different time frame in the life cycle of a bill. Sector 1 of the market represents the one-year bills; i.e., those having seven months to one year to maturity. Sector 2 represents those with a remaining life between three and seven months. And Sector 3 represents those bills with less than three months. (See Figure 10.1) The prices for the bills in each of these categories respond to different factors and key off different points on the yield curve.

Perhaps the best way to explain this process is to follow a one-year bill through its life cycles as it moves from issue to maturity a year later. For purposes of our illustration we will assume a normal, positively sloped yield curve.

Sector 1.   As noted above, section 1 of this yield curve runs from about 180 to 360 days. Thus, this area of the curve reflects the prices, and yields, on the current year bill and all previous year bills auctioned in the past five months.

Once a new 360-day bill begins trading in the secondary market it is quoted on the daily "run." The "run" refers to a quotation of the bid and ask price of the three currently most actively traded bills.

These will almost always be the latest three-month, six-month and one-year bills. Primary dealers automatically quote the "run" as an indication of the relative values of the various sections of the yield curve throughout the trading day. Those bills not on the run are also quoted, but the quotes usually must be requested.

Actively traded bills will trade on 0.02% bid to ask spread, and an "off the run" bill will trade on a 0.04% to 0.10% spread depending on maturity. The average size trade is quite large, with $1,000,000 being the minimum. Five-million-dollar trades are usual and easily transacted without negotiation. Trades of large size are easily transacted with little negotiation and only slight price concessions.

A newly auctioned one-year bill will be actively traded, and quoted on the run for the first month of its life. But after it is 28 days old, a new auction occurs and a new star is born. The new one-year bill replaces the old one on the run. Once no longer quoted actively on the run, that one-year bill begins to trade less actively. This is due partly to the fact that it is no longer on the run, but also because a distribution process takes place and the floating supply in the secondary market decreases rapidly. That bill begins to trade on a yield spread differential to the newest year bill. The spread between the bid and asked price starts to increase.

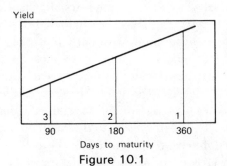

Figure 10.1

Gradually the trading in that bill becomes less influenced by the most recently auctioned one-year bill and begins to fall under the pricing influence of the six-month bills. See section 2 in Figure 10.1. When the bill finally gets into the same month as the newly auctioned six-month bill, it will then begin to trade in direct relation to the current six-month bill.

It is important to keep in mind that bills originally issued as one-year bills are not deliverable on 90-day T-bill futures contracts traded on the IMM. They are deliverable only on the market basket one-year T-bill futures contract traded on the IMM.

Sector 2. This area of the T-bill yield curve is dominated by the six-month bills. The newly auctioned six-month bill begins to trade actively right after the end of the auction period on Monday, until it takes a back seat the next Monday when a new six-month bill is auctioned. During this first week in the life of a six-month bill, there is heavy trading as the distribution process takes place. The bills change hands and gradually many of them end up in the hands of ultimate lenders. Thereafter, that bill begins to trade less actively and soon its value is affected by its growing distance from the latest six-month bill. Gradually the spreads widen and the daily volume begins to decrease.

When the six-month bill gets to be two or three weeks away from having only 90 days left until maturity, its price begins to reflect the trading in the current three-month bill. Eventually it becomes a three-month bill and goes back "on the run" as the 90-day bill.

Sector 3. This is the portion of the bill market dominated by the three-month bill. In general, it encompasses all bills with less than three months to maturity. Thus, this sector will include the new three-month bill and the old one-year and six-month bills that now have three months to run. The ninety-day bill is the most liquid trading of all T-bills. This is mostly because of the large amounts outstanding and the relatively smaller price changes as yields change. Recently auctioned three-month bills trade on a "spread" or roll value against the newest three-month bills. The "roll" refers to the relative value in basis points per week between different issues of bills. This roll, or price spread per week, can reflect either a positive yield pickup when the yield curve is positive, or a give-up of yield when the yield curve is negative. It is not unusual for roll spreads to range from $+5$ basis points to -5 basis points over an interest rate cycle.

As the bill moves toward maturity, its value begins to be more influenced by the short-term cost of overnight money and less by the 90-day values. Thus, 60-day T-bills will trade at yields closely approximating 60-day repurchase agreements. Thirty-day bills will trade at yields approximating those for 30-day money. And during the final days they will trade roughly equal to overnight money.

The spread between the bid and ask also tends to widen as the bill approaches maturity. This widening in the spread results from the decreasing value of a basis point as maturity approaches. To compensate, dealers try to maintain a constant dollar margin by increasing the bid/ask spread.

Some General Trading Guidelines

T-bills have no credit risk between issues. They are all government guaranteed and any bill is a perfect credit substitute for any other. But all T-bills do not trade equally. Some are more equal than others. For example, three- and six-month bills tend to have more liquid trading than one-year bills partly because their supply is larger.

Some T-bills have more attractive maturity dates than others and therefore trade at slight premiums to bills with other maturity dates. For example, the first bill of a new fiscal quarter will generally trade at a slight premium to its neighbors because of its value as window dressing for balance sheet purposes. These bills can be used to effect certain tax benefits that also add to their attractiveness. Late December and late June bills in particular have value for financial statement and tax reasons.

Bills that mature on or near corporate dividend dates also generally trade at a premium to other bills as corporations hold in a T-bill the cash they are accumulating to pay the dividend.

Lastly, the six-month bill that corresponds to the IMM delivery dates for 90-day T-bills generally begins to outtrade the rest of the bills as the 90-day bill auction that corresponds with an IMM delivery date approaches.

The Role of Primary Dealers

The primary dealer has three basic functions in the T-bill market. First, he has an unwritten obligation to participate in the bill auctions. A dealer does not necessarily have to purchase in every auction, but he must submit bids to assure that the bills will be sold.

Second, he must make an active two-sided market under all market conditions and stand ready to buy or sell at the prices he quotes. Of course, he has a good deal of latitude in the prices and amounts he is willing to buy or sell at any one time.

Third, he acts as a conduit for tenders from the public to the Federal Reserve, both in the primary auction bids and when the Fed is buying or selling bills for its own account. To avoid confusion and speed up response time, the Federal Reserve Open Market Desk uses only the 30 Primary Government Bond Dealers, who in turn use their resources to contact other large institutional customers who may want to buy or sell to the Fed.

The Role of the Federal Reserve Open Market Desk

The Open Market Desk plays a very large role in the secondary market. It conducts part of its monetary policy through the T-bill market when it buys or sells Treasury Bills for its own account. Such purchases and sales may be outright or through repurchase and reverse-repurchase agreements.

When the Fed buys bills it adds money to the banking system and reduces the floating supply of bills, thus temporarily strengthening bill prices. When the Fed does repurchase agreements, it temporarily reduces the supply of bills in the market and adds money to the banking system. This also effectively reduces the short-term cost of financing dealer positions. When it sells T-bills or does reverse repos, the effect is the opposite.

The Fed is usually in the market once or twice a week in one of the four ways mentioned above—outright buys, outright sells, repos, or reverse repos.

Second, the Fed also acts as an agent, buying and selling for customers. If the Fed fulfills its customers needs from its own account, there is no immediate change in the supply of bills, but reserves in the banking system are impacted. Conversely, if the Fed fills the customers needs the from marketplace, it affects the supply and demand for bills but has no impact on reserves in the banking system.

Delivery of Cash Treasury Bills

All T-bills sold for regular or normal delivery settle (are delivered) the day following execution. Bills sold for cash delivery settle the same day as the transaction. The Federal Reserve, whether trading repos, reverses, or actuals, almost always trades for cash settlement.

Nearly all deliveries of cash bills occur through the "book entry" system operated by the Federal Reserve. This system is simple and relatively straightforward. Under the book entry system banks that are members of the Federal Reserve hold their securities at the Fed in accounts for which the record keeping is computerized. Thus, each bank has an account at the Fed, and as the transactions occur those accounts are adjusted accordingly. The actual engraved pieces of paper never move from one location to another. If First of Chicago were, for example, to sell bills to Citibank, it would make delivery by sending a wire message to the Fed instructing its computer to debit the First of Chicago's account for x number of bills and credit Citi's account for the same number. Simultaneously, the Fed's computer would automatically transfer money equal to the purchase price of the bills out of Citi's reserve account at the Fed and into First Chicago's reserve account. Almost all transactions in government securities are settled in this way, through simple adjustments of accounts kept at the Federal Reserve.

Individual commercial banks have subaccounts for each of their clients. When they receive notification through the Fed wire that their account has been credited with the appropriate bills, they then, through their internal computerized record keeping systems, credit their customers accounts with the appropriate bills and debit their accounts for the correct funds. If one were to buy a T-bill, his bank would charge his account or honor his check and issue a receipt of ownership saying he owns a specific number of T-bills which they hold for him in their account at the local Federal Reserve Bank.

CHAPTER ELEVEN

Futures in Treasury Bills, Eurodollars, and Certificates of Deposits

THE TREASURY BILL FUTURES CONTRACTS

T-bill futures were first listed for trading on the IMM in January 1976. That first contract called for delivery of Treasury bills with 90 days left until maturity. The contracts were traded for delivery in the months of March, June, September, and December.

Since that time the contracts have been revised to reflect a "market basket" contract. That is, the delivery unit is not restricted to 90-day bills only, but also includes a bill originally issued as a year bill as a deliverable bill into its 90-day bill contract. The purpose of expanding the number of issues eligible for delivery is to relieve the pressure on the cash market at futures delivery time and assure that a sufficient supply of bills is available for delivery.

The "price" of the future is quoted in terms of an exchange-devised index representing the actual annualized T-bill interest yield subtracted from 100. Hence, if you want to know the annual interest yield being represented by a particular futures quote, subtract the quote from 100. For example, an index number of 94.5 represents an annual yield of

125

5.5%. In contrast to interest rates, the index goes down as the contract loses value and vice versa. Almost all newspapers carrying T-bill futures quotes carry the interest yield price as well as the index price. Bids and offers in the trading pit at the exchange must be made in terms of the index, so be sure that you give your orders to your broker in terms of the index. The minimum price fluctuation of the contract is 0.01 of the index or one basis point of annual yield. This is equivalent to $25 on a standard $1,000,000 T-bill futures contract.

As noted earlier, the Fed holds T-bill auctions every week. The last day of trading in T-bill futures for any particular month is the second day following the third T-bill auction of that month. Delivery is the following day.

Delivery is accomplished through banks that are registered with the exchange and are members of the Federal Reserve System. Through them you can have the T-bills delivered to your account in any major city. Futures delivery is a relatively simple procedure and mirrors the action taken when deliveries are made in the cash market.

The futures contract on 90-day T-bills calls for the delivery of bills having 90 days of life remaining. Thus, on delivery you obtain an instrument that will earn interest over the next 90 days. At the time you buy Treasury bills, you pay something less than face value—the difference between what you pay and the face value will be equal to the accrual of the interest during the remaining 90 days.

Keep in mind as you consider trading in financial instruments that there is an inverse relationship between prices and yields. If you expect interest rates to go up, take a short position in the market. If you expect interest rates to go down, take a long position in the market.

Delivery of Treasury Bill Futures

As described in the section on the cash market for T-bills, delivery is made through the "book entry" system. To accomplish delivery on the IMM, the following steps must be completed (delivery is accomplished similarly on the other exchanges):

1. On notice day, the last trading day, notice must be made by the seller to the Clearinghouse of intent to deliver.

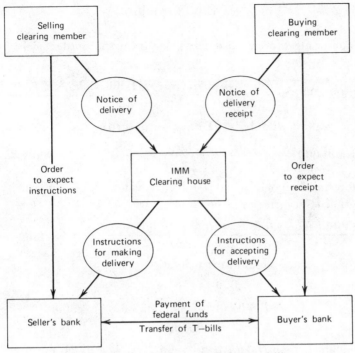

Figure 11.1   Delivery of Treasury bills.

2. "Order to expect" instructions are given to the bank of the seller. The seller instructs his bank that he has sold bills through the exchange clearinghouse. He also instructs them to be ready to wire the T-bills and to accept payment from the clearinghouse via the Fed money wire.

3. The official settlement price on the exchange is converted to a discount yield and from that an actual dollar price is calculated. For example,

settlement (index) price = 94.00

$$100 - 94 = 6\% \quad (6\%, 91 \text{ days to maturity})$$

$$\$984,833.33 = \text{invoice price} \quad (\text{see the next section for formula})$$

4. The exchange clearinghouse contacts the seller's bank to confirm the value of the bills being delivered.

5. Delivery is made. See Figure 11.1 for a diagramatic presentation of the delivery process.

T-Bill Formulas

1. Calculating the actual dollar price from the quoted yield prices.

$$\$ \text{ price} =$$
$$\$1,000,000 - \frac{(\text{days to maturity} \times \text{T-bill yield} \times \$1,000,000)}{360}$$

For example, 6% bills, 91 days to maturity:

$$1,000,000 - \frac{(91 \text{ days} \times 0.06 \times 1,000,000)}{360} = \$984,833.33$$

2. Determining yield when T-bill face value, days to maturity, and actual issue price are known.

$$\frac{\dfrac{(\text{T-bill face value} - \text{actual issue price}) \times 360}{\text{days to maturity}}}{\text{T-bill face value}} = \text{T-bill yields}$$

for example, $1,000,000 × 91 days:

$$\frac{(\$1,000,000 - \$984,833.33)}{\$1,000,000} \times \frac{360}{91}$$

3. Calculating equivalent bond yield. This is a much misunderstood number. It relates the yield on T-bills to the yields on coupon-bearing securities, taking into consideration the amount of the discount from face value and the time until maturity. T-bill yields are calculated on a 365-day basis.

$$\frac{(\text{T-bill face value} - \text{actual dollar price})}{\substack{\text{actual dollar price} \\ \text{to maturity}}} \times \frac{365}{\text{actual days}}$$

For example, 6% yield, $1,000,000 worth of T-bills, with 91 days to maturity:

$$\frac{(1,000,000 - 984,833.33)}{984,833.33} \times \frac{365}{91} = 6.18$$

This formula will cause a slight overstatement of T-bill yield versus coupon-bearing investments when comparisons are made of T-bills over 180 days to maturity, because the coupon instrument will have a coupon interest payment to reinvest after six months. Treasury bills make no six-month interest payments; they only pay 100% of face value at maturity.

Value of a Basis Point

A basis point is a 0.01% change in yield. Thus, a change in yield from 9.00 to 9.02 is a change of two basis points. The value of a basis point varies in direct proportion to the remaining time to maturity of a bill. For example, a 0.01% of yield is worth twice as much for one year as it is for six months. A general rule of thumb is:

0.01 at 360 days per million = $100

0.01 at 180 days per million = $50

0.01 at 90 days per million = $25

Each point is worth $0.2775 per million dollars per day.

THE EURODOLLAR FUTURES MARKET

The great growth of the Eurodollar market and its increasing use by corporations as well as financial institutions prompted the introduction in the summer of 1981 of a contract on Eurodollar time deposits.

A Eurodollar is defined as any U.S. dollar on deposit outside of the United States. This generally means dollar balances on the books of London branches of major world banks. Since these deposits lie outside the U.S., they do not fall under U.S. jurisdiction and, therefore, the regulations such as reserve requirements and maximum interest rate restrictions that govern domestic deposits do not apply to Eurodollars.

The trading of Eurodollar time deposits involves several risks that are not present in the government securities market. First, obviously, Eurodollar deposits reflect private credit; whereas government securities reflect public credit, hence the credit risk associated with the trading of the underlying cash instrument is greater for Eurodollars than for treasury bills. Generally, banks involved in the Eurodollar market place a limit on the size of Eurodollar deposits they will accept from other banks. They analyze each other's credit standing and allocate an internal line of credit for each bank with which they deal. These lines are based upon their perceptions and analyses of the size, financial strength, and reputation of the other party. Another risk that arises in the cash market for Eurodollars is a sovereign risk. That risk is independent of the bank with which the funds are placed and relates instead to the country under whose regulation that bank operates. There is always the risk that a particular country may establish regulations that would affect the movement of bank deposits into or out of that country. This happens particularly when a country's currency is under pressure.

The Eurodollar cash market also includes a forward market in which banks quote rates from today's (spot) date to a future date (forward) for deposits or placements. A typical transaction for a bank interested in improving its yield would be:

1. To borrow dollars from another bank for six months.
2. Lend those dollars to a third party for three months—thus creating a three-month gap between their asset and their liability.
3. After the initial three-month investment matures, reinvest the principal and the interest received for the remaining three months.

Generally, when the bank knows what the initial three-month investment will be, it is then able to calculate the rate it needs on the last three-month segment in order to achieve its break-even rate. It is then in the position to evaluate the alternatives for its second three-month investment. It may decide that the second three-month investment should be a loan to a corporate customer to which it will commit today for drawdown three months hence. It may also decide to close out the position by making a forward deposit commitment, or it could simply wait and take its chances that interest rates move in its favor and will be higher at the end of the first 90-day period.

One thing that happens in these types of forward transactions is that a bank uses up its lines of credit with other banks. It also inflates the balance sheet of the participating bank.

Another way of accomplishing the same objective without using up valuable lines of credit, or inflating the balance sheet, is to use the Eurodollar futures.

For example, assume that in September a bank wanted to price in advance the last three-month portion of a six-month asset which would be funded by a six-month Eurodollar liability. The bank would be interested in protecting against a fall in interest rates from the period beginning the middle of December through the middle of March and would make the following transactions:

1. In September, borrow six-month Eurodollars and, simultaneously, make a three-month loan.

2. In September, buy one IMM Eurodollar contract for delivery in December.
3. In December, receive the money from the maturing asset (loan) and relend that money for three months at the then current interbank rate; and, simultaneously, sell (offset) one Eurodollar contract on the IMM. The proceeds from the futures should be applied to the new asset to get the net investment rate.

Spreads Between CD, T-Bill, and Eurodollar Rates

As noted earlier, Eurodollar and CD rates reflect private credit, while T-bill rates reflect public credit. Generally, because of the credit characteristics of Eurodollars, rates on Eurodollars will exceed the rates on CDs. Further, the spread between Eurodollar rates and CD rates does not remain constant. They respond to a variety of market forces, most of which are unpredictable, and many of which involve political decisions of the U.S. and foreign governments. They also react to changes in currency relationships. A strong dollar will generally result in a narrowing of the spread between Eurodollars and domestic CD rates. An increase in Federal Reserve requirements on domestic CDs will also cause the spread to increase. Lastly, the liquidity of the Eurodollar time-deposit market is frequently less than it is for domestic CD deposits. This is because Eurodollar deposits are usually non-negotiable time deposits while domestic Certificates of Deposit are negotiable. Depositors are willing to receive less interest to gain the ability to raise needed cash in the secondary market, if necessary, prior to the deposit's maturity.

All of these factors also affect the spreads between Eurodollar rates and Treasury bill rates, but to a lesser degree. The T-bill/Eurodollar spreads tend to widen as rates rise and to fall as rates fall.

THE CD FUTURES CONTRACT

Certificates of Deposit (CDs) are short-term interest-bearing cash deposits at banks and savings institutions. In the early 1960s, banks, who were hungry for cash to meet the demand for loans, offered to accept large ($100,000) deposits from corporations who had temporary excess funds. The fixed rates paid on those cash deposits usually were above the Treasury bill rates being offered by the Treasury. Banks quickly learned that not only did these CDs offer the potential for improving the management of their short-term cash needs, but also that they were a means of permanently increasing the size of the bank. Customers, putting their money in CDs, were happy because they had higher yields than the traditional Treasury bills, and also they had greater flexibility with their funds.

CD futures were first offered by the IMM and, as such, became the first private credit instrument to be traded on a futures exchange. The CD futures contract calls for delivery of a 90-day Certificate of Deposit issued by selected major banks (the exchange publishes the list of acceptable banks) with a face value of $1,000,000. In contrast to the Treasury bill futures, the instrument underlying the CD futures is a private credit instrument and the risk associated with private credit instruments is higher than would be the case with a public credit instrument like Treasury bills. Accordingly, the interest rate on CDs is correspondingly higher.

A major difference between pricing CDs and pricing Treasury bills is that the invoice price for Treasury bills is a discount yield, while the invoice price for CDs is an add-on yield. For example, in the case of a 90-day bill with a bank discount yield of 14%, the Treasury bill has an initial value of $965,600—$35,000 less than the maturity value of the bill. A $1,000,000 CD with a bank add-on yield of 14% has a maturity value of $1,035,000—$35,000 more than its initial value of $1,000,000. The formula for computing the invoice price of a 90 day treasury bill is:

$$\text{INVOICE PRICE} = \frac{(1 - 90)}{360} \times \text{the futures yield} \times \$1,000,000$$

The add-on yield formula (principal plus interest at maturity) of a deliverable CD is:

$$\text{INVOICE PRICE} = (\text{maturity value}) \div \frac{(1 + 90)}{360} \times \text{the futures yield}$$

In short, the cash and futures markets for CDs are markets for an instrument quoted on a bank add-on basis which is not a yield directly comparable to the discount yield found in the cash and futures markets for Treasury bills.

The delivery process for domestic CDs also provides considerable flexibility. In the case of the T-bill contract, there is a single delivery day during the deliverable week in the contract month. In CDs any CD of an approved delivery bank written to mature during the second half of the delivery month is deliverable. The effect is that CDs between 2½ and 3½ months to maturity can be delivered.

Price Spreads Between CDs and T-Bills

There is no "normal" spread between CDs and Treasury bill rates. The spread varies with people's perceptions of the relative risk of owning private credit instruments, such as CDs, versus public credit instruments such as Treasury bills. In recent years, there have from time to time been flights to quality as investors feared bank failures or questioned the overall financial strength of CD issuers and were unwilling to accept CD rates at levels comparable to Treasury bills. Further, generally, in periods of rising rates, banks pay an increasingly higher rate relative to the Treasury for money. This fact stems from, first, banks needs for cash to fund strong loan demand typical of a rising rate environment and, second, banks inability to issue unlimited amounts of CDs. The Treasury is not circumscribed by the amount of Treasury bills it can issue, nor does it operate under a limited price scenario. For these reasons the spread between CDs and Treasury bills has varied from nearly zero to more than four points.

Using CD Futures to Hedge

A major problem faced by banks is that corporations all want CDs that mature on the tax date. Corporations are willing to accept lower yields on tax-dated CDs than on nontax-dated.

Corporations can use the CD futures contract to assure themselves of cash on tax day without putting the money in the lower-yielding tax-dated CDs. They can buy a nontax-dated CD from a bank which is eligible to issue deliverable CDs and short (sell) the futures contract. When the futures matures on the 16th day of the contract month, they can deliver the CD in fulfillment of the futures, thus receiving funds to meet their tax obligations.

Any delivery bank can create a deliverable CD at any time and, thus, at a time when the yield curve is advantageous, such a bank could purchase a six-month CD and sell a CD futures contract for delivery three months after the purchase. When the time comes for the maturity of the futures contract, the six-month CD will have only three months' remaining life and will be eligible for delivery on the future. At that point, one could deliver the CD on the futures or repurchase the futures and sell the CD in the cash market.

Table 11.1 Summary of Contract Specifications: Three-Month Eurodollar Time Deposit, Three-Month Certificate of Deposit and 90-Day Treasury Bill

Specifications	Three-Month Eurodollar Time Deposit	Three-Month Certificate of Deposit	90-Day U.S. Treasury Bill
Size	$1,000,000	$1,000,000	$1,000,000
Contract grade	Cash settlement	1) "No-name" CDs. Deliverable banks announced 2 business days before 15th day of delivery month. Deliverable CDs determined by polling of dealers 2) CDs must mature between 16th and last day of the month 3 months after delivery month 3) Deliverable maturity range approx. 2½ to 3½ months 4) CDs with no more than 185 days accrued interest 5) Variable rate and discount CDs are deliverable if and when yields are equivalent to "no-name" run	1) Treasury bills with 91 days to maturity
Yields	Add-on	Add-on	Discount
Months traded	Mar, Jun, Sep, Dec.	Mar, Jun, Sep, Dec	Mar, Jun, Sep, Dec,

135

Table 11.1 Summary of Contract Specifications: Three-Month Eurodollar Time Deposit, Three-Month Certificate of Deposit and 90-Day Treasury Bill (*Continued*)

Specifications	Three-Month Eurodollar Time Deposit	Three-Month Certificate of Deposit	90-Day U.S. Treasury Bill
Size	$1,000,000	$1,000,000	$1,000,000
Minimum fluctuation in price	.01 (1 basis pt)($25/pt)	.01 (1 basis pt)($25/pt)	.01 (1 basis pt)($25/pt)
Limit move	1.00 (100 basis pts)($2,500) No spot month limit	.80 (80 basis pts)($2,000)	.60 (60 basis pts)($1,500)
Last day of trading	2nd London business day before 3rd Wednesday	Last business day *before* last delivery day	2nd day following 3rd weekly Treasury bill auction in contract month. (Effective with Jun '83 contract, the day before the first delivery day)
Delivery date	Last day of trading	15th through last day of month	1st Thursday after 3rd weekly bill auction in the delivery month

CHAPTER TWELVE

The Treasury Note and Bond Market

TREASURY NOTES

Treasury notes are coupon-bearing securities issued by the Government with maturities of not less than one year and not more than ten years. The timely payment of interest and principal on such notes is fully guaranteed by the government. Interest is paid twice each year in six-month intervals.

Note Cycles

Notes are sold in a variety of cycles similar to the T-bill auction cycles noted earlier.

Two-Year Note Cycle.   Notes are issued each month with a 24-month maturity. Every month, a week or so before the month's end, the Treasury offers a new two-year note for sale that is dated to mature at the end of the month 24 months hence.

Four-Year Note Cycle.   In the last week of the quarter, the Treasury sells a note that is dated and matures at month's end 48 months hence. These notes eventually become two-year notes and trade in consonance with newly issued two-year notes.

Five-Year Note Cycle.   In April, July, October, and January the Treasury auctions five-year notes. These notes are auctioned at the end of the month and are dated and mature on the 15th of the month.

Refunding Cycle.   In addition to the note auctions mentioned above, the Treasury engages in fund raising and refundings in the middle month of each quarter, February, June, September, and December. During these periods the Treasury sells a short note of three to four years maturity and another note with a maturity between five years and ten years. The exact maturities depend on market conditions. A long-term bond, usually maturing in 15 to 30 years, is also sold during these refunding periods.

All of the note cycles were begun in the middle 1960s when William Simon was Secretary of the Treasury. They were part of an effort to regularize the issuance of debt and minimize the market impact of concentrating the selling of a huge amount of debt.

TREASURY BONDS

Treasury bonds are coupon-bearing securities issued and guaranteed by the U.S. government. Bonds are issued in two different cycles.

Fifteen-Year Bond Cycle.   Each January and July, at month's end, 15-year bonds are auctioned with settlement and maturities on February 15 and August 15.

Refunding Cycle.   Every quarterly refunding recently has included a long-term bond with maturities from 25 to 30 years. These bonds usually have a call protection feature that is five years less than maturity. Consideration has also been given to issuing even longer bonds, with 40-year maturities, if market conditions permit.

Flower Bonds

Flower bonds are issues that, when held by a decedent and being part of his estate, are redeemable at par if used to pay federal estate taxes. These bonds are often in great demand and the amount held in public hands is constantly decreasing as they are turned in to the Treasury for estate tax purposes. Some of the bloom was taken from the flower bonds by the Tax Reform Act of 1976. Under this law the difference between the purchase price and the par redemption price could be taxed as ordinary income, depending on how long the bond had been held. The following is a list of all flower bonds outstanding:

3.50%—11/15/80	4.125%—5/15/89–94
3.25%—5/15/85	3.50%—2/15/90
4.25%—8/15/87–92	3.00%—2/15/95
4.00%—2/15/88–93	3.50%—11/15/98

Treasury Bond Authority

By statute Treasury bonds are limited to a maximum coupon of 4.25% and a maturity of not less than ten years. Originally everything over five years had to be a bond and fell into the 4.25% limitation. This limitation was changed to seven years in 1967 and ten years in 1976. In 1971 Congress authorized the Treasury to sell ten billion dollars of bonds without regard to coupon rate. This authority is to be reviewed annually by Congress and a new amount authorized. While Congress has always provided the new authority, it has sometimes delayed the authorization, thus raising concern that it may not always continue to grant blanket increases in the future. Fear of "crowding out" the private sector from the long-term debt market by the Treasury is often cited by Congress as a reason for the foot-dragging.

METHOD OF SALE FOR BONDS AND NOTES

The Auctions

Auctions for bonds and notes are held in much the same manner as auctions for T-bills. The Federal Reserve System acts as agent and bids must be submitted by 1:30 P.M. EST on the day designated as auction day. Bids are submitted differently, however, as notes and bond bids are denominated by yield. The Treasury accepts the yield bids, awards the noncompetitive tenders, then allocates bonds to the highest yield bids until all have been awarded. After that the weighted average competitive bid is calculated and used as the noncompetitive award price. This average price (yield) also becomes the basis for setting the coupon rate on the new issue. The coupons are set to the nearest one-eighth of a point, which allows the average price to be less than par. For example if the average price were 11.65%, the coupon would be 11.625%. The high, low, and average *dollar* price are then calculated from this coupon price based upon the high, low, and average yields bid in the auction.

The Dutch Auctions. In recent years the Treasury on two occasions used the Dutch auction method to sell Treasury bonds. This method allocated to all successful bidders bonds at the lowest accepted price. Bidding is carried on in the same manner as before but after the high, low, and average bids have been determined, all bids, including noncompetitives, are confirmed at the low price.

Subscription Issues

In 1976 and early 1977, the Treasury sold issues on a subscription basis only. They set a coupon rate, which was a concession to the market, and allowed everyone to subscribe to a maximum amount of $500,000. The higher rate attracted many individuals and smaller institutions and kept dealers from buying large amounts to cover shorts they had created. The issues were heavily subscribed and the after-markets were very active. This method of sale is used to attract money from individuals and small institutional investors who would not be willing to purchase all the new debt issues at then current prices.

Rights Issues

Rights issues of new securities were very popular in the early 1970s when budget deficits were relatively small. In order to participate, however, an investor had to hold a maturing note or bond. Payment for new refunding purchases could be made only by presenting maturing notes or bonds. In this type of refunding the coupon was designated by the Treasury when the refunding plans were disclosed.

While all three of the above-mentioned methods of sales were used in the 1970s, it is unlikely that they will be used in the very near future unless the market stabilizes and the size of the deficit is reduced.

The Secondary Market

The secondary market for Treasury notes and bonds is broad and deep. Unlike the T-bill market, there are, in the secondary market, many dealer participants other than the Primary Dealers Association. The primary dealers are a majority of the active market makers but many corporate bond dealers are also actively involved in the long and intermediate government bond markets.

The growth of the secondary market began in the middle 1970s with the regular issuance of long-term debt with current coupons. The market had previously consisted of flower bonds and an occasional small issue. When investors became aware of the availability of a strong, secondary market they began to purchase government bonds on a regular basis. This added a great deal of liquidity to the market for long-term securities.

Over $3 billion in long-term bonds are traded every day by the primary dealers alone.

Pricing and Delivery

Prices for notes and bonds are quoted in dollars, with increments of one thirty-second of a dollar being the norm. Spreads between bid and ask prices are usually two thirty-seconds on short notes, and four thirty-seconds on longer bonds. Each thirty-second is worth $31.25 per one hundred thousand dollars of notes or bonds.

When delivery of any note or bond is made, the dollar price quoted is multiplied by the face amount to get principal amount or price. Then a calculation is done to figure how much accrued interest is owed to the seller. Since the Treasury pays interest every six months, adjustment must be made when a note or bond is sold between coupon dates. The seller must always deliver a bond that has all outstanding coupons attached. If the notes and bonds are in book entry form, then the coupons are already attached. The method of computing the sellers accrued interest is to figure total interest earned from the last coupon date.

The formula is as follows:

$$\text{ACCRUED INTEREST} = \frac{\begin{array}{c}\text{number of days}\\\text{from last}\\\text{coupon payment}\end{array} \times \text{coupon rate} \times \text{face amount}}{365 \text{ days}}$$

The accrued interest is added to the principal amount to determine the total invoice price. This method of accrued interest calculation is the same for futures as it is for cash.

The Bank Range

The bank range is that part of the yield curve where commercial banks usually concentrate their purchases of Treasury notes. This range encompasses the notes in the two- to seven-year range. Because the liabilities of banks tend to be very short, it is prudent for banks to tend to concentrate their fixed income investments in this relatively short maturity range. Therefore, the note market from two to seven years usually reflects the capabilities and attitudes of commercial banks. When bank "liquidity" is low, this area of the market suffers disproportionately from tight money policies.

THE TREASURY BOND FUTURES CONTRACT

The CBT T-bond contract is the most actively traded of all futures. The T-bond futures contract trades on the basis of a hypothetical bond issue created by the contract specifications.

The Exchange constructs this hypothetical bond issue by:

1. Setting a standard coupon rate of 8%.
2. Establishing a minimum maturity date. The CBT can use any bond that is not callable for at least 15 years from the *date of delivery,* if callable; or if not callable, bonds that do not mature for at least 15 years from *date of delivery.* Because of the Treasury settlement dates of February 15 and August 15, the most recently issued

15-year T-bonds fall just short of deliverable specification for the CBT March and September contracts. No maximum is set on maturity for bonds that may be delivered into the contracts.

The futures are traded on dollar prices as any other security would be traded. The yield of the security is set by the forces of a free market and the dollar price resulting is the dollar price quoted on the exchange.

Converting the Exchange Price to a Cash Price

The CBT uses a "factor" method of converting exchange prices to equivalent prices for actual cash government bonds. For a short time the NYFE also traded a T-bond contract. That contract reflected a 9% coupon, 20-year maturity, and yield maintenance method of pricing. Since it is no longer actively traded, it is not included in this exposition.

The Factor Method. The CBT publishes a list of factors covering each possible deliverable coupon (see Table 12.1) for use in adjusting different coupon rates and maturity dates to equate with the 8% exchange standard. This ensures that every coupon, regardless of whether its rate is higher or lower than 8%, will receive a fair and equal price if it is delivered or accepted for settlement of a contract. This also adjusts for the ten-year possible range of maturity between eligible bonds.

To understand how this factor system works, consider two different bonds both with a CBT price of $80,000 for the March 1980 contract:

1. Issue 7⅝ of 2/15/2002–07. Time from call date until delivery date of March 20, 1980 = 21¾ years.
2. Issue 10⅜ of 11/15/04–09. Time from call date until delivery date of March 20 = 24¾ years.

The factor for the 7⅝ with 21¾ years is 0.9614.
The factor for the 10⅜ with 24¾ years is 1.2540.
The factor is then multiplied by the exchange price to get the correct principal value for each bond.

80 (exchange price for March 80 futures) × 0.9614 (factor) = 76.912 for 7⅝ of 07.

80 × 1.2540 = 100.32 is the price for 10⅜ of 2009.

The total invoice price is found by multiplying the dollar price by the face amount. ($100,000 × 79.912 = $799,120.00) The accrued interest from the last coupon date is then added.

To illustrate how maturity affects the price of the cash bonds, assume the 7⅝ of 2/15/02–07 were to be delivered into the June 1980 contract instead of the March. The factor would then be 0.9618. Assume the price of June CBT T-bond futures to be 80.00, the same as March futures in the above example:

$$80 \times 0.9618 = 76.944$$

One can easily see how the factor adjusts each issue for maturity as well as coupon.

This method of calculation equalizes the "basket" of deliverable issues so that the contract price will usually reflect the yield of the cheapest traded coupon eligible for delivery. To date, that has always been the most current coupon with the longest maturity. It has maintained this consistency of maturity even through changes in the yield curve.

FACTORS AND WEIGHTING A HEDGE

As will be explained in Chapter 15, one needs to weight a hedge in order to get the correct dollar value relationships between the cash and futures markets. The conversion factors referred to above become the correct weighting factor in a hedge. Hence, a conversion factor of 1.4269 means that one should use 1.4 futures contracts for each $100,-000 of bonds being hedged.

DELIVERY OF TREASURY BOND CONTRACTS

Delivery of T-bonds is made through the Fed "book entry" system in the same manner as delivery of T-bills.

Table 12.1 Prices to Yield 8.000% Conversion Factor for Invoicing

Term	7%	7 1/8%	7 1/4%	7 3/8%	7 1/2%	7 5/8%	7 3/4%	7 7/8%
				Coupon Rates				
15	0.9135	0.9243	0.9352	0.9460	0.9568	0.9676	0.9784	0.9892
15-3	0.9126	0.9235	0.9344	0.9453	0.9562	0.9671	0.9780	0.9889
15-6	0.9121	0.9231	0.9340	0.9450	0.9560	0.9670	0.9780	0.9890
15-9	0.9112	0.9222	0.9333	0.9444	0.9555	0.9666	0.9776	0.9887
16	0.9106	0.9218	0.9330	0.9441	0.9553	0.9665	0.9777	0.9888
16-3	0.9098	0.9210	0.9323	0.9435	0.9548	0.9660	0.9773	0.9885
16-6	0.9093	0.9206	0.9319	0.9433	0.9546	0.9660	0.9773	0.9887
16-9	0.9084	0.9198	0.9313	0.9427	0.9541	0.9655	0.9770	0.9884
17	0.9079	0.9195	0.9310	0.9425	0.9540	0.9655	0.9770	0.9885
17-3	0.9071	0.9187	0.9303	0.9419	0.9535	0.9651	0.9766	0.9882
17-6	0.9067	0.9183	0.9300	0.9417	0.9533	0.9650	0.9767	0.9883
17-9	0.9059	0.9176	0.9294	0.9411	0.9528	0.9646	0.9763	0.9881
18	0.9055	0.9173	0.9291	0.9409	0.9527	0.9645	0.9764	0.9882
18-3	0.9047	0.9166	0.9285	0.9404	0.9522	0.9641	0.9760	0.9879
18-6	0.9043	0.9163	0.9282	0.9402	0.9521	0.9641	0.9761	0.9880
18-9	0.9035	0.9156	0.9276	0.9396	0.9517	0.9637	0.9757	0.9878
19	0.9032	0.9153	0.9274	0.9395	0.9516	0.9637	0.9758	0.9879
19-3	0.9024	0.9146	0.9268	0.9390	0.9511	0.9633	0.9755	0.9876
19-6	0.9021	0.9143	0.9266	0.9388	0.9510	0.9633	0.9755	0.9878
19-9	0.9014	0.9137	0.9260	0.9383	0.9506	0.9629	0.9752	0.9875
20	0.9010	0.9134	0.9258	0.9381	0.9505	0.9629	0.9753	0.9876
20-3	0.9004	0.9128	0.9252	0.9377	0.9501	0.9625	0.9749	0.9874
20-6	0.9000	0.9125	0.9250	0.9375	0.9500	0.9625	0.9750	0.9875
20-9	0.8994	0.9119	0.9245	0.9370	0.9496	0.9621	0.9747	0.9873
21	0.8991	0.9117	0.9243	0.9369	0.9495	0.9622	0.9748	0.9874
21-3	0.8984	0.9111	0.9238	0.9364	0.9491	0.9618	0.9745	0.9871
21-6	0.8981	0.9109	0.9236	0.9363	0.9491	0.9618	0.9745	0.9873
21-9	0.8975	0.9103	0.9231	0.9359	0.9487	0.9614	0.9742	0.9870
22	0.8973	0.9101	0.9229	0.9358	0.9486	0.9615	0.9743	0.9872
22-3	0.8967	0.9095	0.9224	0.9353	0.9482	0.9611	0.9740	0.9869
22-6	0.8964	0.9093	0.9223	0.9352	0.9482	0.9611	0.9741	0.9870
22-9	0.8958	0.9088	0.9218	0.9348	0.9478	0.9608	0.9738	0.9868
23	0.8956	0.9086	0.9217	0.9347	0.9478	0.9608	0.9739	0.9869
23-3	0.8950	0.9081	0.9212	0.9343	0.9474	0.9605	0.9736	0.9867
23-6	0.8948	0.9079	0.9211	0.9342	0.9474	0.9605	0.9737	0.9868
23-9	0.8942	0.9074	0.9206	0.9338	0.9470	0.9602	0.9734	0.9866
24	0.8940	0.9073	0.9205	0.9338	0.9470	0.9603	0.9735	0.9868
24-3	0.8935	0.9068	0.9201	0.9334	0.9466	0.9599	0.9732	0.9865
24-6	0.8933	0.9066	0.9200	0.9333	0.9466	0.9600	0.9733	0.9867
24-9	0.8928	0.9061	0.9195	0.9329	0.9463	0.9597	0.9730	0.9864
25	0.8926	0.9060	0.9194	0.9329	0.9463	0.9597	0.9731	0.9866
25-3	0.8921	0.9055	0.9190	0.9325	0.9459	0.9594	0.9729	0.9863

Table 12.1   Prices to Yield 8.000% Conversion Factor for
Invoicing (*Continued*)

	Coupon Rates							
Term	7%	7 1/8%	7 1/4%	7 3/8%	7 1/2%	7 5/8%	7 3/4%	7 7/8%
25-6	0.8919	0.9054	0.9189	0.9324	0.9460	0.9595	0.9730	0.9865
25-9	0.8914	0.9050	0.9185	0.9321	0.9456	0.9592	0.9727	0.9863
26	0.8913	0.9049	0.9184	0.9320	0.9456	0.9592	0.9728	0.9864
26-3	0.8908	0.9044	0.9180	0.9317	0.9453	0.9589	0.9725	0.9862
26-6	0.8906	0.9043	0.9180	0.9316	0.9453	0.9590	0.9727	0.9863
26-9	0.8902	0.9039	0.9176	0.9313	0.9450	0.9587	0.9724	0.9861
27	0.8900	0.9038	0.9175	0.9313	0.9450	0.9588	0.9725	0.9863
27-3	0.8896	0.9034	0.9171	0.9309	0.9447	0.9585	0.9722	0.9860
27-6	0.8895	0.9033	0.9171	0.9309	0.9447	0.9585	0.9724	0.9862
27-9	0.8890	0.9029	0.9167	0.9306	0.9444	0.9583	0.9721	0.9860

THE TEN-YEAR TREASURY NOTE FUTURES

High and increasingly volatile interest rates, plus high inflation, caused investors in the late 70s and early 1980s to be reluctant to commit funds to the purchase of long-term fixed-income securities. Investors preferred to keep their investments liquid and in short-term maturities to maximize return. Consequently, the U.S. Treasury and large corporations had an increasingly difficult time in selling long-term debt. Instead they turned to issuing more intermediate-term debt of a 7- to 10-year maturity. For example, the amount of new 10-year corporate bonds issued now exceeds one third of the total new debt issued. As recently as 1980, such bonds accounted for only about 20%.

At the Treasury, the amount of marketable debt in the 5- to 10-year maturity range grew from $50 billion to $65 billion in the 18 months between December 1979 and July 1981. Even more dramatically, the face value of new issues of 7- to 10-year notes increased 52% from December 1980 to November 1981. The Treasury has now made the 10-year note a permanent part of its quarterly financing package, and has initiated a regular quarterly auction for 7-year notes. This wave of new intermediate issues has made the 10-year maturity a focal point of cash market trading. Average daily dealer transactions in the 5- to 10-year range now total over $3.5 billion.

The CBT's 10 year Treasury futures contract is based on a security with a face value (par amount) of $100,000 maturing in 6½ to 10 years. Its 8% coupon corresponds to the coupons on the CBT's Ginny Mae and Treasury bond contracts. Thus the 10-year Treasury futures offers market participants a natural compliment to the CBT's other financial futures.

Converting Cash Prices to Futures Prices

Although the CBT's 10-year Treasury note contract is based on a 8% coupon, in reality various coupons on instruments with maturity ranging from 6½ to 10 years are deliverable on the contract. Each auction of 7- to 10-year notes, brings a new list of deliverable notes and each eligible coupon maturity has a different value. The key for hedging purposes and for delivery purposes is that all values must be related to one futures price; hence, just as in the Treasury bond futures, the CBT uses "conversion factors."

These conversion factors equate the value of the note with a coupon other than 8% to the futures settlement price. In any delivery month, each deliverable issue will have a specific conversion factor that reflects its coupon and time left to maturity at that date. See Table 12.2 for some sample conversion factors for the March 1983 T-note contract.

· Thus, a seller delivering any one of these eligible notes calculates the invoice amount for a particular note issue by multiplying the futures settlement price by the appropriate conversion factor and adding the accrued interest. The buyer then holds an investment with the yield

Table 12.2   *T-Note Conversion Factors*

Coupon	Maturity	Mar '83
14 ½	July 15, 1989	
10 ¾	Nov. 15, 1989	1.1373
10 ¾	Aug. 15, 1990	1.1488
13	Nov. 15, 1990	1.2780
14 ½	May 15, 1991	1.3787
14 ⅞	Aug. 15, 1991	1.4091
14 ¼	Nov, 15, 1991	1.3802
14 ⅝	Feb. 15, 1992	1.4109
13 ¾	May 15, 1992	1.3640
11 ⅞	Oct. 15, 1989	1.1935
10 ½	Nov. 15, 1992	1.1642

approximately equal to the yield he would have received had he paid the settlement price and received an 8% coupon. For example, if a seller delivers 13% notes against one 10-year Treasury futures contact for June 1984 at a settlement price of 74, the principal invoice amount would be: settlement price of 74 times the conversion factor of 1.2975 times the par value of $100,000.

Cheapest to Deliver

A buyer who stands for delivery of Treasury notes when his futures contract expires should remember that the seller chooses which note to deliver and when in the delivery month to tender it. The long must accept whatever the short chooses, when he chooses to deliver it, as long as the note being delivered meets the contract specifications. By looking at which notes are eligible for delivery, one can calculate which note is cheapest to deliver at any particular time.

A rule of thumb for identifying which note is cheapest in the cash market is to divide the cash price for each deliverable issue by the appropriate conversion factor. This procedure, however, is only a guide. Other factors also affect which note a seller would select to deliver. Since relationships among notes change every day, it is important to recalculate the cheapest-to-deliver on a regular basis.

Hedging with a 10-Year Note

As noted previously, one of the most important concepts in evaluating the effectiveness and efficiency of a hedge is the concept of basis. Basis refers to the difference between the price of the cash instrument being hedged and the futures price. The process of hedging replaces the overall risk of absolute price change with the risk of relative price change as reflected in changes in the basis. A changing basis can contribute either profits or losses to a hedged position, but the overall fluctuation in the basis should be much less than the absolute fluctuation in the cash price or the futures price.

It is important to note that in calculating the basis for coupon issues, one needs to convert either the cash price or the futures price in order to get a common comparison of the two prices. The cash price may be a high coupon issue with a large dollar value, while the futures price in the case of 10-year Treasuries (and Ginnys and Bonds as well) is always based on the dollar value of an 8% coupon. If one were to take the "raw" basis between two instruments, one might find a relationship as follows:

Cash Price	94–16
Futures Price	73–16
Raw Basis	21–00

For a better comparison one should divide the cash price by the appropriate conversion factor (this requires putting the cash price into decimal form as follows: $94.5 \div 1.3165 = 71.7812$ or 71–25). In that instance one will get a basis of -1.23:

Converted Price	71–25
Futures Price	73–16
Converted Basis	−1.23

Put on the converted basis, one is then in a much better position to evaluate the potential effectiveness and efficiency of a hedge.

A strengthening basis refers to a basis that becomes increasingly positive or less negative. It reflects growing profits from the futures side of a short hedge because it means that the futures price is dropping faster than the cash price.

A weakening basis refers to a basis that becomes more negative or less positive. It reflects growing losses on the futures side of short hedges because it means that the futures price change is greater than the cash price change.

CHAPTER THIRTEEN

The Government National Mortgage Association

GNMAs are a unique debt instrument created in 1970 to increase the flow of funds to the secondary mortgage market. The Government National Mortgage Association is a division of the Department of Housing and Urban Development and carries out the mandate of the Housing Act of 1968. Its three basic functions are (1) to maintain a secondary market for FHA and VA mortgages by buying and selling government guaranteed mortgages, (2) to manage and liquidate its portfolio of mortgages purchased prior to 1968, and (3) to approve and guarantee mortgage-backed securities issued against pools of FHA and VA mortgages.

WHAT ARE GNMAs?

The GNMA takes pools of existing FHA and VA mortgages presented to it and issues a certificate that guarantees the principal and interest from that pool will be paid to the certificate holder.

The GNMA pass-through is the most common type of GNMA certificate, and is the one used as the standard security for futures contracts.

151

The modified pass-through certificate guarantees the purchaser prompt payment of principal and interest received from a pool of mortgages. If payments of principal and interest are not received from the mortgages, the GNMA will pay promptly.

The originator assembles a pool of mortgages in the following two ways:

1. Through direct issuance of mortgages to home buyers, builders, or developers.
2. Through commitment to purchase the mortgages produced by other lending institutions or mortgage bankers.

Once the originator has assembled the mortgages (he has to have at least $1,000,000), he transfers them to a custodian bank that in turn issues pool documents attesting to the pool's presence in the bank, whereupon the originator requests a guarantee of the pool by GNMA. The originator can request a "commitment" from GNMA prior to actually placing the mortgages with the custodian, but GNMA will not issue the certificate until the mortgages are held by the custodian. The originator also has responsibility to arrange for the service of the pool. Sometimes he does this directly. Other times he will sell the servicing rights to another institution. The servicing institution collects the principal and interest payments, maintains the financial records, and pays the certificate holders. Service fees and GNMA guarantee fees are equal to 0.5% of coupon interest.

After the pool has been formed and guaranteed, the originator usually seeks a buyer for the pool. He may sell it in the cash forward market, hedge it in the futures market, or he may pay an investor to stand by to purchase the GNMA at a later date.

Sometimes an originator will offer to sell a pool before he has it in final form. In such situations the originator with interest rate commitments from lenders can assure a buyer of the makeup of a pool. Lenders who make such commitments to originators are subject to risk during the period between commitment and closing of the mortgage. If the market interest rates for GNMAs increase during this time the lender would be subject to a loss. Conversely, if the rates should decline he will have a gain. To avoid such risks lenders can use the futures to hedge. Of course they can also protect themselves through the forwards market and by timing their sales as closely as possible to the date of commitment to borrowers.

THE GNMA CERTIFICATE AND ITS CHARACTERISTICS

When an investor purchases a GNMA Pass Thru certificate the GNMA issues a certificate to the investor evidencing that the holder has an ownership share in a pool of FHA or VA mortgages. The GNMA certificate contains a complete description of the pool. The following elements are covered on the certificate:

1. *Face Value.* The certificate states the original principal value of the pool or individual investment. All GNMA pools must have at least $1,000,000 of mortgages in them, but a pool may be distributed among many different investors. The minimum investment is $25,-000 and rises in increments of $5,000.
2. *Factor.* The factor is the *percentage* of unpaid principal still remaining on the mortgages that comprise the pool backing the GNMA certificate. The factor is multiplied by the face value to determine the current principal balance of the pool.
3. *Current Principal Balance.* The current principal balance is the aggregate amount of unpaid principal outstanding on mortgages in a certain pool. When figuring the dollar value of a GNMA, the current principal is multiplied by the dollar price to compute principal amounts.
4. *Coupon.* The coupon on the GNMA is the rate of interest that the purchaser will receive. The coupon is automatically 0.5% less than the standard FHA/VA rate in effect at the time of issuance. This 0.5% is paid to the servicing organization (0.44%) and to GNMA (0.06%) for a guarantee fee. As the mortgage rate for FHA/VA mortgages changes, the coupons on new GNMA pass-throughs change. Thus, there are GNMAs outstanding with different coupon rates.
5. *Pool Number.* Each certificate has a pool number that identifies the exact pool of mortgages backing the certificate.
6. *Date.* The certificate also gives the date the pool was originated and the date the pool will mature.

Payment Provisions

Payments of principal and interest to the certificate holder or "owner of record" are made monthly. GNMA guarantees payment in case of a default by the borrowers. The first payment is made 45 days after the initial issue date. Subsequent payments of principal and interest are made no later than the fifteenth calendar date of the month following the month in which collection from the borrowers was made.

Any prepayments are also made to the certificate holders on a pro rata basis upon their receipt by the servicer. Prepayment occurs when mortgages are prepaid by borrowers or when borrowers default on their loans. When FHA/VA loans go into default, the loan is repaid in full by the FHA/VA agencies. Any shortfalls resulting from delay in payments between default and repayment are paid by GNMA. This gives a GNMA certificate a double government guarantee: FHA/VA guarantees the mortgages and GNMA guarantees timely payment of principal and interest.

All payments are accompanied by a remittance notice that states the amount of principal being paid, the amounts of prepayments being made, and the amount of interest being paid.

Record date for payment on a GNMA certificate is the last day of each month.

MATURITY YIELDS OF GNMAs

The maturity of a GNMA is considered to be 12.5 years, which represents the average life of a 30-year mortgage.

Yields or rates of return on GNMAs are the subject of many arguments among experts. The problem with accurately assessing the rate of return on a GNMA stems from two sources: (1) the fact that, unlike other fixed-income securities, monthly payments include return of principal, and (2) the large prepayments that take place in some mortgage pools. The two most usual ways to measure the return of GNMAs are Pass Through or GNMA yield, and the corporate bond equivalent.

The GNMA yield or pass-through yield makes four basic assumptions:

1. For the first 12 years there are no prepayments or defaults. The investor receives all interest and scheduled principal payments on time.
2. The investor is able to reinvest the principal and interest payments at the same rate as the coupon on the GNMA. This is known as

compounding an "internal rate of return." The same concept is used in rate-of-return calculations for almost all fixed-income securities.

3.   The investor is able to reinvest his payments monthly.
4.   At the end of 12 years the total amount of unpaid principal is prepaid.

GNMA yield is the yield referred to in the cash and futures market when yields are quoted for purposes of "yield maintenance" contracts. Most of the business is contracted among dealers and in mortgage auctions. When these are held, dealers and all financial publications use the pass-through or GNMA yield as the standard.

Corporate Bond Equivalent

The corporate bond equivalent method adjusts the pass-through yield to a comparable yield for other fixed-income securities. Two adjustments must be made. First, since interest payments are not received until the fifteenth of the month, a negative adjustment must be made to account for the loss of reinvestment income. Second, a positive adjustment is made to account for the fact that the GNMA has monthly payment with reinvestment of principal and interest. This contrasts with the normal six-month interest payment on fixed-income securities. The amounts of these adjustments is a function of the level of interest rates and the subsequent reinvestment rates.

The corporate bond equivalent rate is often used by investors when comparing yields on GNMAs to other investments. Table 13.1 shows the "add on" or adjustment to pass-through yield that provides the corporate bond equivalent yield.

THE EFFECTS OF PREPAYMENTS

The mobility of the U.S. population makes prepayment of mortgages very common. As borrowers sell their homes they pay off their mortgages. Defaults, although not common, also happen. When either of these events occur they cause the GNMA holder to be paid back principal faster than expected, thus changing the expected return for the period the investment was held.

Table 13.1

If the GNMA is between	To get corporate bond yield add	If the GNMA is between	To get corporate bond yield add
7.72–8.01	0.13	14.01–14.17	0.42
8.02–8.30	0.14	14.18–14.33	0.43
8.31–8.58	0.15	14.34–14.49	0.44
8.59–8.85	0.16	14.50–14.65	0.45
8.86–9.11	0.17	14.66–14.81	0.46
9.12–9.37	0.18	14.82–14.97	0.47
9.38–9.62	0.19	14.98–15.12	0.48
9.63–9.86	0.20	15.13–15.28	0.49
9.87–10.10	0.21	15.29–15.43	0.50
10.11–10.33	0.22	15.44–15.58	0.51
10.34–10.55	0.23	15.59–15.73	0.52
10.56–10.77	0.24	15.74–15.88	0.53
10.78–10.99	0.25	15.89–16.03	0.54
11.00–11.20	0.25	16.04–16.17	0.55
11.21–11.41	0.27	16.18–16.31	0.56
11.42–11.62	0.28	16.32–16.46	0.57
11.63–11.82	0.29	16.47–16.60	0.58
11.83–12.01	0.30	16.61–16.74	0.59
12.02–12.21	0.31	16.75–16.88	0.60
12.22–12.40	0.32	16.89–17.01	0.61
12.41–12.59	0.33	17.02–17.15	0.62
12.60–12.77	0.34	17.16–17.29	0.63
12.78–12.96	0.35	17.30–17.42	0.64
12.97–13.13	0.36	17.43–17.55	0.65
13.14–13.31	0.37	17.56–17.69	0.66
13.32–13.49	0.38	17.70–17.82	0.67
13.50–13.66	0.39	17.83–17.95	0.68
13.67–13.83	0.40	17.96–18.08	0.69
13.84–14.00	0.41		

Prepayment can adversely affect the investor if the GNMAs were originally purchased at a premium, because it shortens the investment's life. However, if the original purchase price was at a discount, the investor would be receiving his money sooner than expected. Thus his yield would be higher than originally anticipated by the standard "pass-through yield."

The amount of prepayment is studied and analyzed each year by HUD. From these studies a "normal FHA experience," indicating the probability of a mortgage being prepayed, is developed. The study is conducted on a national as well as on a state-by-state basis. The Financial Publishing Company furnishes a book of tables indicating the average prepayment experience for every group of mortgages outstanding. When the factor for any particular GNMA pool is compared to the tables, one obtains the payment experience of that pool versus the average pool with similar coupons and maturity.

The data in Table 13.2 compare the GNMA 8.5% pools with various prepayment experiences. For example, all GNMA pools issued two years, 11 months ago should on average (100% column) have a factor of 0.9115. Those 8.5% GNMAs with higher factors have had fewer prepayments, and 8.5% GNMAs with factors less than 0.9115 have had greater than normal prepayments. The early prepayment history of a GNMA pool is often an indication of the total prepayment experience.

Experience in recent years has shown that the higher coupon GNMAs are prepaying at a much faster rate than lower coupon GNMAs. This suggests the weakness in calculating yield on the pass-through method, since such a method does not take account of prepayment before 12.5 years.

THE CASH MARKET FOR GNMAs

The market for GNMA pass-throughs began in the early 1970s to supplement the secondary market for mortgages. The first secondary market was the GNMA cash market.

GNMAs are very actively traded in the cash market through a group of dealers who act as principals to the trade. They are market makers who provide a bid or ask for investors seeking to participate in the cash market. Quotes are provided in increments of one thirty-second of a dollar. The spread between the bid and ask generally ranges from four thirty-seconds to eight thirty-seconds, depending on the coupon rate associated with a particular GNMA.

Standbys

A GNMA standby commitment is an agreement whereby one party commits to "standby" to receive a GNMA from another party. The

Table 13.2 8½% Pool Rate Decimal Balance Table[1]

DECIMALS BASED ON FHA MORTGAGE MORTALITY EXPERIENCE

Years	Months	300% FHA	200% FHA	150% FHA	125% FHA	100% FHA	75% FHA	50% FHA	0% FHA
0	1	0.9974	0.9981	0.9984	0.9986	0.9988	0.9989	0.9991	0.9995
0	2	0.9947	0.9961	0.9968	0.9972	0.9975	0.9979	0.9982	0.9989
0	3	0.9921	0.9942	0.9952	0.9957	0.9963	0.9968	0.9973	0.9981
0	4	0.9894	0.9922	0.9936	0.9948	0.9950	0.9957	0.9964	0.9978
0	5	0.9868	0.9903	0.9928	0.9929	0.9938	0.9946	0.9965	0.9972
0	6	0.9842	0.9883	0.9904	0.9915	0.9925	0.9936	0.9945	0.9967
0	7	0.9815	0.9864	0.9888	0.9900	0.9813	0.9925	0.9936	0.9961
0	8	0.9789	0.9844	0.9872	0.9886	0.9900	0.9914	0.9927	0.9955
0	9	0.9762	0.9825	0.9856	0.9871	0.9888	0.9903	0.9918	0.9949
0	10	0.9736	0.9805	0.9840	0.9857	0.9875	0.9892	0.9909	0.9943
0	11	0.9709	0.9786	0.9824	0.9843	0.9862	0.9881	9899	0.9938
1	0	0.9682	0.9765	0.9807	0.9827	0.9848	0.9869	0.9890	0.9832
1	1	0.9608	0.9713	0.9766	0.9783	0.9819	0.9845	0.9872	0.9926
1	2	0.9534	0.9662	0.9726	0.9758	0.9790	0.9823	0.9855	0.9920
1	3	0.9459	0.9610	0.9685	0.9723	0.9761	0.9799	0.9837	0.9914
1	4	0.9385	0.9558	0.9645	0.9688	0.9732	0.9776	0.9820	0.9908
1	5	0.9312	0.9506	0.9604	0.9653	0.9763	0.9752	0.9802	0.9901
1	6	0.9238	0.9455	0.9564	0.9619	0.9674	0.9729	0.9784	0.9895
1	7	0.9164	0.9403	0.9523	0.9584	0.9645	0.9706	0.9766	0.9889
1	8	0.9090	0.9852	0.9483	0.9549	0.9615	0.9682	0.9749	0.9883
1	9	0.9016	0.9800	0.9443	0.9514	0.9586	0.9659	0.9731	0.9876
1	10	0.8942	0.9248	0.9402	0.9479	0.9557	0.9635	0.9718	0.9870
1	11	0.8869	0.9197	0.9362	0.9444	0.9528	0.9612	0.9695	0.9853
2	0	0.8794	0.9144	0.9320	0.9409	0.9498	0.9587	0.9877	0.9857
2	1	0.8709	0.9083	0.9872	0.9368	0.9463	0.9559	0.9656	0.9850
2	2	0.8624	0.9022	0.9224	0.9326	0.9429	0.9581	0.9635	0.9844
2	3	0.8540	0.8961	0.9176	0.9285	0.9394	0.9594	0.9614	0.9837
2	4	0.8455	0.9800	0.9128	0.9243	0.9359	0.9476	0.9593	0.9830
2	5	0.8370	0.8840	0.9080	0.9202	0.9324	0.9448	0.9572	0.9824
2	6	0.8285	0.8779	0.9032	0.9169	0.9289	0.9419	0.9551	0.9817
2	7	0.8201	0.8718	0.8984	0.9119	0.9255	0.9391	0.9530	0.9810
2	8	0.8116	0.8657	0.8935	0.9077	0.9220	0.9363	0.9509	0.9803
2	9	0.8032	0.8597	0.8887	0.9036	0.9185	0.9335	0.9488	0.9795
2	10	0.7947	0.8536	0.8839	0.8994	0.9150	0.9307	0.9487	0.9789
2	11	0.7863	0.8475	0.8791	0.8913	0.9115	0.9279	0.9445	0.9782
3	0	0.7778	0.8414	0.8743	0.8910	0.9080	0.9251	0.9428	0.9775
3	1	0.7689	0.8348	0.8690	0.8864	0.9041	0.9219	0.9490	0.9768
3	2	0.7601	0.8282	0.8637	0.8818	0.9002	0.9188	0.9876	0.9761
3	3	0.7512	0.8216	0.8584	0.8772	0.8963	0.9156	0.9353	0.9754
3	4	0.7424	0.8151	0.8531	0.8726	0.8924	0.9125	0.9329	0.9746
3	5	0.7335	0.8085	0.8478	0.8680	0.8885	0.9094	0.9305	0.9739
3	6	0.7247	0.8019	0.8425	0.8634	0.8846	0.9062	0.9281	0.9731
3	7	0.7159	0.7953	0.8372	0.8588	0.8807	0.9081	0.9258	0.9724
3	8	0.7071	0.7888	0.8320	0.8542	0.8769	0.8999	0.9284	0.9715
3	9	0.6983	0.7822	0.8267	0.8496	0.8730	0.8968	0.9210	0.9709
3	10	0.6895	0.7757	0.8214	0.8450	0.8591	0.8935	0.9185	0.9701
3	11	0.6807	0.7691	0.8161	0.8404	0.8652	0.8905	0.9162	0.9894
4	0	0.6720	0.7625	0.8108	0.8358	0.8613	0.8823	0.9138	0.9686

Table 13.2   8 ½% Pool Rate Decimal Balance Table¹ *(Continued)*

		DECIMALS BASED ON FHA MORTGAGE MORTALITY EXPERIENCE							
		300%	200%	150%	125%	100%	75%	50%	0%
Years	Months	FHA	FHA	FHA	FHA	FHA	FHA	FHA	FHA
4	1	0.6635	0.7559	0.8054	0.8310	0.8572	0.8839	0.9113	0.9678
4	2	0.6550	0.7493	0.7999	0.8262	0.8531	0.8806	0.9087	0.9670
4	3	0.6465	0.7426	0.7944	0.8214	0.8480	0.8772	0.9062	0.9662
4	4	0.6380	0.7360	0.7890	0.8186	0.8448	0.8789	0.9336	0.9854
4	5	0.6295	0.7294	0.7835	0.8118	0.8439	0.8705	0.9012	0.9846
4	6	0.6210	0.7228	0.7781	0.8070	0.8367	0.8672	0.8985	0.9838
4	7	0.6126	0.7161	0.7726	0.8022	0.8326	0.8723	0.8959	0.9630
4	8	0.6041	0.7095	0.7672	0.7974	0.8285	0.8604	0.8934	0.9622
4	9	0.5957	0.7029	0.7618	0.7926	0.8244	0.8571	0.8903	0.9618
4	10	0.5872	0.6963	0.7563	0.7878	0.8203	0.8537	0.8882	0.9605
4	11	0.5788	0.6897	0.7509	0.7830	0.8152	0.8504	0.8856	0.9596
5	0	0.5703	0.6831	0.7454	0.7782	0.8120	0.8470	0.8831	0.9588
5	1	0.5624	0.6765	0.7399	0.7733	0.8378	0.8435	0.8804	0.9579
5	2	0.5545	0.6700	0.7344	0.7634	0.8036	0.8400	0.8777	0.9571
5	3	0.5466	0.6635	0.7289	0.7635	0.7993	0.8365	0.8750	0.9562
5	4	0.5387	0.6571	0.7234	0.7585	0.7951	0.8339	0.8723	0.9553
5	5	0.5309	0.6506	0.7180	0.7537	0.7909	0.8295	0.8676	0.9545
5	6	0.5280	0.6441	0.7125	0.7488	0.7867	0.8260	0.8669	0.9536

¹The mortgage rate for borrower is 1/2% greater because of service charge, the decimal is the proportion of original pool still unpaid according to assumptions as to experience for elapsed time. It thus corresponds to decimal published by GNMA

buyer who is standing by makes a commitment to purchase a GNMA from the seller at a specific price on a specific date. The price is negotiated at the time of commitment. Some of these commitments contain a yield maintenance clause that allows the seller to deliver any GNMA coupon he wishes to the buyer, but only at the yield specified in the original commitment. However, the seller cannot force the buyer to pay more than par for any coupon unless otherwise negotiated at the time of commitment. This type of contract is known as a "par cap" contract.

For example, suppose a person commits to "stand by" to receive 12.5% GNMA at a price of 98⁸/₃₂, and no negotiations were made with regard to paying more than par. The 98⁸/₃₂ price reflects a yield of 12.70%. In this case, the seller could, at the time of exercising the standby, deliver any of the coupons at the prices shown in Table 13.3. However, if rates were to rise and the current coupon change were to represent 13%, the seller would not be paid more than par (100) for the 13%. A yield of 12.704 on a 13% coupon equates to a dollar price of

$101^{8}/_{32}$. The seller would be forced to deliver another GNMA against his standby or lose the $1^{8}/_{32}$ premium.

The GNMA Dealers Association has been unable to arrive at a consensus on whether the par cap clauses should be abolished or endorsed. Consequently, the par cap restrictions are currently negotiated from dealer to dealer.

The seller pays a "commitment fee" to the buyer for the right to make delivery in the future. The commitment fee is usually cash, but may be a strike price lower than the current market value of the current GNMA coupon.

The standby market in GNMAs has been subject to many problems, most of which stem from the overextension of buyers. This has led to financial problems as a number of institutions have been forced into bankruptcy.

Standbys had originally been written for time periods of a year or more but recently sellers have been unwilling to pay fees to standby buyers for periods of less than six months.

THE PASS-THROUGH FORWARD MARKET

The GNMA forward market is a dealer market. Although standbys can be negotiated between any two parties, the forward cash market revolves around dealers who "make" the market.

In the forward market participants make commitments to buy or sell to one another at specific prices for future settlement, without commitment fees. Forward markets rarely are active for commitments longer than six months. The newest regulations from the Federal Reserve

Table 13.3

GNMA	Price	Yield
12.5%	98 $^{8}/_{32}$	12.704
11.5%	92 $^{9}/_{32}$	12.704
10.5%	86 $^{13}/_{32}$	12.704
10%	83 $^{15}/_{32}$	12.704
9.5%	80 $^{18}/_{32}$	12.704
9%	77 $^{23}/_{32}$	12.704

Table 13.4   Normal Standby Commitment

Seller	Buyer
Pays commitment fee	Receives commitment fee
Receives right to sell to buyer at strike price on current coupon	Must pay the strike price for the current coupon (current at the time of commitment) if seller exercises his options
Receives right to sell another coupon to buyer at the same yield as the pass-through yield of the current coupon at the strike price	Must purchase a different GNMA coupon at a price that will return the same yield as the current coupon at the strike price
Cannot deliver a coupon different from the current coupon at a price that exceeds par or 100	Does not have to pay a premium for any GNMA coupon that might be delivered
The GNMA pool must have a factor of at least 0.997499.	Will receive a GNMA pool with a factor of at least 0.997499
If the size of the standby is $1,000,000, can deliver only two separate GNMA pools that add up to 1,000,000.	If the size of the standby is $1,000,000, will receive no more than two separate GNMA pools that add up to 1,000,000
If the standby is for less than 1,000,000, only one pool can be used.	If the standby is for less than 1,000,000, will receive only one pool
Risk is limited to the commitment fee, plus the possibility buyer will be unable to make payment at delivery time.	*Risk is unlimited*
Receives no margin.	Pays no margin

Board, Federal Deposit Insurance Corp., and the Comptroller of the Currency limit commercial banks, savings banks, and S&Ls to a maximum commitment of 150 days. Thus, they cannot enter into a contract to deliver or receive a GNMA pass-through certificate that would mature in 150 days or more.

Yield Maintenance Contract

The forward market trades in yield maintenance contracts, which are very similar to the contracts in the standby market. The buyer purchases the current coupon at a specific price for delivery in a specified month. The yield of that current coupon at the agreed-upon price is the "yield maintenance" price the buyer has committed to pay in the future. There is no strike price above which the agreement is "in the money." There is no standby provision. The buyer contracts to buy at a particular price and the seller contracts to sell at that price.

If, for example, the current coupon is 11.5% and the price for June delivery was 89²⁄₃₂, the yield would be 13.290. Regardless of the direction interest rates moved in the interim, both parties would be obligated to settle the contract at a yield maintenance rate of 13.290.

Par Cap Contracts

Yield maintenance contracts often contain an added convenant that limits the dollar price paid by the buyer. This is known as a "par cap limitation."

Most forward contracts contain par cap conditions. Under these par cap agreements the seller is prohibited from delivering a coupon to the seller at a price in excess of par. And an 11.5% yield maintenance contract cannot be fulfilled with a 12% GNMA at any price higher than par. Many GNMA dealers have begun to make the par cap provisions optional or are refusing to deal in par cap forward contracts. The reason for this is that the par cap provision creates added risk for dealers when rates are moving up sharply.

For example, assume a dealer sells, on a forward agreement, 11.5% GNMAs at a price of 94⁷⁄₃₂ to yield 12.3%. If rates rose sharply and the Federal Home Loan Bank raised the base lending rate for FHA/VA loans to 13%, then the current GNMA coupon would become 12.5%.

Assume the seller goes to another dealer and covers his short by buying a 12.5% GNMA at a yield of 13.5. This would equate to a price of 87³⁰⁄₃₂.

He would deliver the 12.5% GNMA to his original customer, but because of the par cap restrictions he would not receive more than 100 for it. The original buyer purchased a 12.3% yield. The new coupon of

Table 13.5   Forward Market for GNMAs

Seller	Buyer
Pays no fees	Receives no fees
Sells at a specific price for current coupon with yield maintenance provisions	Purchases GNMAs at a specific price for current coupon with yield maintenance provisions
Cannot deliver under the yield maintenance agreement at a price higher than 100 (optional par cap agreement)	Will not have to pay higher than par for optional GNMA coupons under the yield maintenance contract
GNMA pools delivered to the buyer must have an average factor of at least 0.9974999	Receives GNMA pools with an average factor of at least 0.9974999
If the size of the GNMA contracted for is $1,000,000, can deliver two GNMA pools that add up to $1,000,000 and have an average factor of 0.997499	If the size of the GNMA contracted for is 1,000,000, can deliver two GNMA pools that add up to $1,000,000 and have an average factor of 0.997499
If the commitment is for less than $1,000,000 only one GNMA pool may be used	If the commitment is for $1,000,000 only one GNMA pool may be used
Risk to market exposure is unlimited	Risk to market exposure is unlimited
Risk that the buyer will not be solvent at the time of delivery is an additional uncertainty if the market is lower than the trade price	Risk that the seller will not make delivery if the market price improves over the original price
No margins are usually paid or received	No margins are usually paid or received
Liquidity often restricted by credit limitations in regard to existing or potential buyers	Liquidity often restricted by credit limitations in regard to existing or potential sellers
Regulators limit the length of contracts for many potential buyers	Regulators limit the length of contracts for many potential sellers

12.5% would reflect a price of $100\tfrac{5}{32}$, so the seller would lose $\tfrac{5}{32}$ of his profit and the buyer would gain 0.5% in yield.

The "par cap" restriction favors the buyer to the detriment of the seller, but the par cap is vital to continued existence of the forward market. The reason is that, as noted earlier, premium prices substantially lower the returns to the investor in GNMAs when prepayments at par cause his principal to be paid back faster than the assumed 12.5 years. If rates were to fall, it would be expected that more prepayments would occur as old mortgages were refinanced. In such a situation buyers would be hesitant under a non-par cap condition to make a commitment to take a future delivery of GNMAs, unless they could do so at substantial discount to alternative fixed-income securities.

THE GUARANTEED COUPON MARKET

Many dealers make markets to buy or sell GNMAs without a yield maintenance agreement. They simply quote a firm price to buy or sell GNMAs and guarantee the delivery of a specified coupon at settlement of the trade. This market is highly speculative and the dealers take the risk that there will be or will not be enough of a particular coupon available to meet standards.

CHAPTER FOURTEEN

The GNMA Futures Market

The futures market for GNMAs offers the following three key elements not available in the cash forward market:

1. An exchange environment where large numbers of buyers and sellers lend depth and liquidity to the market and where buyers and sellers have anonymity and an umbrella of regulations and surveillance that helps protect the participant from abuse.
2. Standardized contracts with the terms clearly defined.
3. A clearing corporation that provides financial integrity to the transactions and reduces the credit risks associated with forward markets.

The GNMA futures market is the oldest of the interest rate futures, having been started in October 1975 on the CBT. The market was an almost immediate success as both volume and open interest increased rapidly and steadily during the first few years of its existence. The concept of futures markets was new to GNMA cash dealers but the concept of forward settlement dates had been a part of their life for over five years prior to the beginning of the GNMA futures market.

In the exchange environment two types of GNMA contracts emerged: the CDR, or Collateralized Depository Receipts contract, and the CD, or Certificate Delivery contract.

THE COLLATERALIZED DEPOSITORY RECEIPT CONTRACT

The CDR contract was the original GNMA contract devised by the CBT and remains the most actively traded of all GNMA contracts. It is used extensively for hedging GNMA commitments and also for intermediate term debt instruments of all types.

CHARACTERISTICS OF THE GNMA CDR

The CDR is a yield maintenance contract based upon an 8% GNMA with a 30-year maturity prepaid in 12 years. The yield calculations are pass-through or GNMA yields.

The Receipt

The CDR is a document signed by a depository that attests that a CDR originator[1] has deposited $100,000 minimum principal balance of GNMA 8s (8% coupon). Only an originator can create CDRs, and originators are classified as such by the CBT. An originator must be bonded, the amount of the bond depending on the number of receipts that are to be originated.

The originator places pools of GNMAs with a depository bank and has the GNMA pools re-registered in the name of the depository or its nominee. Once the re-registration takes place the originator gives the depository a CDR to sign that verifies there is $100,000 principal balance minimum of GNMA 8% certificates, or their equivalent, in safekeeping. Thus, when delivery of the CDR contract takes place, the buyer of the contract receives a certified depository receipt entitling him to obtain from the depository $100,000 worth of GNMA 8% pass-through certificates or their equivalent. This last phrase is important.

---

[1] A CDR originator, as distinguished from a *GNMA cash originator*, is one who is registered at the exchange as an organization that can originate the CD receipt in order to accomplish delivery on the futures.

THE CDR—A YIELD MAINTENANCE CONTRACT

The CDR contract is a yield maintenance contract. Coupons other than 8% coupons can be delivered, but to be acceptable for delivery they must provide a yield equivalent to that of a principal balance of $100,000 of GNMA 8s, calculated at par under the assumption of a 30-year certificate prepaid in 12 years.

This means that if a seller were to deliver a GNMA with a coupon less than 8% he would have to deliver more than $100,000 face value. If the coupon being delivered were higher than 8% the seller would deliver less than $100,000 face value.

The data in Table 14.1 indicate the face value amount to be delivered given a particular interest rate, in order to provide a yield equivalent to a GNMA 8%. This aspect is very important to the hedger who might want to make delivery of a GNMA pool to the CDR contract. If the coupon to be delivered is larger than 8%, the hedger will have to sell more CDR contracts than the face value of his GNMA. For example,

Table 14.1*

GNMA interest rate	Amount equivalent to $100,000 principal of GNMA 8s	GNMA interest Rate	Amount equivalent to $100,000 principal of GNMA 8s
6	116,702	10	87,088
6.25	114,362	10.25	85,686
6.5	112,100	10.5	84,324
6.75	109,913	10.75	83,002
7	107,797	11	81,718
7.25	105,751	11.25	80,470
7.5	103,771	11.5	79,258
7.75	101,855	11.75	78,079
8	100,000	12	76,934
8.25	98,203	12.25	75,819
8.5	96,463	12.5	74,735
8.75	94,777	12.75	73,680
9	93,143	13	72,654
9.25	91,559	13.25	71,654
9.5	90,023	13.5	70,680
9.75	88,534	13.75	69,732
		14	68,808

*Financial Publishing Co., Publication 736, Revised, p. 5.

a hedger who wished to deliver $1,000,000 of 12.5% GNMAs could only present $74,735 of principal for each CDR contract. Therefore, the seller needs to short an average of 13.38 contracts for every million dollars of cash GNMA 12.5%. If a hedger wanted to deliver $1,000,000 of 6.5% GNMAs, he would need to sell only an average of 8.92 contracts ($1,000,000 ÷ 112,100 = 8.92).

Par Cap

There is no par cap provision in the CDR contract. Any price is eligible for delivery. This is important. The buyer, or receiver, of a CDR who exercises his right to redeem the CDR and receive the actual cash GNMAs may receive any GNMA without regard to coupon or price.

The absence of a par cap in the CDR specifications puts the buyer at a slight disadvantage if the pools backing a CDR have large premiums. This would discourage a buyer from redeeming his CDR and taking possession of the underlying GNMAs, because premium coupons encourage fast prepayment of principal.

A Perpetual Obligation Without Principal Payment

The CDR is a perpetual obligation of the originator to maintain the principal balance in the deposit account at $100,000 of GNMA 8%, or its equivalent. As the GNMAs that back or collateralize a CDR generate principal payments, the originator receives them and must reinvest these monies in GNMAs to keep the deposit account up to $100,000. The holder of the CDR does not receive the principal payment directly and therefore does not receive the benefits of reinvestment that he normally would if he owned an actual GNMA.

The CDR holder receives $635 per month in interest regardless of the coupon rate on pools in the deposit account. When such rates are high and GNMA pools containing higher current coupons are used for collateralizing CDRs, buyers will often surrender their CDRs and obtain the underlying GNMAs to receive the benefits of higher current incomes and faster prepayments usually associated with higher GNMA rates.

CDRs Have a One-Year Life

On the last interest date prior to the CDR becoming one year old the holder must present the originator with the CDR for renewal. At that time, the originator has the right to replace the old CDR with a new CDR originated by himself or another originator. He would do this in declining rate markets, because as rates go lower he can take out some profit and replace the old GNMAs with current coupon GNMAs.

The Number of Pools in a CDR

A CDR deposit account may contain as many pools of GNMAs as necessary for the seller of the futures to meet his principal requirements. This means that a holder who surrenders a $1,000,000 CDR to the originator may receive a delivery unit that would not be eligible for delivery into the cash market or the CD futures market. The cash and CD markets limit the number of "pieces" or pools that a seller may deliver per $1,000,000 of principal value to two separate pools.

DELIVERY

The opportunity to make and take delivery is a key element in any futures contract and is the aspect of futures trading that assures that cash and futures prices converge when the futures contract matures. The delivery process for the CDR contract is completely different from the delivery process for cash GNMAs, and is somewhat more difficult to complete. Because of the difficulty of delivery terms, the CDR contract has relatively few deliveries. The contract is used extensively by hedgers who do not wish to make or take actual delivery of GNMAs, but rather are seeking to protect themselves from adverse price movement.

Figure 14.1 shows the steps to be followed by the various parties to accomplish delivery

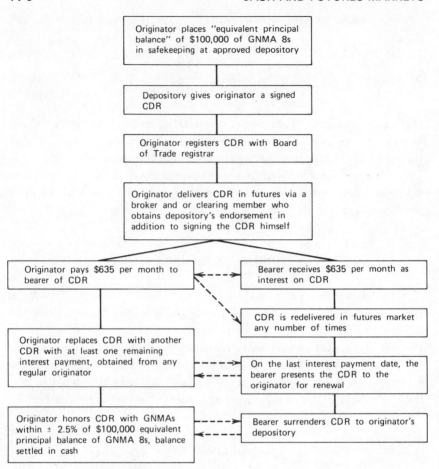

Figure 14.1 Schematic diagram of origination, delivery, and surrender of CDRs. (*Making and Taking Delivery of Interest Rate Future Contracts*, 2nd rev. ed., Chicago Board of Trade, 1977, p.23)

COUPON SLIPPAGE

Coupon slippage or "price compression" refers to differentials in price changes as yields change on fixed-income securities. In other words, different coupons have different absolute dollar price changes associated with the same change in yield. This phenomenon is very important when hedging with a yield maintenance contract. Therefore, a hedger using the CDR must be sure to get full coverage in dollars when yields change sharply.

Table 14.2 shows absolute dollar changes when yields move from 9% to 10% for coupons ranging from 6% to 12%. As one can see, higher coupons have greater absolute dollar changes than lower coupons for the same rate changes. If an investor hedged a 12% GNMA with a yield maintenance CDR when rates were 9% and they then moved to 10%, he would have an opportunity loss of $1^{32}/_{64}$, or the difference between $7^{53}/_{64}$ and $6^{21}/_{64}$.

When hedging or using fixed-coupon yield maintenance contracts, one should take into consideration coupon slippage as part of the basis calculation. A larger futures hedge should be used when hedging higher coupon GNMAs, and a smaller hedge when hedging lower coupon GNMAs.

It is important to note also that the concept of coupon slippage applies to *all* yield maintenance contracts, not just GNMAs.

The severity of coupon slippage is affected also by the maturity of the security. For example, a bond with an 8% coupon and five years to maturity will have a different "coupon slippage" than a bond with an 8% coupon and 15 years to maturity. For those readers interested in exploring this idea further, *Inside the Yield Curve* by Homer and Liebowitz (Englewood Cliffs, N.J.: Prentice-Hall, 1979), contains an excellent exposition.

In GNMAs, unlike normal fixed-income bonds, volatility increases as coupon increases if yield changes and maturities are equal. Slippage

Table 14.2*

Certificate Rate (%)	Price to Yield 9%	Price to Yield 10%	Change in Price
6	79–15	73–42	5–37
7	85–57	79–60	5–61
8	92–45	86–24	6–21
9	99–40	92–60	6–44
10	106–43	99–38	7–05
11	113–50	106–21	7–29
12	120–62	113–09	7–53

*Financial Publishing Co., Publication 736 Revised, p. 6.

increases with maturity if coupon and yield are the same. Slippage in the higher yield ranges are greater than slippages in the lower yield ranges.

In summary, coupon slippage is dependent on three factors: the coupon, the level of interest rates, and the maturity of the security.

THE CERTIFICATE DELIVERY FUTURES CONTRACT

As noted earlier, the CDR futures contract has certain features that inhibit delivery. The Certificate of Delivery (CD) contract was designed to correct some of those problems. As of this writing, the CD contract has had so little trading and the prices have sometimes been so much at variance with the cash prices that it is debatable whether the CD contract has actually added much to the marketplace.

LIQUIDITY

The CDR futures contract has much greater liquidity than any of the CD futures contracts. This is due to the fact that most originators and commercial users find that the CDR is a better contract for hedging. The CDR has no par cap restriction or limitation on numbers of deliverable pools. This insulates the CDR contract from some of the supply factors that arise in the origination process, and from the effects that potential rate changes have on the possible supply of GNMAs available to meet the delivery specifications of a par cap requirement. These factors often cause the CD and cash markets to trade at substantially different prices from older GNMAs in existing portfolios.

Mortgage banks and mortgage originators use the CD contracts as a means of selling inventory when the prices of the CDs are higher than comparable prices in the cash market. Because the cash market does not require margins, and the futures markets do, the originators have tended to use the CD futures contract only when the price of a CD futures is considerably higher than the cash market.

DIFFERENCES BETWEEN THE CASH AND FUTURES MARKETS FOR GNMAs

The GNMA futures market offers something for everyone. Speculators, hedgers, and originators can all find a GNMA futures contract that is right for their needs. But they must know and fully understand the contract specifications of the particular contract they choose. The specifications of the various GNMA contracts will determine future relative price actions and are the important determinant of the basis relationship between the cash market and futures.

There are few important differences between cash and futures in regard to delivery procedures.

Failure to Deliver

The futures markets do not tolerate a failure to deliver on time or in good form. A "fail," as it is called by cash traders, occurs when one of the parties *temporarily* fails to meet the time or current form requirements as specified in the original agreement. When this happens in the cash market, the delivery is delayed and the offending party loses interest on the investment until a "good" delivery is completed. The loss of interest is usually sufficient inducement to discourage fails in the cash market.

In the futures market there is no accommodation for a fail. A late delivery, or one in incorrect form, is considered to be a default on contract specifications. The defaulting party is subject to substantial fines from the exchange as well as the loss of interest.

Thus, if one is planning to make delivery in the futures market it is imperative that the seller have his GNMAs in position to give proper delivery. Otherwise the failure can be costly.

Time Difference in the Delivery Process

The CDR contract stipulates that the seller must deposit his cash GNMAs prior to the actual settlement date. Most clearing members require that the GNMAs be delivered to them prior to the actual required delivery day to ensure against failure to deliver on the part of the seller. The CDR delivery process takes four days. Thus, the seller has to finance the certificates for at least those four days, and this cost must be calculated into the cost of using the futures market as a means of disposing of inventory. This extra financing cost is not necessary when delivering to a cash market dealer.

Number of Pools in Delivery Unit

The CBT contract does not limit the number of pools that are deliverable per delivery unit; it allows the seller to deliver as many pools as he wishes to meet his commitment, regardless of the size of the commitment. The cash market limits the seller to two pools per $1,000,000, and to one pool when the amount to be delivered is less than $1,-000,000. This means that the buyer who takes delivery on the CBT may find that the pools delivered may not comprise good delivery in the cash market. This would severely reduce the secondary market potential for his newly purchased GNMAs.

CASH FLOW AND FUTURES CONTRACTS

The futures market demands daily settlement of losses and gains. Thus, using a futures contract can have a very real impact on the cash flow of a buyer or seller. If a mortgage banker were to sell short a contract on a futures exchange and the market were to go lower in price between the time of sale and the time of delivery, the banker would be paid his profits daily in cash. By the same token, if the price rises between time of sale and time of delivery, the banker must deposit his daily losses in cash.

This is not the case in the cash market. There the seller receives his profit on settlement date. The positive cash flow of the futures can be quite valuable when rates paid on short-term money are high and the seller reinvests his profits daily. However, a period of negative cash flow in the futures can cause problems for the seller who has not planned his cash flow needs correctly. The cash market might not lower his losses, but it would not cause him cash flow problems prior to delivery.

PART FOUR

Hedging Uses and Techniques

CHAPTER FIFTEEN

The Concept of Hedging

Several years ago the CFTC decided it was time to develop a modern definition of the concept of hedging. A casual perusal of the statistics on users of futures markets had revealed that many corporations who could hedge were not doing so. A little reflection revealed why.

The traditional and "text book" concept of hedging was so narrow as to severely limit the use of the markets for risk shifting purposes. The old definition simply precluded many legitimate uses of the market for managing price risk. For example, unless one had the nearly identical product in the cash market as was reflected in the futures market, it was frequently not considered a hedge by the federal government. Boards of directors of major corporations were regularly advised by their legal counsel that unless their use of these futures markets coincided directly with the narrow definition used by the federal government, their futures positions would not be treated as hedges by the IRS.

Thus, the federal government's definition of hedging was severely hampering the opportunity for the business community to use the markets for the precise purpose for which they had been developed.

In order to satisfy the niceties of the law and to assure the proper technical expertise would be brought to bear in developing the new definition, the CFTC held a series of hearings around the U.S. titled "What is Hedging?" Scholars of all sorts, chief executive officers of major corporations, experienced commercial users of futures markets, professional commodity speculators, and a lot of others were invited to these meetings to speak their mind and to answer the question. After hundreds of hours of hearings, thousands of pages of testimony, and dozens of days spent in analyzing the information, the new definition was ready. The following is the new definition:

(1) *General Definition.* Bona fide hedging transactions and positions shall mean transactions or positions in a contract for future delivery on any contract market, where such transactions or positions normally represent a substitute for transactions to be made or positions to be taken at a later time in a physical marketing channel, and where they are economically appropriate to the reduction of risks in the conduct and management of a commercial enterprise, and where they arise from:

(i) The potential change in the value of assets which a person owns, produces, manufactures, processes, or merchandises or anticipates owning, producing, manufacturing, processing, or merchandising.

(ii) The potential change in the value of liabilities which a person owes or anticipates incurring, or

(iii) The potential change in the value of services which a person provides, purchases or anticipates providing or purchasing.

Notwithstanding the foregoing, no transactions or positions shall be classified as bona fide hedging for purposes of section 4a of the Act unless their purpose is to offset price risks incidental to commercial cash or spot operations and such positions are established and liquidated in an orderly manner in accordance with sound commercial practices and unless the provisions of paragraphs (2) and (3) of this section and sections 1.47 and 1.48 of the regulations have been satisfied.

(2) *Enumerated Hedging Transactions.* The definition of bona fide hedging transactions and positions in paragraph (1) of this section includes, but is not limited to, the following specific transactions and positions:

(i) *Sales* of any commodity for future delivery on a contract market which do not exceed in quantity:

(A) Ownership or fixed-price purchase of the same cash commodity by the same person; and

(B) Twelve months' unsold anticipated production of the same commodity by the same person provided that no such position is maintained in any future during the five last trading days of that future.

(ii) *Purchases* of any commodity for future delivery on a contract market which do not exceed in quantity:

(A) The fixed-price sale of the same cash commodity by the same person;

(B) The quantity equivalent of fixed-price sales of the cash products and by-products of such commodity by the same person; and

(C) Twelve months' unfilled anticipated requirements of the same cash commodity for processing, manufacturing, or feeding by the same person, provided that such transactions and positions in the five last trading days of any one future do not exceed the person's unfilled anticipated requirements of the same cash commodity for that month and for the next succeeding month.

(iii) Sales and purchases for future delivery described in paragraphs (2)(i) and (2)(ii) of this section may also be offset other than by the same quantity of the same cash commodity, provided that the fluctuations in value of the position for future delivery are substantially related to the fluctuations in value of the actual or anticipated cash position, and provided that the positions in any one future shall not be maintained during the five last trading days of that future.

(3) *Non-Enumerated Cases.* Upon specific requests made in accordance with section 1.47 of the regulations, the Commission may recognize transactions and positions other than those enumerated in paragraph (2) of this section as bona fide hedging in such amounts and under such terms and conditions as it may specify in accordance with the provisions of § 1.47. Such transactions and positions may include, but are not limited to, purchases or sales for future delivery on any contract market by an agent who does not own or who has not contracted to sell or purchase the offsetting cash commodity at a fixed price, *provided* that the person is responsible for the merchandising of the cash position which is being offset.

In short, a bona fide hedge requires the future position to be economically related to the cash position and designed to reduce the risk of managing a commerical enterprise.

TRADITIONAL HEDGING THEORY

Traditional hedging theory emphasizes the risk avoidance potential of futures markets. Hedgers are envisioned as taking futures positions exactly equal and opposite of the position they have in the cash market. For example, a holder of $10 million in Treasury bonds would protect himself against a decline in price by selling short $10 million of Treasury bond futures. When the inventory was sold the futures contracts would be repurchased, canceling the previous short position.

Traditional theory states that spot and futures prices generally move together so that the gains or losses in the futures market will be offset by the gains or losses in the cash market. In traditional theory the concept of "basis," defined as the difference between futures prices and spot prices, is most important. A hedge is traditionally viewed as perfect if the change in the basis is zero or if the expected basis is realized. In reality, such perfect hedges are rare. Further, the theory of adaptive expectations suggests that if futures prices reflect market expectations they should not normally match changes in cash prices. This theory implies that any change in the spot price will be accompanied by a proportional but not necessarily equal movement of the futures prices.

In other words, the basis will be likely to change. It is clear that in reality the basis does change, and therefore most traditional hedges are not perfect. The traditional or conventional practice of illustrating hedging with a hypothetical example, in which the price of the futures bought or sold as a hedge rises or falls by the exact amount that the spot price rises or falls, is a mistaken notion.

Holbrook Working, considered by many the dean of economists working in the area of futures trading and hedging and the economist most responsible for developing the underlying concepts of futures and hedging, has challenged the view of hedgers as pure risk minimizers and instead emphasized expected profit maximization. In his view, hedgers function much like speculators. Since they hold positions in the cash market as well, they are concerned with relative, not absolute, price changes. Instead of expecting cash and futures prices to move together, he argues that most hedging is done in *expectation* of a change in the spot/futures price relationship. Holders of a long position in the cash market would, according to Working, hedge if the basis was expected to fall and would not hedge if the basis was expected to rise. Hedgers thus are, in effect, speculating on the basis.

PORTFOLIO HEDGING THEORY

Johnson and Stein integrated the concept of risk avoidance, the heart of traditional theory, with Workings' expected-profit maximization theory. They argued that one buys and sells futures for the same risk return reasons that one buys or sells any other portfolio assets. While traditional theory argued that hedgers should always be completely hedged, portfolio theory suggested why hedgers would hold both hedged and unhedged actual commodity stock. In the portfolio theory model, cash and futures market holdings are not viewed as substitutes. Instead, spot market holdings are viewed as fixed and the decision is how much of these actual stocks to hedge. Thus, the question comes down to a comparison of the expected return on an unhedged position versus the return on a portfolio that includes both cash market holdings and futures market holdings. In the latter case, the portfolio may be either completely or partially hedged and there is no presumption as in traditional theory that the position in the futures market is exactly equal and opposite to the position in the cash market.

In today's world actual practice suggests that the portfolio theory of hedging is more widely accepted than the traditional theory. That does not mean that the concept of basis is irrelevant. It is still the heart of risk neutralization. Portfolio theory only makes more explicit the need to calculate and evaluate risk exposure and make the decision on how much risk is desirable prior to the application of the concept of basis. The new CFTC definition of hedging reflects portfolio theory of hedging and so do the modern day accounting procedures explained in Chapter 19. It is with these concepts of basis, risk evaluation, and risk tolerance in mind that the following sets forth the decision-making steps in a hedging program.

WHO HEDGES AND WHY

The purpose of hedging in interest rate futures is to establish in advance a particular rate of interest for a specific period of time. Borrowers may seek to establish a specific cost of money to protect themselves from higher interest costs and to enhance the success of business decisions involving factors sensitive to interest rates. Lenders seek protection against lower rates.

Portfolio managers and holders of fixed income securities can hedge to protect the value of their assets from erosion during periods of rising interest rates. Lenders and investors with cash can hedge against declining rates by buying futures at current high yields.

Hedging provides the portfolio manager with a great deal of flexibility in investment choices and in timing his purchases and sales. This is especially pertinent for investment managers operating under a corporate policy of not selling a security that has a current principal loss, as the futures profit helps offset the decline in asset value, and thus significantly broadens the portfolio manager's available alternatives.

Mortgage bank and savings and loan institutions can use the GNMA futures markets to hedge both the mortgages they plan to hold and the mortgages they currently hold.

Builders can lock in construction loan costs and protect themselves from higher mortgage rates through the use of futures.

Corporations can use futures to protect against higher borrowing costs and higher sinking fund costs while at the same time smoothing out their cash flow.

MAKING THE HEDGING DECISION

Hedging should be looked upon as a process of risk management that involves decisions as to whether, when, and how to utilize the futures markets. As with any tool, its benefits hinge on the skill with which it is used. To do an intelligent and informed job of hedging one must consider two fundamental criteria: the economic outlook and the economic practicability of a hedge. The following questions will aid one in making the hedging decision. These questions apply whether one is hedging in the forward markets or the futures markets; hedging lumber, wheat, or interest rates.

Question 1. What is the risk exposure?

The objective in answering this question is to quantify the loss that would be incurred if there were no hedge. To answer this question one needs to go far beyond the simple accounting calculation of how much money is involved. The answer also includes analysis of the outlook for interest rates, the estimation of the size of the rate change, and the probability of its occurrence.

Once the determination has been made as to the probable direction and size of the rate change and the probability of it's occurrence, one can plug the numbers into a simple mathematical expectation model and arrive at a quantification of risk exposure associated with not hedging.

Question 2. Is the risk affordable?

Frequently one will find that the answer to Question 1 on risk exposure will be such that one can bear the risk without hedging. That decision should be based on the relative size of the risk compared to the capital of the entity taking the risk. If the risk is small and the capital of the firm is large, management may decide that it is a risk not worth covering. On the other hand, if the risk is quite large relative to the capital of the firm the banker may insist that the firm hedge.

Question 3. Is the risk hedgeable in the futures markets?

The answer to this question is found largely through analysis of the correlation of price movements in the cash instrument (from which the risk emanates) and the relevant futures contract. It is necessary to draw a distinction between correlations between rates and correlations between price movements. It is entirely possible to have a high correlation between rate changes of a given cash instrument and a futures contract and still have a very low correlation in prices. For example, the value of .01 change in the rate for 90-day T-bill futures is $25. The value of .01 change in the rate for a six-month CD is $50. Hence, if one were using T-bill futures to hedge risk incurred in a six-month CD, one should use twice the dollar equivalent in the futures markets to reflect the risk associated with the cash market position. The important point here is to hedge dollar equivalency, not dollar equality.

Whether the appropriate correlation for a reasonable hedge is .80 or .90 depends on the discretion of the individual manager. It is possible that a manager may conclude that a 70% correlation gives him a high enough probability that he will transfer a sufficient amount of risk through the hedge to make it worthwhile.

Even in instances where the correlation is not high and the basis is unstable but the volatility in the cash-market instrument is high, a hedge with a low correlation will be much preferred over no hedge at all. For example, if it is normal for commercial paper to trade within a range of 25 to 150 basis points over T-bills, one might think that T-bill futures would be a poor mechanism for hedging commercial paper rates. However, the volatility of commercial paper rates is such that a 300 point change is a highly probable occurrence. One can easily see that the 125-point basis exposure that would accompany the hedge is much preferred over the 300-point exposure of the nonhedged position.

Question 4. What is the basis relationship?

Basis is the single most important concept in hedging. Basis is defined as the difference between the price of the futures contract and the price of the instrument held in the cash market.

All successful hedgers know and understand their basis. They study how and why it changes and make their decisions to hedge or not to hedge based upon their expected basis action. Indeed, hedging has been defined as speculating on the basis.

Basis is explored in depth later. Suffice it to say here that one cannot do an effective job of hedging without a knowledge of the size and stability of the basis.

Correlation analysis, as noted above, measures the stability of the basis relationship. Regression analysis can be used to measure the size of the basis relationship and to give a sense of the probability that it will change significantly.

Question 5. What are the costs of hedging?

The costs of hedging can be categorized into two major categories. The first comprises execution costs. Execution costs are reflected in the difference between the bid and the asked prices in the market. For example, if one bought a contract and immediately resold it, he would give up the spread between the bid and ask. Another aspect of execution costs is basis risk, which refers to the potential loss that may result in the total hedge transaction as a result of an adverse movement in the basis.

The second group of hedging costs can be called transaction costs. These include commissions paid to brokers and opportunity costs associated with the interest foregone on money posted as margins.

Question 6. What are the tax implications of the hedge?

This question highlights the importance of having an accountant helping to devise the hedging and strategy plan. Generally, all monies made or lost on hedges are considered ordinary income. But because of the complexity of the IRS codes and the fundamental questions surrounding the definition of a "hedge," it is most important that your accountant provide an opinion on whether a particular transaction qualifies under the IRS code as a hedge. If it does, the income or loss could be considered ordinary. A number of instances may arise, particularly in the "cross-hedge" situation, where the IRS may question the validity of the transaction as a hedge. In order to put the best light on the transaction for tax purposes, the accountant should set forth the criteria necessary to assure the IRS that the transaction does qualify as a hedge.

Once one has reviewed each of these aspects, one can put all the variables into a decision-making framework and quantify some of the uncertainties. A simple mathematical expectation model serves to illustrate the point.

Measuring the Probabilities

1. What is the probability of a change in interest rates? For example, 90%.
2. What is the probable size of the rate change? For example, 15%. (Note that a rise in rates from 10% to 11.5% is a 15% change.)

3. By multiplying 90% by 15%, we come up with an expected value for not hedging of -13.5%.

Transaction Cost

The transaction costs should be totaled and expressed as a percentage of the principal value of the assets or liabilities to be hedged; for example, 3%. A percentage cost must also be generated for basis risk as measured by an imperfect price correlation potential; for example, 5%. The best measure of this potential cost should be found in historical price correlation between the cash item being hedged and the appropriate futures contract. Adding these two factors together, we derive a cost factor in this example of 8%.

Decision

The final decision step compares the expected cost of not hedging with the expected cost of hedging. In this case, the 13.5% expected cost of not hedging outweighs the 8% expected cost of hedging. So hedging is appropriate.

THE CONCEPT OF BASIS

As mentioned earlier, "basis" refers to the difference between the price of the cash instrument being hedged and the futures price. Theory has it that if the expected basis associated with the hedge is realized, the hedge is theoretically perfect. Another way of putting it is that the closer the value of the futures contract moves in concert with the price of the commitment being hedged, the more perfectly the futures transaction acts as a substitute for the cash transaction (which is the definition of a futures hedge).

CROSS HEDGES

If every financial instrument in the cash market had a futures contract that exactly mirrored its characteristics, the futures markets would generally yield very good hedges. But in the real world hedging must be accomplished by using existing futures contracts that have similar price fluctuations with the cash market instrument being hedged, but that show a price movement variance (basis instability) because the underlying deliverable item for the futures contract is different from the cash market instrument being hedged. These imperfect matches of the futures contract to the cash instrument are known as "cross hedges."

An example of a cross hedge is the use of T-bill futures contracts to hedge a commitment in another money market instrument—CDs, BAs, commercial paper, prime rate, and so on. Another example would be the use of Treasury bond futures contracts to hedge a different long-term asset or liability, such as corporate bonds, permanent construction financing, or other long-term investments and loans.

Basis instability typically results from the differing impact of changes in supply and demand on the futures contract, the deliverable cash market security, and the item being hedged. The important point is that the cost associated with basis instability inherent in a cross hedge is usually much less than the expected cost of not being hedged at all.

The potential efficiency for a hedge can be measured by correlation analysis. If the price of the instrument being hedged in the cash market has a high positive correlation with prices in the futures market, one would expect the hedge to work out very well, because gains in the futures market will offset losses in the value of the cash instrument, and vice versa.

In financial futures, basis relationships should really be analyzed from two standpoints: (1) the group context and (2) an individual context.

The group context is important because certain groups of securities, such as AA industrial bonds, have price characteristics that cause them to be generally highly correlated or not so highly correlated with a particular futures market or contract. Hence, one would get some idea of how the basis for an individual issue of AA industrial bonds would act by looking at the group generally.

The individual context is important because, after all, it is an individual commitment that is being hedged. In analyzing why the basis changes in an individual context, one must consider the following factors:

1. *Credit Worthiness.* If the credit rating of the cash instrument is not as high as the credit worthiness of the instrument reflected in the

futures contract, the correlation in price movement will be reduced.

2. *Maturity.* The maturity of the instrument being hedged relative to the maturity of the instrument represented in the futures contract is important. The closer their maturities, the more they reflect the same time-value judgments.

3. *Liquidity.* The liquidity of the cash instrument and the liquidity of the futures market are both meaningful. The more liquid the market for the cash instrument, the less basis variation one would expect. Some futures contracts are also more liquid than others, and so provide a more reliable basis estimate.

4. *Supply and Demand Factors.* If a cash instrument has a limited supply, the chances are that the basis relationship will be more volatile than a situation where these is a large supply of the cash instrument around. Similarly, certain cash instruments have peculiarities in their demand factors that are not present in the futures market and cause basis variation.

ANALYZING GROUP BASIS CHANGES

There are a number of factors that cause the basis to change on individual issues as a result of group influence. Among them are:

1. *General Economic Conditions.* Securities of different credit quality will fluctuate differently under the same economic conditions. In periods of increasing rates, securities with lower credit ratings will decline faster than securities with higher credit ratings. They will also rise faster in easy money or declining-rate markets. Therefore, before you enter into your cross hedge, study how the different periods of past economic conditions influence the general basis for groups of securities with different quality ratings.

2. *Cyclical Effects.* Some securities perform differently from others as one moves through the interest rate cycle. In a "boom" economy federal government borrowings should decline as tax revenues increase and budget deficits run to relatively smaller levels. During tight money, however, organizations issuing debt instruments operate in different ways. They develop new types of debt instruments to fund expansion and they switch emphasis among different types

of issues in order to raise money in the most efficient way. One therefore needs to look carefully at the relative supply of the new securities being issued and whether they will cause fundamental changes in rate relationships.

3. *Institutional Segmentation of Markets.* This situation is also a key consideration in calculating group basis. Different industry groups rely on different types of securities for raising money. As a result, the economics of a particular industry can cause the securities that industry relies on to perform differently. For example, GNMA futures will generally react sharply in periods of disintermediation while corporate bonds react very little. During a liquidity squeeze commercial banks may demand large amounts of money through the CD markets, while the T-bill market may be very attractive to foreign central banks. Thus, one needs to know which institutional investing groups are most likely to have an impact on the price of the cash instrument being hedged *and* the instrument represented in the futures contract.

4. *Administered Rates Versus Free Market Rates.* It is important to note that the prime rate is an administered rate. It may change significantly while the T-bill and commercial paper rates—which are fundamentally free markets—remain relatively unchanged. So if one is trying to use the T-bill market for hedging the prime rate, he needs to be aware of the effect of the difference between administered rates and free market rates. GNMAs may experience severe distortions, when base minimum lending rates for FHA and VA mortgages lag behind changes in conventional mortgages, for the same reason. The FHA and VA mortgage rates are administered rates, while the GNMA rate is mostly a free market rate.

When one looks at basis one must be aware that the individual factors are also reflected in the group action. If you are hedging a new issue, say a AA bond, and do not know how it will act relative to the group of AA bonds, then the best guide you can use is the correlation between the futures and the group. If it is a seasoned issue with a good price history, you should review the price relationship of the individual securities to the group as well as to the futures. Then be aware that even if an individual issue trades with a much better correlation to the futures than does the whole group, over any given period of time the group influence may dominate.

Armed with an understanding of what causes basis to change, one is then ready to consider more fully the concept of dollar equivalency hedging.

DOLLAR EQUIVALENCY

Dollar equivalency refers to the process of structuring the hedge in such a way that one gets equivalent dollar movement in the two (cash and futures) positions even if the per-unit dollar changes in the two are not equal. This is accomplished by adjusting the number of contracts bought or sold in the futures position so that a 1% change in yield in the futures instruments will yield the same dollar value as a 1% change in the yield associated with the cash position. In order to do this a hedger must be aware of the dollar value of a 0.01% change in yield (one basis point) in each position. The rate sensitivity adjustment is normally measured through regression analysis. The "beta" coefficient is the correct weighting factor.

The longer the time left to maturity, the more dollar principal risk exposure there is in a basis point change in yield. For example, a .01% change in a 90-day T-bill contract will yield a $25 change in principal value. A six-month instrument will change $50 for every .01% change in yield. Hence, if one were hedging a $1,000,000 six-month commitment, one would use two 90-day T-bill contracts in order to effect dollar-equivalent hedging.

When hedging liabilities one frequently finds that the maturity of the loan (liability) being hedged does not match the maturity of the deliverable item on the futures contract. This mismatching can be adjusted for by increasing or reducing the number of contracts in the futures position. To understand this, consider the following. Assume a $1,000,000 floating rate loan for one year, with the rate tied to the prime rate. This loan could best be hedged by using 90-day CD or Eurodollar futures. If one were to use dollar-for-dollar hedging—that is, a $1,000,000 90-day CD futures contract to hedge the $1,000,000 loan—one would find that each basis point move in the futures contract would result in only a $25 change in principal value while each basis point move in the loan would result in a $100 change in the principal value. Thus, one would want to hedge on a 4-to-1 ratio (4,000,000 in futures value to $1,000,000 in cash position) at the start of the hedge.

However, as time passes and the one-year loan becomes a 270-day loan, a one-point change in the yield rate on the loan would be equal to only $75, while the one point change in the CD contract would still be equal to $25. Hence, one would need to adjust the hedge to a 3-to-1 ratio. Similarly, when the loan has 180 days until maturity, the cost of a 1% increase in the yield for the remainder of the life of the loan would be $50 per million and one should adjust the number of contracts to a 2-to-1 ratio. At 90 days the cost of a 1% change in yield would be $25 per million for the loan as well as for the futures position. Therefore, a 1-to-1 ratio would be appropriate. The correct strategy to use in such a situation would be to short four contracts on day one and retire them proportionately over the life of the loan. In this way one would keep an approximate dollar equivalency between the two positions.

Weighting a Coupon Hedge

Most people who are involved in hedges will not be doing direct hedges, but rather will be doing what are called cross hedges. A cross hedge is an instance where the instrument reflected in the futures contract and the instrument being hedged in the cash market are not identical. They may vary by maturity, credit worthiness, market liquidity, coupon, et al. In such instances, it is usual that the cash and futures markets will not move exactly in unison. In other words, the basis will vary because of fundamental differences between the cash instrument and the futures contract. In these cases hedgers should weight their hedge, using a greater or lesser number of futures contracts than the face value of the cash item being hedged.

The purpose of the weighting is to achieve the same dollar value change in the two markets, irrespective of rate change. For example, in the case of the 10-year Treasury futures contracts, weighting is necessary when hedging an instrument with a coupon other than 8%, which is the standard coupon reflected in the contract. For the same change in yield, coupons other than 8% will change in price by a different dollar amount. A small increase in interest rates for an 8% coupon might lose only $100 dollar of value, while a 13% coupon would lose $130. To compensate for this, then, when hedging a 13% coupon, one would use 1.3 times as many futures as the amount being hedged. A quick method of determining this weighting ratio is to use the conversion factor furnished by the exchange for the specific coupon and maturity being hedged. The ratio would equal the par amount of the cash instrument divided by 100, multiplied times the conversion factor.

In summary, it is crucial to remember that, in order to obtain the most efficient hedge, one needs to consider the dollar equivalent change in the futures position versus the cash position associated with the same change in yield in both positions. In order to obtain that dollar equivalency, one needs to monitor and adjust the size of the futures position on a periodic basis.

HEDGING AND THE PRICE STRUCTURE OF THE FUTURES MARKET

The price structure of a futures market can refer to two relationships: the price relationships between different delivery months for the same futures contracts, and the relationship between different futures instruments (i.e., bonds and bills). Since the latter has already been discussed in the section explaining yield curves, we will not dwell on that aspect here. Instead, this section will deal with the price relationships between futures contracts for the same deliverable instrument.

IDENTIFYING UNDERVALUE AND OVERVALUE

Among the questions frequently asked by hedgers are: How do I know which futures month to use for placing a hedge? Should I be short hedging in December or June? Should I be long hedging in September or December?

These questions are not unlike the questions asked by spread traders: Which month is undervalued relative to another month? Which month is overvalued relative to the other months?

The answers to these questions are largely influenced by two major elements: "cost-of-carry," and expectations about future the cost of carry and of levels of interest rates. At any single point in time either of the elements may be dominant. Most of the time the two work together.

"Cost of carry" refers to the net cost of owning a cash investment for a given period of time. It is not dissimilar to the cost-of-carry concept familiar to traders of storable agricultural commodities such as wheat and corn. In those instances, the cost of carry includes storage, insurance, interest, and transaction costs.

In the case of financial instruments such as 90-day T-bills, cost of carry represents the net interest differential between the interest earned on the 90-day cash investment and the cost of borrowing the initial money needed to pay for the 90-day bill.

Consider the situation where one can borrow money for 90 days at 10%. Assuming all else equal, if 90-day T-bills return 12%, the cost of carry is a positive 2%. On the other hand, if 90-day bills return only 8%, then the cost of carry is a negative 2%.

Determining the correct rate to use as the cost-of-borrowing rate is obviously a key to determining the true cost of carry. Normally, one would use repo rates as the cost of borrowing. Repos, as mentioned earlier, are "sale and repurchase agreements." One sells an instrument such as a 90-day T-bill and as part of the same transaction agrees to repurchase the bill at a later date and at a specified price. The buyer, and later reseller, of the bill in effect makes a loan to the seller for the time of the repo agreement, because he pays for the bill at the time of purchase but receives the money back when the repo agreement matures and the bill is returned to the original holder. The rate of interest charged on the loan is stipulated in the transaction. In the case of a repo on T-bills priced on a discount basis, the rate is implied in the price.

Repo transactions normally span very short periods of time, such as one to five days. Nevertheless, 30-day repos are not unusual. Regular quotes on them are available. Repos covering longer periods of time such as 60 or 90 days are also available, but the quotes must be requested from a dealer.

As a substitute for using the repo rate as a means of estimating the cost of carry, one can use the cash yield curve. If it is normal—that is, upward sloping to the right—the cost of carry is positive. If it is inverted the cost of carry is negative.

Once one knows the cost of carry for a cash market investment, one can then determine whether the futures contracts are dear or cheap relative to each other and to the cash market alternative. If the net cost of carry is negative (the repo rate or the equivalent borrowing rate is more than the yield on the cash instrument), then one should expect futures to sell at a premium to the cash market instrument.

Conversely, if the net cost of carry is positive, the futures should sell at a discount to the cash market.

The logic behind this is as follows. Assuming all else is equal, if one can borrow money at 12% to purchase a $1,000,000 T-bill that over the next 90 days will yield 10%, then one has a net loss of 2%, or $55.55 per day. Over 90 days, this would be $4999. Since one basis point in yield (1/100 of 1%) is worth $25 for a $1 million principal value 90-day security ($1,000,000 × 0.0001 × 90/360), this $4999 loss result from a 2% negative carry over a three-month holding period represents 199 basis points yield loss ($4999/25 = 199). Therefore, this 90-day futures contract should theoretically be worth 199 basis points more than the cash (spot) price.

In such a situation, one will not borrow money to buy bills as an investment. The only people who will hold bills are those who are required by management policy or legal stipulations to do so. Others would be better off (by 2%) to buy a futures contract, if it can be bought to provide at maturity an instrument yielding anything in excess of 8%. Thus, one will bid for T-bill futures until their price rises to the point of an 8% yield.

Conversely, if the cost of carry is a positive 2% (cost of borrowing is 10% and the yield on T-bills is 12%), then an investor will borrow as much as he can to buy bills. However, since an alternative to borrowing to buy the bills today is to buy a bill for future delivery, an investor

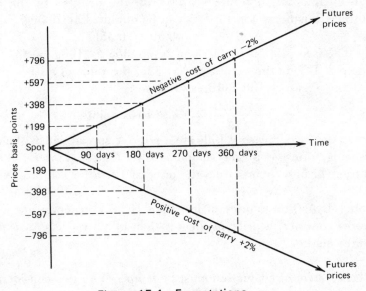

Figure 15.1 Expectations.

will lower his bids on T-bill futures to reflect the 12% rate (see Figure 15.1).

The formula for determining the corresponding futures value for a specific cost of carry in the cash market is as follows.

Step 1. Determine the net cost of carry for the cash instrument being considered. This is obtained by subtracting the cost of financing for the holding period from the bond equivalent yield (or yield to maturity) on the cash security. Then calculate total income for the period held.

Step 2. Convert the net cost of carry to a corresponding dollar value by dividing the total amount of net income earned or lost by the value of a basis point. In the case of T-bonds or GNMA's divide the net income by the value of 1/32, or $31.25.

Step 3. Add the appropriate dollar price adjustment from Step 2 to the current spot price of the cash security.

Step 4. Compare the theoretical futures price against the actual futures price. An illustration of this evaluation would be:

Step 1. A six-month bill has a yield of 10.25 and a bond equivalent yield of 10.85%, there are 45 days till the delivery of the futures contract. Financing for 45 days can be obtained at 10.50%. Then
$$10.85 - 10.50 = 0.35$$
$$0.35\% \text{ for 45 days} = 0.0035 \times 45/365 \times 1000 = 431.50$$
Step 2. Divide the net income by $25, the value of a basis point on a 90-day Treasury Bill Futures Contract:
$$\frac{\$431.50}{\$25} = 17.26 \text{ basis points.}$$
Step 3. Since Treasury Bills are a positive spread versus the cost of financing, futures contracts should be lower than spot prices. Therefore subtract 17 basis points from the price of 10.25 for a futures value of 10.08.

Step 4. A futures price of less than 10.08 reflects an undervalued futures contract, a price of greater than 10.08 reflects an expensive futures market.

This system of evaluation must be tempered by two considerations; first, when contracts are evaluated over long periods of time the financing costs are difficult to lock in; it may even be difficult to get a reliable quote on what they should be. Second, in further out contract months the market will begin to anticipate different financing rates and expectations play a large role in futures prices. These expectations will become more dominant as longer term financing becomes more difficult to obtain.

By plugging the appropriate numbers into the formula, one has a means of comparing futures to futures and futures to cash, and in this way identifying potentialy dear or cheap futures prices.

In summary, you would be willing to pay more for a futures contract if it helped offset an income loss arising from a negative yield carry. You would also pay less for a futures contract that would not earn the positive carry received by owning a cash market security.

EXPECTATIONS

The cost of carry is a convenient technique for estimating the value of a particular future relative to other futures and to cash instruments. But the futures market frequently reacts to forces other than cost of carry. One of those other forces can be lumped under the heading of "expectations." If market participants expect cost of carry or absolute interest rates to change significantly from their current levels, those expectations may overwhelm cost-of-carry considerations.

Without considering expectational factors, price curves for futures would be the linear summation of the current cost of carry as shown in Figure 15.1. When expectations are added to the futures pricing curve, the straight price line described above changes to a curved line that shows the effects of expectations. See Figure 15.2 for an example.

The comparatively smaller price changes between delivery months reflect expectations that the cost of financing will decline in the future.

To evaluate the "cheap" or "expensive" relative value of a particular month, draw both a futures and a cash market yield curve. (See Figure 15.3.) Then, adjust the differential $(B-A)$ for cost of carry. If the dollar amount resulting from the cost of carry is greater than $B-A$, then the December T-bill contract used in this example would be cheap when compared to the cash instrument. If, however, the cost of carry is less than $B-A$, the December T-bill contract would be expensive versus the cash market. When looking at cost of carry for farther-out contracts,

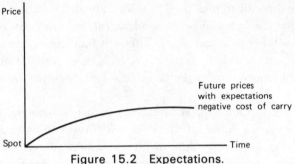

Figure 15.2   Expectations.

be sure to use the appropriate cost of financing—not the overnight repo rate, but the 30-, 90-, or 120-day repo rate.

In summary, this method of cost-of-carry and expectation analysis gives one an idea of the relative value of various futures contracts and helps guide one in selecting the better months for placing hedges.

CONVERGENCE OF CASH AND FUTURES PRICES

The last element of the price structure to be discussed here is the concept of "convergence." Since futures prices are a function of the cost of financing and expectations, the closer the date of maturity or contract expiration, the less the effect of expectations. The closer the delivery date, the less the futures will fluctuate from spot. In fact, the price of an expiring futures contract will equal the price of the deliverable cash market security at the close of trading on the contract expiration date. This effect can substantially impact the performance of a hedge depending on the shape of the futures yield curve.

For example, in a positive-carry market, the price curve for futures will lie below the current spot price. Figure 15.4 displays positive-carry futures price curves at two points in time.

In this situation, the cash price of the 90-day T-bill dropped from *A* to *B,* resulting in a downward shift in the "futures price curve" over the September/December period. A short hedge in the December contract would have produced a profit of *C–B,* but this would not have equalled the loss in the cash market *(A–B).* Under these circumstances, a better hedge would have been achieved by shorting the March contract because it is on the flatter part of the price curve. The rate of

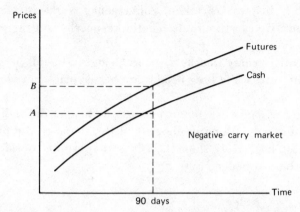

Figure 15.3 Futures and cash market *price* curves.

convergence declines in the more distant contracts as the price curve flattens out. Thus, short hedges using nearby contracts in a positive-carry market can produce less efficient hedges than the more distant contracts.

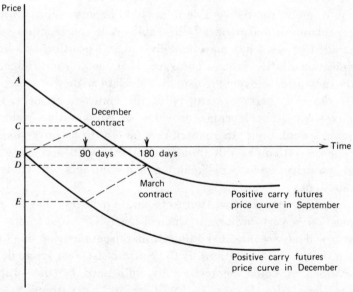

Figure 15.4 Price curve for futures. *A–B*, loss in cash; *C–B*, profit from hedge if December contract is used; *A–C*, net loss using December hedge; *D–E*, profit from hedge if March contract is used; (*A–B*) − (*D–E*), net loss using March hedge.

When long hedges are taken, convergence works in favor of the hedger in positive carry markets. Therefore, nearby contracts should be used.

For negative carry markets, short hedges should be placed in nearby contracts, while long hedges are better placed in more distant futures.

Convergence can work for or against the hedger depending on the nature of the hedge (long or short) and the shape of the price curve (positively or negatively sloped). It is an important consideration on how and when to hedge.

CONTRACT SPECIFICATIONS AND HEDGE EFFICIENCY

Once a futures contract has been selected, one should study the contract's specifications carefully to determine if there are any provisions that may make it trade differently from cash. In this type of study there are two major areas of concern.

First, does the contract have specifications for a "market-basket" delivery, whereby the deliverable item could be any security within a broad spectrum of maturities? Deliverable grade specifications should be examined to see what may be delivered if a position was held to the expiration of the futures contract. If it has a wide range, does the contract price movement usually correlate with the same maturity? If the cash market maturity of the contract changes, it can play havoc with the leverage or value of comparative yield/price basis point calculations. In general, contracts with a conversion "factor" type of settlement will trade consistently with a constant cash market maturity, while yield maintenance contracts will trade with less consistency.

Second, is the contract written to facilitate delivery? The answer to this question is very important when using GNMA contracts. Some contracts will have severe aberrations from the cash market due to their contract delivery specifications. If the contract has restrictive delivery specifications, it could be technically influenced by the supply of GNMAs eligible for delivery or by "par cap" regulations. So, when possible, use a contract that does not present the added risk of delivery distortions.

"Cheapest to Deliver"

Since bids and offers on the trading floor are based on the cash value of the cheapest issue to deliver, being able to identify that issue and to track its price in the cash market is a key factor in effective market strategy. It is also important to remember that price relationships change during the life of a contract. Consequently, the coupon that is currently cheapest should be identified periodically.

The most precise technique for identifying cheapest to deliver uses the "holding period return" or the "implied repo rate": the rate that determines a trader's break-even financing costs for cash/futures arbitrage. These transactions keep prices in both markets "in line" because traders buy cash securities and sell futures contracts if the return on the combined transaction is greater than the cost of financing or carrying the securities until the delivery date. Because this method takes into account accrued interest earned during the holding period it is more accurate than simply dividing the deliverable issues' cash price by the appropriate conversion factor.

The implied repo rate reflects break—even financing costs. Hence, the cheapest coupon to deliver will generally, though not always, have the highest implied repo rate.

To calculate the implied repo rate for deliverable coupons: (a) multiply the futures price by the appropriate conversion factor; (b) add interest accrued on the deliverable security up to the delivery date. This figure equals the futures invoice amount. Next take the futures invoice amount (the amount received for delivering the security); (c) subtract the security's total cost—cash price plus accrued interest from the futures invoice amount; and, (d) divide the difference by the total cost and annualize—the result equals the implied repo rate.

$$\text{IMPLIED REPO RATE} = \frac{\substack{\text{Total Cost} \\ \text{Invoice Price}}}{\text{Total Cost}} \times \frac{365}{\text{Days to Delivery}}$$

Cheapest for the March Delivery

In the recent past, the cheapest issue has generally been one of the high coupon securities. Using the implied repo rate and prices on February 17, 1983, the issues shown in Table 15.1 were cheapest to deliver

Table 15.1 Cheapest to Deliver

Issue	Cash Price (Yield)	Futures Price (Converted to A Decimal)	Conversion Factor	Implied Repro Rate
Treasury Bond	14% of 2011	122.000 (11.30%)	74.281	1.6313	5.40%
10-Year Treasury Note	13 ¾% of 1992	114.781 (11.15%)	83.469	1.3640	4.72%
2-Year Treasury Note	14 ⅝% 0f 1985	108.625 (9.76%)	96.789	1.1154	8.10%

against the upcoming March 1983 deliveries in bonds 10-year notes, and 2-year notes. We have assumed delivery will occur on March 31. In general, positive yield curve environments make it advantageous to carry the deliverable issue to the end of the month.

EXAMPLES OF BASIC HEDGES

For illustrative purposes here, hedges are categorized by the position taken in the futures market.

The Long Hedge

A long hedge can be used to protect against falling yields. If a money manager believes that current investment rates offered in the futures market will exceed the yields forecast for the cash market on the contract expiration date, a long hedge would effectively lock in the present futures market yield for that investment date. If the yields on that date prove to be less than the futures rate available today, the long hedge will increase an investor's return by that differential. Consider the following example.

An investor may wish to lock in today's prices for long-term government bonds. Should the securities be purchased in the cash market and financed for six months? Or does it make more sense to purchase a U.S. T-bond futures contract for delivery in six months? The following example illustrates how an investor faced with this decision should make his analysis.

- In September, the price of $9\frac{1}{8}$, 2009 U.S. Treasury bonds is $100\frac{1}{32}$.

- The price of the June T-bond futures contract on the CBT is $88\frac{19}{32}$; the conversion to a cash price on $9\frac{1}{8}$ 2009 would be $88.59375 \times 1.1267 = 99\frac{26}{32}$. In this case it is cheaper to buy June futures at an effective cost of $99\frac{26}{32}$ than pay $100\frac{1}{32}$ in the cash market.

    When adjusted for cost of carry, the futures are even more attractive.

- The yield on the cash $9\frac{1}{8}$ 2009 at $100\frac{1}{32}$ is 9.12%. The cost of carry of $9\frac{1}{8}$ T-bonds of 2009 is $11\frac{1}{4}$ on 9/15/79. This is a negative carry of 2.125% annualized, or \$5.82 per day. During the 280 days between September and June, the cash positions would lose 280 × \$5.82 = \$1,629, or $1^{20}/_{32}$. Thus, the real cost of the cash bond is $101^{20}/_{32}$ versus $99^{26}/_{32}$. June futures are $1^{26}/_{32}$ cheaper than buying the cash instrument and carrying it until June.

- This example indicates that the market is expecting a positive carry, or lower financing cost, between September and June. Therefore, the spot is valued higher than the futures contract. The relationship between cash and futures changes as expectations about futures financing costs change. Consider this same example one month later, in November.

- The price of $9^{1}/_{8}$ T-bonds for 2009 is $88^{25}/_{32}$. The price of June T-bond futures on the CBT is $80^{23}/_{32}$. Using the factor pricing system of the CBT, the price of $9^{1}/_{8}$s on the CBT is actually 80.-71875 × 1.1267 = 90.9458 or $90^{30}/_{32}$. Which is the cheaper price to pay for $9^{1}/_{8}$ of 2009 for delivery in June 1980, the spot price of $88^{25}/_{32}$ or $90^{30}/_{32}$ for a June future? Let's find out.

- If you purchase the spot, your financing cost—or opportunity cost of money—would be 12.5% to June 1980. The yield on $9^{1}/_{8}$s at 88 $^{25}/_{32}$ is 10.35%. Therefore, one would lose 2.15% (annualized) or \$5.89 per \$100,000 per day. In the 232 days between November and June, the negative carry would cost \$1,366 or $1^{11}/_{32}$. When this is added to $88^{25}/_{32}$, the adjusted price would be $90^{4}/_{32}$.

- On this basis, the futures market is expensive relative to the cash market. The $^{26}/_{32}$ premium for the futures reflected investors' uncertainty that they could continue to finance themselves between November and June at a rate of 12.5%. If the investor is sure of his financing cost, he would be better off not to use the futures market, but instead to purchase the cash instrument and continue to finance that cash position.

The Short Hedge

In a rising interest rate environment, shorting futures against an inventory of financial assets hedges the inventory against the loss of value that would result as interest rates rise. A short futures position would yield a profit as rates rise. The erosion in the value of the cash market asset would be hedged to the extent of the profit made on the futures.

Short Hedge Against Liability Issuance

Let's assume that on October 5 a regional financial institution commits to make a loan on October 12 at a specified interest rate. The institution determines the interest rate for the loan based on its expected costs. It plans to issue $50 million in six-month liabilities to finance the loan. To protect itself from a major increase in its cost of funds between the time the loan is agreed to and when the funds are raised, the institution enters into a short hedge.

The steps followed are:

	Cash market	Basis	Futures market
October 5	Commits to sell $50 million CDs due April 12.80	2.61	Sell $100 million* CD futures for March 10.19
October 12	Sells $50 million CDs due April 13.80	2.73	Buy $100 million CD futures for March 11.07
	-100	-12	88

Each basis point for futures = $\$25 \times 88 \times 100 = \$220,000$
Each basis point for CDs = $\$50 \times 100 \times 50 = \underline{\quad 250,000}$
$ -\$30,000$

Loss reduced from $250,000 to 30,000

Note: As the CDs are issued, the futures position should be liquidated proportionately.

---

*Assume a 1.00 beta coefficient.

When the institution agreed to a specific interest rate on October 5, it was long six-month liabilities because it had locked in its charge for funds, but not its cost. It then sold three-month CD futures as its short hedge. On October 12, the "long" position in the cash market was liquidated by the issuance of the liabilities. At the same time, the short hedge in CD futures was covered. The important items to note in this example are:

1. This was a *cross hedge.* The cash market instrument (a regional bank's CDs) was not the same as the underlying futures contract instrument (CDs from a major bank).
2. The *basis,* the difference between prices (rates) of cash and futures, moved adversely, thus, the hedge only protected the institution for 88 of the 100-point increase in liability rates (the basis widened by 12 points). Basis risk is an integral part of any hedging decision, thus the correlation of cash to futures must be examined. This is most important for a cross hedge, since the underlying cash instruments are different.
3. Determining the *dollar equivalent* of a 0.01% (one basis point) move in rates between cash and futures is vital. In this example, each basis point of liabilities per million dollars was worth $50, while for the three-month CD futures, $25. Therefore, $100 million in futures were used to offset the $50 million cash position.

Cash Flow Implications of Hedging

Cash flow considerations are important factors that can work for or against the hedger. The cash flow implications of hedging arise as a result of the daily cash settlement procedures of the clearinghouse, wherein each day the losses from the previous day are collected from the losers and passed on to the gainers. For example, when a mortgage banker sells production into the futures market and interest rates rise, the mortgage banker will have a positive cash flow as he receives the profit daily on his short futures position. This occurs because the clearinghouse marks-to-market daily and pays all profits in cash on the next day. The value of the cash thus received from the clearinghouse makes the futures market an attractive alternative in rising rate markets. In declining interest rate markets, the sale of the futures contract would have adverse effects on cash flow. The loss in value would have to be paid daily by the mortgage banker to the clearinghouse as interest rates declined. In the cash and forward markets profits are not realized on a cash basis until settlement and delivery of the physical securities. Thus, cash flow considerations are negligible in the cash market.

The futures market hedger will recoup this variation margin when the cash transaction is consummated. But the use of cash will be lost until settlement day and this constant cash outflow could cause cash flow problems. The "losses" on the actual cash securities are paper losses to the hedger. The total profit or loss earned on the transaction for the hedger comes from the difference between the price paid for futures and the price received or paid for cash securities.

To illustrate, assume a mortgage banker purchases mortgages from lenders, originates a GNMA, and hedges by selling GNMA futures contracts. He intends to deliver on the futures contract. In this case, the following steps are taken:

1. Mortgage banker purchases 14% mortgages from lenders at a price of 99.00.
2. Mortgage banker warehouses mortgages and originates 13.5% GNMA.
3. Mortgage banker sells new GNMA 13.5 to futures market at an equivalent price of 100.00 for delivery in 60 days. Price of futures is $68^{27}/_{32}$. Profit "locked in" on trade is $10,000.00.
4. Interest rates go higher during the 60-day period and prices of GNMA futures go lower, declining to $65^{27}/_{32}$.

Over the 60-day period between step 3 and settlement the mortgage banker would have been paid $30,000 cash from the futures clearinghouse that he would have used or reinvested in short-term securities. However, on settlement date the price received for the GNMA would only be $65^{27}/_{32}$ or a bond equivalent price of $95^{31}/_{32}$. The price paid to the original lender remains 99.00, but the exchange only pays $95^{31}/_{32}$, or a loss of $30,000. As one can see there was no real profit or loss from selling on the futures exchange in this example, only a temporary gain in cash flow.

Now assume the reverse happens and interest rates go lower during the period between step 3 and settlement day, and the price increases to, say, $71^{27}/_{32}$.

To the mortgage banker this would be a mark-to-market loss on the futures of $30,000 that he would have paid to the clearinghouse over the 60-day period. The loss in futures is offset by the profit made from the difference between cash and futures prices and the mortgage banker is left with his original $10,000 profit. However, he lost the use of $30,000 as interest rates fell.

This concept of cash flow gain or loss applies to all futures market contracts, and is an important consideration in evaluating the cost of hedging.

INTERNAL ORGANIZATION FOR HEDGING

The internal organization of the decision-making machinery for a firm is quite important. The hedge decision should be a part of a firm's total management strategy. It's important that the top people in the firm, including the president and the board of directors, be aware of how and why the futures market is being used for hedging. If they understand the theory of hedging and that hedges do not always work out perfectly, the chances of futures trading becoming an integral and useful part of the management decisions of the firm are much greater.

Some firms establish committees to review the basic economic data, estimate risk exposures, set the hedge policy, and monitor the results. The actual implementation of the hedge is often delegated to an individual.

In all cases there should be a close liaison between the comptroller of the firm and the man having responsibility for the hedging, because hedging is basically a financial operation and, as we have seen, can have an important effect on the cash flow of the firm. It can also be used advantageously for tax purposes.

The internal organization and record keeping aspects of a hedging program are discussed in greater detail in Chapter 21.

In summary, hedging cash market financial commitments can reduce interest rate risk, create more certainty in business planning, and optimize the use of money, either for a borrower or for a lender/investor. Depending on the forecast for the direction of interest rates, hedging with futures can increase the profitability of your money management efforts.

CHAPTER SIXTEEN
Hedging Strategies for Various Industries

FINANCIAL CORPORATIONS

The very essence of financial institutions is that they are leveraged corporations that borrow money to invest in financial instruments or to reloan at higher rates of return. The difference between the cost of money and the rate of return on assets, minus operating expenses, is the firm's profit. This spread between cost and return is the lifeblood of the financial institution and must be maintained if the corporation is to survive. This profitability is dependent partly upon the firm's ability to forecast cost of money and rates of return in advance and position the corporation to take advantage of, or avoid being harmed by, changes in interest rates that affect that spread. Financial futures can be used to protect one or both sides of their transactions.

Financial futures offer a unique opportunity to hedge the fluctuations in the value of fixed-income securities caused by changes in interest rates. Interest rates have risen to record levels in recent years, eroding the value of investment portfolios and increasing the cost of borrowing money. No business operates without firsthand knowledge of the cost, or value, of money. It is imperative that they know the cheapest place to get money—whether from banks, the credit markets, or the equity market—and, conversely, the best place to invest excess cash. Financial futures offer a method of assuring, usually within a small range of error, interest rates at a specific level. Through interest rate futures, a rate of return on investments can also be established, again within some small margin of error.

This chapter takes a look at some basic strategies for hedging. For simplicity, industry groups, where they have the widest application, are used to illustrate various strategies and concepts of hedging. However, many of the strategies used in one industry group are applicable to other groups.

COMMERCIAL BANKS

Commercial banks are the epitome of financial corporations. Their business is to borrow large sums of money from their depositors and reloan the money to others at higher rates. A bank may loan money to the public in the form of business loans or consumer loans, or it may loan the money to governmental bodies through the purchase of Treasury notes, bonds, or bills.

A bank gets in trouble when its borrowers default on loans, or the cost of money borrowed from depositors is more than the return from its loan portfolios. The latter problem usually occurs when a bank mismatches the maturity of its fixed-income assets with the average maturity for deposits. Usually, in these cases, banks purchase assets that have maturities longer than the average life of its liabilities. As rates rise, the liabilities mature and are reissued to the same or a different depositor at a higher cost to the bank. The return on the investment portfolio thus remains fixed while the cost of "rolling over" the liability increases, causing a decrease in the profit spread. If rates continue to rise, and the maturity of the assets is too long, the spread will become negative and the bank will begin losing money. Likewise, if a bank makes fixed-rate loans, it is subject to the risk that the spread will go against it unless it locks in a cost of money to fund the fixed-rate loans. A fixed rate of return on an asset could be especially costly if funded by a variable rate liability. A bank should use financial futures to hedge that portion of its balance sheet that is mismatched in maturity between assets and liabilities, or that portion of its balance sheet that is fixed in terms of rate of return.

A bank may also wish to hedge the spread between assets and liabilities when the spread difference is changing because of different market forces operating in different money markets. Banks sometimes find the cost of funds increasing faster than the rates of returns on assets. This differential in rates of change can also be hedged.

A bank must be very careful, however, not to increase its risk through hedging. This can happen when a bank's assets and liabilities are matched naturally by maturity and liquidity. A hedge may disturb this natural match and cause an imbalance. Many banks have a great portion of their balance sheets already in a natural hedge. For example, short-term variable rate commercial loans are balanced against short-term variable rate liabilities, such as demand deposits and certificates of deposits. Any hedge that would lock in, or sterilize, one side of the balance sheet without affecting the other side of the balance sheet could be creating more risk than it is averting. Hedging should be practiced when the hedge evens out the maturity differences between the asset and the liability, or evens out liquidity.

Hedging Assets

When a bank finds itself with a portfolio of fixed-rate assets and financing costs that are rising, it may wish to hedge those assets. Two ways of doing so are to hedge the cost of financing or to hedge the portfolio from further price erosion. Since the bank cannot always easily identify the exact source of funds used to finance a portfolio, it often chooses to hedge the asset itself.

The fixed-income securities in a portfolio can be hedged by shorting an appropriate amount of interest rate futures contracts. As the level of interest rates increases, the price of the fixed-income securities will decline. The offsetting short position in the futures market should show a similar price decline, but this price decline will generate a profit since the bank was short futures contracts that declined in value. The profit from the hedge is then used to adjust the cost of the fixed-income asset to a lower cost (higher yield). The higher yield on the asset then works to maintain the spread between the cost of funds and the return on assets.

For example, assume a bank owns $10,000,000 worth of 30-year U.S. government Treasury bonds, 10.375% coupon with a maturity of 11/15/09. Assume the bank purchased these bonds at par and wishes to protect them from a price decline as interest rates rise. To hedge the

bank should short 100 U.S. Treasury bond contracts against the ten
million 10.375% Treasury Bonds. We have assumed:

Long	Short
$10,000,000 10.375%	100 U.S. T-bond contracts
T-bonds 11/15/09	Sept 1980 CBT
	Price $82.10
Price 100	
Book yield 10.375%	

Interest rate rise for long bonds to 11.5%

Price of 10.375 $900,000	Price of futures $72.10
loss on 10.375 $100,000	Profit on futures $100,000

Adjust book value of 10.375% 11/15/09 by
_____ profit from futures

New book cost _____
New book yield _____

In this example the bank has effectively *unlocked* the return on a
fixed asset, thus matching the unlocked cost of liabilities that finance
this asset.

In this simple example we illustrated a perfect hedge—U.S. Treasury
bond futures contracts versus cash Treasury bonds—with no basis
change. It is unusual for hedge situations to be so clean and to work
out so well. (See Chapter 15 for discussions on basis, dollar equivalency,
and convergence.)

In hedging a bank's spread it may be easier to hedge the cost of
money than to hedge particular assets. Hedges against the cost of
liabilities can be carried out using CD and T-bill futures contracts, since
they closely coincide with the nature of a bank's liabilities.

Locking in the Cost of Funds

In hedging liabilities a bank is attempting to protect itself against a rise
in the cost of funds. When a bank begins to experience an increasing
cost of money and is concerned that liability costs are rising faster than
asset returns, it may choose to protect its spread.

For example, assume there is a bank with $50 million of negotiable certificates of deposit having an average maturity of 90 days. Assume also that at the end of that 90 days the portfolio would normally be rolled over into new certificates at the then current rate. If the bank fears that it will not be able to roll into 180-day paper at favorable prices it could hedge to establish today its liability prices for that 90-day period between the maturity of the liability and the maturity of its assets. To accomplish this the bank would short 50 90-day CD futures contracts. If rates rise 100 basis points equally in the CD cash and CD futures markets, the profit from the futures will offset the increased cost of rolling over the liabilities for 90 more days.

CD rates on day 1 15.00%	Futures prices on day 1 86.50
CD rates on day 90 16.00%	Futures prices on day 90 85.50
Increased cost of writing $50 million of 90-day CDs on day 90 versus day 1 = $125,000	Profit on short position in 50 CD futures contracts = $125,000

The profit from the CD futures contract would lower the book cost of the liability, thus maintaining the spread.

This same technique is applied when hedging the total liability portfolio of the bank. A short futures position taken against a "long" money position will effectively lock in that cost of money for as long as the hedge is maintained—if the buying basis and the selling basis remain constant. As the basis (the price difference between the futures contract and the liability) changes, the number of contracts shorted should be increased or decreased depending on the amount necessary to maintain dollar equivalency. If liability costs begin to rise in yield faster than CDs, more contracts would have to be shorted to maintain dollar-for-dollar gains and losses between the cash and futures sides of the hedge.

Hedging When Rates Are Falling

Commercial banks usually make nice profits as rates rise, because the rates of return on most of their assets (commercial loans) are administered higher on a same-day basis. While the return on assets goes up on day one, the cost of liabilities does not change until the liability matures and is refunded at the new higher rates. This lag in timing between price changes usually allows a healthy bank a windfall profit. The longer the average life of a liability portfolio in rising rate markets, the greater the windfall.

However, when the market turns down, the rates at which the liabilities roll over does not fall as fast as the prime rate, which is administered down. Therefore, banks need to hedge their liabilities by "unlocking" the fixed cost of their liabilities as they lower the return on their variable rate assets.

To unlock the costs of the liability portfolio a banker would purchase futures contracts that coincide with the maturity of his existing portfolio of CDs or other variable rate liabilities. As rates move lower, the profit on the futures contract would offset the cost of being in higher rate CDs as the return on assets decreases.

For example, assume a bank with a CD portfolio of $50,000,000 and an average maturity of 180 days. When rates begin to decline, and the prime is being lowered, the banks would purchase 90-day CD futures contracts. (If the average maturity on the liabilities were to decline, the number of contracts should also decline; if the average maturity were to remain at 180 days, the number of contracts would remain unchanged. This adjustment is done to maintain dollar equivalency in the two positions). This would effectively unlock the maturity of the portfolio and give it a floating rate cost based on the daily price of the 90-day CD contract. This type of hedge unlocks the costs of funds, opening the portfolio to immediate lowering of costs if rates go lower; but it also precludes any opportunity profits if rates go higher, because the "cheap" money already purchased would be offset by the loss on the long position in CD futures.

Another strategy can be employed when rates are expected to peak in the near future. For example, liability managers shun the longer term liabilities and attempt to keep the maturity of their liability portfolio as short-term as possible when rates are expected to decrease in the near future. This preference usually causes the yield curve to have an inverse slope with near-term rates being considerably higher than longer rates. (See Figure 16.1.)

Banks don't want to buy the longer term money and lock in higher liability costs for long periods of time as rates begin to fall. Therefore,

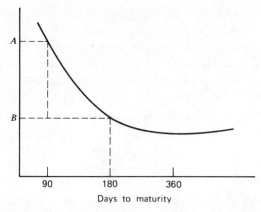

Figure 16.1   Yield curve with an inverse slope.

they tend to bunch their purchases of money into the shorter maturities, causing short-term money to be bid for very aggressively by banks. To take advantage of this type of yield curve a bank would buy the longer term money—180 days in Figure 16.1—and pay price *B* for it. This would be substantially cheaper than buying the 90-day money at price *A*. It then purchases 90-day CD futures in an equal amount. The short position of the 180-day CDs versus the long position in 90-day CD futures in effect reduces the exposure of the banks CD position to 90 days while allowing it to pay the lower 180-day rate. If rates were to go lower, the profit from the futures contract would be applied to the difference between 90-day CD rates on day number 90 of the hedge, minus the 180-day rate from day one. To illustrate, consider the following:

Assume that on day 1 90-day CD rates are 16.00% and 180-day CD rates are 15.00%.

Step 1.   Purchase the money for 180 days by selling $10,000,000 in certificates of deposit.
Saving 1% for 90 days on $10,000 equals $25,000.

Step 2.   Buy 90-day CD futures contracts.

Assume that rates do indeed move sharply lower 90 days later and that the new 90-day CD rate is now 13.75%.

Since the CDs purchased earlier are locked in at 15.00% for another 90 days, they cannot be rolled into another 90-day CD. Thus, the opportunity cost is $31,250 for the next 90 days.

However, if the CD futures have also improved in price by 125 basis points, the profit on the long position will be $31,250. To summarize:

Saving on original CD position	+$25,000
Opportunity loss after 90 days	−$31,500
Profit on CD futures position	+$31,500
Net saving	$25,000

(*Note* that the assumption made in this example was that the basis did not change—a rather unrealistic assumption, as mentioned several times before. Nevertheless, as also noted, the variation in the basis is likely to be a lot less than the variation in absolute price.)

The important concept illustrated above is that a hedger can take what the yield curve gives him and then use the futures market to tailor the maturity of his liability to fit his needs. This concept works equally well with asset hedging.

Another use of interest rate futures is in pre-refunding existing assets when rates are falling. Many times a bank will have securities maturing over the next six months and would like to reinvest those monies at current rates rather than at rates that might prevail at the time of maturity. The bank portfolio manager has three choices. First, the bank could sell the securities now and reinvest in longer maturities at current rates. This is possible only if the bank is willing to take the losses on the income statement in the current quarter. Second, the bank could borrow the money in the federal funds market or the CD market, or purchase longer term securities and finance them until the maturity of the current assets. This alternative has some possible disadvantages, however. In financing a new position, the bank could end up paying a higher reserve requirement for a marginal purchase that it financed. Also, the bank's limits on portfolio size may limit new purchases and, finally, the longer security could be at a negative carry versus the cost of short term money used to finance the longer asset. Third, the bank could purchase interest rate futures. If the bank picks this alternative, it should decide on the maturity range. Then it should pick a futures contract or contracts that would give the same dollar value price appreciation if rates move lower. If rates go lower between the time the hedge is put on and reinvestment, the hedger's profit on the futures helps lower the cost of investments. If rates go higher the investors do not receive the benefits from reinvesting at higher rates, as the losses on the futures would offset any increase in income from higher rates and lower prices at reinvestment.

All of these examples are straightforward strategies designed to illustrate various basic concepts in the use of futures contracts for hedging. Although not specifically noted in each case, each example assumes that the correlation between the cash and futures positions are high (so that the risk of basis change is low) and that the hedger uses the correct dollar equivalency factors in matching his cash and futures positions.

There are many other variations in the uses of futures by a bank for hedging. As the reader applies the concepts explained here and in the other chapters on strategies, he will begin to see the other applications, and the basic elements of hedging will become more apparent.

THRIFT INSTITUTIONS

As a group thrift institutions have generally relied on savings deposits as a main source of borrowed money. Their assets tend to be longer term investments in mortgages with relatively small, highly liquid portfolios of short-term investments. This type of asset and liability mismatch, short-term borrowing and long-term investment, is a classic textbook formula for financial disaster.

As short-term interest rates have risen since the early 1970s, deposits have moved out of thrift institutions and into the money market funds or other short-term investments. As thrift institutions began losing savings deposits, they devised new methods of attracting deposits to fund their long-term loans. After supplying their depositors with toasters and electric drills, there was nothing left to do but compete for deposits by matching the higher interest rates being paid by alternative investments. Regulatory authorities cooperated by allowing thrift institutions to raise rates to regular depositors, create new types of savings instruments, and allow NOW accounts or demand deposits that pay interest.

The new savings instruments have had a significant long-run impact on the thrift institutions. They were very well received by the public and their use became widespread. However, because they locked thrift institutions into a bidding war with other financial institutions for short-term deposits, in the final analysis this new solution only added to the mismatch of assets and liabilities. Unlike other financial institutions, as interest costs on short-term borrowing rise the return on existing assets remains constant. As short-term interest rates rise, the profit spread between investments and borrowing narrows and eventually becomes negative, due in large part to the increasing costs of the variable rate borrowings that have been made. Thrift institutions could use the financial futures market to hedge these variable borrowing costs and lock in a cost of funds for their fixed-rate assets and protect their profit spread.

How Issuers Can Hedge Money Market Certificates

The money market certificate pays a varying interest rate. Every week the issuer changes the interest rate paid, based upon the average price paid for 180-day T-bills at the most recent weekly auction of bills. As T-bill rates increase, the cost of borrowing money through the sale of money market certificates increases proportionately.

This type of commitment lends itself to effective hedging through the T-bill futures contracts. It can be almost a direct hedge, except that T-bill futures are based on 90-day T-bill rates while the money market certificate is based on 180-day bill rates. This creates two problems. A change in the price of a 90-day bill will return only half as many dollars as the same change as the price of 180-day bills. And, second, the basis between 90-day T-bill futures and six-month T-bills is not always constant.

Taking these facts into consideration, a savings bank or S&L could hedge against the risk of higher interest costs by shorting twice as many 90-day T-bill contracts as it has millions of dollars of certificates outstanding. This would establish, within a small margin, the cost of interest in advance of the adjustment on the certificate. As the interest rate on T-bills in the cash market rises, the price of T-bill futures should decline. The profit from the short position in futures will help offset the increased cost of borrowing when the money market certificates are repriced.

For example, assume a savings bank has $25 million in money market certificates outstanding. If bill rates go higher between now and when those certificates are repriced, they'll have to pay the higher rate for the next six months. Assume that it is November, and the $25 million worth of money market certificates yield 12% and are due May 1, 1980. If the interest rate rises between November and May to say, 13%, the savings bank, when it reprices its money market certificates, would sustain an increased cost of borrowing for the next six months of $125,000. Assume, however, the savings bank had sold short 50 90-day Treasury bill contracts on November 1 at 12%, and that interest rates climbed 100 basis points for a profit of $125,000 on the short position. As long as the savings bank leaves its short position intact in the futures market, it has locked in the 12% rate that was prevailing at the time the hedge was transacted. The gain on the T-bill futures short position offsets any increase in borrowing costs, but not on a one-for-one basis because of commissions on the futures transactions.

What if interest rates moved in the opposite direction? What if they fell to 11% on 180-day T-bills instead of climbing to 13%? In this situation the savings bank would have lost $125,000 on its short position in the futures market. But on May 1 it would have repriced the money market certificates at 11%, reducing the interest cost by $125,-000. In effect, the costs for the second six-month period would have been the same as for the original six-month period. The bank avoided the risk of having to pay 13% or more, and also gave up the opportunity for a windfall gain if rates fell. At any time during the intervening period between November 1 and May 1, the savings bank could have lifted the hedge by buying back 50 90-day T-bill futures contracts for the same months it had previously sold. This would unlock the interest rate level previously fixed, and allow the new rate to decline from that date forward. Of course, this sort of selective hedging leaves the savings bank at risk again.

Hedging Other Savings Banks Liabilities

Another important source of funding for thrifts has been the "jumbo" certificate of deposit. This is a certificate of deposit of at least $100,000. The rates of these certificates are administered by the savings banks in much the same way as a commercial bank administers the rate paid on its certificates of deposit. In order to attract money for these types of certificates, the banks must pay a rate that is at least as good as and often better than most commercial banks for similar maturities. The higher rates are sometimes necessary because the thrift institutions usually have less capital than commercial banks and the secondary market for their certificates is usually less liquid.

The rate paid on jumbos is not directly related to T-bill rates as in the previous example. It is more closely related to the rate paid by other savings banks and commercial banks for certificates of deposit. Thus, the secondary CD market is a better barometer of interest costs for jumbo certificates than is the T-bill market. Therefore, the hedging of jumbos would be done in CD futures. Similar to the preceding hedge, this type of hedge would be a short hedge; that is, a hedge in which the futures market side of the hedge results in a short position and the cash market part of the hedge results in a long position. The savings bank is long money. The contract month shorted would be the one that best coincides with the maturity of the CDs anticipated to be written. It is conceivable that the interest rates on CDs will rise more than interest rates on CD futures. In this situation, because the hedge is a cross hedge, the cost of writing new CDs may not be completely offset by the profits on the futures contract. In other words, there could be some basis risk. If changes in the basis are not anticipated or are inadequately compensated for through adjustments in the number of futures contracts shorted, the hedge will not be efficient.

PENSION FUND MANAGERS IN THE FINANCIAL FUTURES MARKETS

Pension fund managers in recent years have become more active in the management of the assets under their control. There are several uses of the futures market that enable them to increase the return on their assets and to increase the liquidity of the portfolios that they manage. Let's look first at increasing the return on pension investments through the use of futures.

Many times in the recent past the yield curve has been negatively sloped. That is, higher rates have been paid on the shorter end of the market than on the longer end of the market. This is characterized by a downward sloping yield curve. If a pension fund manager has money to invest, he's faced with a difficult decision. Does he make a long-term investment at a lower rate, where he might have potentially greater appreciation in price in the future, or does he maximize his immediate return by purchasing shorter term money market instruments? By using the futures market the pension fund manager can have the best of both worlds. He can invest his cash in short-term money market certificates earning a higher current yield, but not lose the advantage of capital appreciation available in the long-term market. He can do this through the simultaneous purchase of a long-term bond futures contract and high-yield short-term cash investments. The purchase of the long-term futures contracts locks in today's current prices on long-term bonds. When this is coupled with the purchase of money market securities, the portfolio manager has the luxury of having a high short-term return on current investments and, through the futures market, the benefit of capital appreciation if long-term rates decline. The money manager is assuming that sooner or later the inverted yield curve will return to a normal yield curve and as it does he will gain on both ends of the portfolio.

There is one important drawback to this type of strategy. In a market with a negatively sloped yield curve the prices for futures contracts will be higher than prices on similar securities in the cash market. Thus, unless the manager assumes he will have a stable basis, he has to compare the premium paid to purchase securities through a futures contract against the extra current income earned on the short-term investment.

For example, if 90-day certificates of deposit offer the investor 17% and long-term bonds are yielding 13%, an investor could earn 4% more income in the CD than in long-term bonds. But if long-term rates were to decline and the basis were to change accordingly while the investor was in the CDs, the higher prices paid later for long-term bonds could quickly wipe out or even exceed the short-term return differential between CDs and bonds. Four percent per million for 90 days is worth $9863.00 per million in extra income. If the premium on a Treasury bond future 90 days from settlement is less than $9863 ($3\frac{1}{32}$) it would make sense to pursue this type of strategy. If the premium paid for futures was greater than $3\frac{1}{32}$, it would be better to buy long Treasury bonds in the cash market and avoid the short-term investment.

Assume, however, that futures prices are below $3\frac{1}{32}$ premium and the investor purchases 90-day certificates of deposit and goes long Treasury bond futures. If during the time of this hedge long-term rates actually declined, the investor would make a profit on the Treasury bond futures contract. But because of lower long-term rates, the investor would have to pay more for long-term fixed-income securities. The profit from the futures would be applied to the new purchase price, thus lowering it back toward the level that existed on the day the futures position was initiated.

If long-term interest rates were to rise during this period, the investor would lose money on the futures contract. The loss would be no greater than the loss would have been if a cash purchase of long bonds had been made assuming a stable basis. The investment prices will be lower at the end of 90 days when this strategy ends and this lower reinvestment price will offset the loss on the futures position.

This technique actually reduces total loss because the extra income earned on the short-term investment will partially offset any losses that might occur when interest rates rise.

A slight variation of this strategy is to sell an existing portfolio in the cash market, purchase higher yielding short-term investments, and repurchase the equivalent of the original position in the futures market. This strategy allows a portfolio manager to increase current return and still hold a portfolio of longer term investments which over time he feels will be good investments. All of the basis and dollar equivalency risks described in previous chapters are inherent in this strategy, however. And the manager has to ask: Does the short-term pickup in yield make up for the premium paid on the futures contracts, plus any transaction costs?

This strategy of using the futures market to alter the maturity of a portfolio works best with a portfolio of GNMAs and long-term Treasury bonds provided that in the GNMA futures one uses a contract where the pools delivered will be of a known standard and in the case of Treasury bonds a factor type contract that equalizes the prices of all potential delivery items is used. It should be noted that with this strategy one need not actually take delivery of the securities purchased through the futures contract. Instead the futures contract is used as a temporary substitute to guarantee an investment price at the maturity of the short-term investment.

If the cash portfolio is composed of securities other than GNMAs or U.S. government Treasury bonds, then one has a cross hedge situation and an increase in basis risk. As noted earlier, picking the proper contract, the correct number of contracts, and the correct month are most important in reducing basis risk. Thus, if corporate bonds were sold from the portfolio or their purchase delayed, one would need a good understanding of the nature and extent of the price relationship between Treasury bond futures and the corporate bond market. If the spread between corporates and government bonds were to change during the short-term investment period, the futures position would not give you the same return as holding the original position in corporate bonds.

The futures market can also be used to increase the liquidity of a long-term investment portfolio and to cut the time lag between decision processes and the execution of those decisions. Market conditions do not always allow the portfolio manager sufficient time to quickly and efficiently execute the strategies he has devised. Often a portfolio manager may decide to purchase a block of a certain type of security but will find that security unavailable in the market at that time. Even if the securities were available in the market, the size he desires to purchase may affect the prices.

A simple method of overcoming this problem is to purchase futures contracts that are closely correlated in price movement with the security he wishes to buy in the cash market. This allows the manager time to accumulate the securities in the cash market without being subject to the full risk of a change in market prices. As the cash securities are purchased, the manager would sell the futures contracts that he had previously purchased. The profit and loss from those futures contracts would then be applied to offset the change in the purchase price of the cash market securities. In this way the portfolio manager can reduce the time between decision and execution and be more efficient in the cost effectiveness of his cash market purchases. In short he uses the futures as a temporary substitute for his cash market transactions.

The same strategy would apply when a portfolio manager wished to sell from his fixed-income portfolio. On the date the decision to sell was made the portfolio manager would sell futures contracts into the market. Then as he was able to sell off the securities the futures contracts would be covered. This type of strategy might be especially applicable when the securities to be purchased or sold are not actively traded. Note however, that once again, this strategy involves a cross hedge. Most of the time the securities being purchased or sold would not be the securities that underly the corresponding futures contracts. Therefore, it would be important to know the basis and the beta and to monitor it to maximize the efficiency of the hedge.

HEDGING BY INSURANCE COMPANIES

Insurance companies that have fixed-income securities can use the futures market to hedge the depreciation of their assets as interest rates go higher. They can also use the futures market to increase the liquidity of their portfolios and cut down execution times using the techniques explained earlier.

However, *life* insurance companies have a unique problem that futures can help overcome. Any losses taken by life insurance companies in their fixed income portfolios must be charged against accumulated surplus. When this surplus is reduced it directly lowers the amount of insurance a company can write. Because of this, it is not always feasible for life insurance companies to swap existing holdings of fixed-income securities in their portfolios for higher yielding securities when interest rates are increasing. As interest rates go higher the prices of securities they already own decline. Swapping into the higher coupons would force them to take this loss against accumulated surplus.

Futures can be used to help solve this problem. When rates begin to go higher, a life insurance company could sell futures contracts short against their existing portfolio. As rates continued to move higher the profits from the short position in futures contracts would help offset the losses on the existing cash position. When swaps of lower coupon securities for higher yielding coupons became attractive they could be transacted with no net loss charged against surplus. As cash securities were sold and loss taken, futures short positions would be covered. This strategy allows insurance companies to improve the yields of their fixed-income portfolios in periods of higher interest rates.

In this type of hedge program it should not be necessary to identify futures contracts to be used for each particular cash position. The overall exposure of the portfolio should be analyzed by categorizing the securities into their major groups. See Table 16.1 for an example of a grouping of securities for a hedge program.

Once the issues are grouped by maturity, the average quality of each group would need to be determined, as well as the average maturity. Once these two factors are known one is then in a position to do the

Table 16.1   Breakdown of a Fixed-Income Portfolio in Hedgeable Groups

Maturity	Type of instrument	Type of futures
0–2 years	U.S. Treasury bills U.S. Treasury notes and bonds U.S. agency issues Commercial paper Bank liabilities	90-day Eurodollar deposits 90-day Certificates of Deposit 90-day Treasury bills
2–6 years	U.S. Treasury notes and bonds U.S. agency issues Corporate bonds and notes	U.S. Treasury notes
7–12 years	U.S. Treasury notes and bonds Corporate debt U.S. agency issues GNMA pass throughs	GNMA futures U.S. Treasury note
12–30 years	Corporate debt U.S. agency issues U.S. Treasury bonds	U.S. Treasury bonds

correlation studies and begin the process of calculating basis and dollar equivalency ratios.

Failure to go through these steps could result in overhedging a portfolio and create great risk for the portfolio manager.

After the portfolio was properly hedged and when attractive, yield improvement swaps became possible, the manager would select the issues to be sold and unwind the futures contracts that coincided with that particular security group.

MORTGAGE BANKERS

The mortgage banker can use the futures market in a variety of ways to hedge the financing cost of warehousing mortgages, to hedge the selling price of his GNMA production, and to hedge the cost of mortgages in the pipeline.

Hedging the Finance Cost of Warehousing

Mortgage bankers who are collecting mortgages with a view toward creating a pool and originating a GNMA usually need to finance part of the mortgages until the closings of all the mortgages. During the period prior to completion of a pool, the mortgage banker borrows money to finance mortgages already purchased. These loans are usually made by commercial banks at a rate based upon the prime rate.

When interest rates keep moving higher, the mortgage banker's costs of warehousing keep increasing. To protect against this, he can hedge by selling Eurodollar futures or 90-day CD futures, whichever provides the most efficient basis against the bank loan. As short-term rates work higher the short futures position should offset the increased financial costs.

Sell Production

When a mortgage banker has accumulated a pool of mortgages and wishes to originate a GNMA pass through and then sell that pass through, he can use the futures market as a temporary substitute, and as an alternative marketplace if later it should be more economical to give delivery. The futures market offers a mortgage banker advantages not available in other marketplaces. When the GNMA is sold, the mortgage banker need not be concerned that the buyer will be able to honor the commitment, as the exchange clearinghouse stands behind the purchase. The futures contract is standardized, so terms of sale do not fluctuate from dealer to dealer.

INDUSTRIAL CORPORATIONS

Nonfinancial, or industrial, corporations can use the futures markets to hedge the cost of borrowed money. Bank loans, commercial paper, and long-term borrowing costs can be established in advance at acceptable levels. This can work to lower the cost of borrowing and increase certainty in business decisions by reducing a very important uncertainty: interest costs.

Hedging the Prime Rate

A variable prime rate loan can be hedged to protect against changes in interest rates. Correlation studies show that the best contracts to use are either the Eurodollar contracts or the CD contracts. There are some difficulties in doing so, however. One reason for the difficulty is the fact that the prime rate is not always highly correlated with futures price movements; the prime rate is administered while futures prices are not. Another reason is that the futures contract and the cash asset may not mature at the same time. This uncertainty in basis and lack of coincidence in maturity of the cash and futures positions presents significant problems.

Both of these problems can be compensated for by (a) selling a series of consecutive contract months and retiring the contracts as the loan approaches maturity or (b) selling an adequate amount of one futures month that matures after the loan matures and retiring contracts as the loan ages. The first technique helps to smooth basis change risk because the futures contracts cover a wide maturity range. The second is sometimes preferable because it reduces transaction costs and in rising rate markets the longer term contract will outperform shorter term contracts. Each technique is illustrated below.

The Multicontract Technique of Hedging

Assume that, as a result of correlation studies, T-bills have been picked as the best vehicle for hedging a variable rate bank loan against a rise in rates. If the price spreads between various T-bill futures contracts had been fluctuating sharply, it might be difficult to pick one contract month to short and maintain a good basis relationship. In such case a string of different months could be shorted to average out the maturity of the futures contract.

The following is an example of this type of hedge. (This concept was introduced earlier in our discussion of spreads, but it's important enough to bear repeating.)

On August 15, a corporation borrows $10 million for one year at the prime rate. The corporation expects the prime rate to rise over the next year, or at least part of that year. The loan agreement stipulates that the interest rate of the loan changes on the same day the lender changes its posted prime rate.

The key consideration is that the amount of money owed will depend not only on changes in the prime rate, but on *when* those changes occur. If the bank raises the rate on the tenth day of the loan, the borrower must pay the increased rate for the next 355 days. If the rate changes on day 150, the borrower pays the higher rate for only 215 days. The trick is to be fully hedged, but not overhedged, for every day of the life of the loan. This calls for the hedger to establish dollar equivalency at the outset, and then maintain it by reducing the size of the short position in futures proportionately over the life of the loan.

To accomplish this, the corporation should, on day one of the loan, short five times (assume a 1.2 bite) as many millions of dollars worth of CDs—or 90-day Eurodollar contracts—as they have millions of prime-rate loan dollars. Each 0.01% increase in one 90-day T-bill futures contract returns only $25, while each 0.01% increase in cost of a one-year loan is $100 per million. As the loan moves toward maturity, the value of each 0.01% change in the futures contract remains $25, while the dollar value of a .01 change in loan interest declines. Table 16.2 shows these values for the loan. The five contracts sold on day one of the loan would be covered on a proportional basis with the declining maturity of the loan.

On August 15, when the loan was made, the corporation would short 13 September futures contracts, 13 December contracts, 12 March contracts, and 12 June contracts. Just prior to the settlement of the each contract month, the corporation would roll that contract month into the next contract month. During the periods between roll overs the corporation would cover the shorts to match the declining maturity,

Table 16.2   Dollar value per
0.01%

Time left to maturity	Cost per $1 million of loan
90 days	$25
180 days	$50
270 days	$75
360 days	$100

always covering them in the closest contract month. The corporation would liquidate the last ten contracts over the time remaining between the last contract month and the maturation date of the loan. Hence, between August and September the hedger should offset three September futures, buying one every nine days (every seven days because 50 contracts must be retired over 365 days, and 365/50 = 7.03 days). On September 19, just prior to the September contract settlement, the hedger would roll the remaining September contracts into the December contract by purchasing September contracts and shorting more December contracts. This process of retiring contracts every seven days will keep the proper balance until the loan matures, assuming there is no basis change.

The Single Month Method

A single contract month of CDs could also be used to hedge the loan. The hedger could short 50 September CD futures contracts and retire one of the contracts every seven days. This would reduce the commission costs, but could increase the basis risk. If the spreads between months are changing rapidly, the September futures contracts could outperform or underperform the rest of the market, causing severe basis problems.

However, there are two times when such a one month strategy pays off. First, when the cash market yield curve is negatively sloped and futures prices are at considerable premiums to cash, it makes sense to lump all shorts into the nearby futures contract, because the convergence of the premium to spot will work in favor of the short. This positive aspect more than overcomes the problem of concentration. It does, however, increase commission cost as the remaining short positions must be rolled into the next contract month more frequently.

A second type of single contract month hedge is to short the closest month following the maturity of the loan. The contracts would be retired proportionately until maturity of the loan. There are two advantages to this strategy. First, the strategy precludes the necessity of rolling into new contract months. This not only reduces brokerage commissions but cuts down operational expenses and bookkeeping expenses. Second, if the market for CDs rallies on a short-term basis, the more distant futures months often will gain less than the front months.

This can reduce the opportunity costs of the hedge. In other words, the basis will be more stable, or is more likely to work in the hedger's favor.

Hedging the Prime at Different Stages of the Business Cycle

There is no "right" technique to hedge variable rate bank loans, but market volatility and the stage of the business cycle must be taken into consideration. There is also no "right" type of futures contract to use as the short side of the hedge. Often T-bills will be the best type of futures contracts to short; at other times commercial paper contracts are best, because they will correlate better with prime rate changes.

The keys to picking between bills and commercial paper lie in two fundamental considerations. First, corporate liquidity is very important. In the early stages of an increasing rate cycle, corporate liquidity is usually high and commercial paper will not always correlate with the prime rate changes. In the later stages of a cycle corporations get squeezed for cash and commercial paper and prime rate loans tend to follow one another closely. During this time bank loans are taken down as an alternative to commercial paper loans. Second, T-bills and T-bill futures are investment vehicles, and investor expectations play a large role in their pricing structure. Therefore, in the first stages of a rising interest cycle, T-bills will usually decline as fast as or faster than the prime rate, as a result of investor expectations of higher rates. However, toward the last stages of an interest rate upswing, investors often anticipate the actual peak and drive the prices of T-bills higher while the prime rate remains unchanged.

In general Treasury bill futures therefore make better hedge vehicles in the beginning and middle stages of a rising interest rate cycle, and commercial paper makes a better vehicle in the later stages of the cycle.

Hedging Commercial Paper Costs

Commercial paper costs can be hedged in much the same way a commercial bank hedges the costs of certificates of deposit. It is actually easier to hedge commercial paper costs than CDs, because the commercial paper contract is less of a cross hedge with an individual commercial paper issuer than specific certificates of deposits are with 90-day T-bill futures. The techniques of hedging would be the same as for CDs, but caution must be used in the commercial paper futures market because of the lack of liquidity in the contracts. Until liquidity increases substantially, the basis risk of using T-bill contracts to hedge commercial paper may be less than the transaction costs in the commercial paper futures market.

Smoothing Out Seasonal Cash Flows and Increasing Returns on Investments

The futures market can be used by the corporate treasurer to even out the investment returns of excess cash. Usually a corporation is limited to the rates extant in the money market at the time the cash is on hand. Also it is subject to the vagaries of the market when it must sell securities whose maturities are longer than the period the cash is available. This either limits the maturity of the investment to the life of the cash or opens the corporation up to security losses.

Lock in Rates for Future Dates

The corporation that knows when it will be receiving cash may invest at any time prior to actually receiving the cash by purchasing futures contracts. The purchase of futures fixes the return at today's futures rates. When the cash arrives and investments are made in the cash market, their performance is adjusted by the profits or losses from futures. A corporation need not take delivery of a security purchased by a long commitment in a futures contract. It is looking for the price appreciation *as if* it had made the cash investment on the day the futures contract was purchased.

The opposite is true for the corporation that has a portfolio and wishes to sell today because of an expected market decline. The corporation may not want to realize the loss on its books, and also may not need the cash at this time. It could instead sell futures contracts against the cash position. As the futures prices declined, the profit from the short would offset the loss in value of the portfolio from the day the hedge was placed.

Increasing the Return of Short-Term Investments

Corporate treasurers often have money for specific periods of time and are limited to making investments for that specified period of time. By using interest rate futures along with cash investments, the treasurer can increase this return for the period held. This can be accomplished by taking the best possible yield in the cash market, then tailoring the maturity of that investment to match the life of the cash. This is very similar to the technique of the liability manager of a bank using the yield curve for CDs to his advantage.

If the highest short-term yield available were 180 days but the corporation had cash for only 90 days, it could purchase the 180-day instrument and sell short a 90-day CD contract. If at the end of 90 days prices in the money market had declined, the corporation would lose money on selling the 180-day investment to raise cash. However, to the extent that prices in the futures market declined equally, the corporation would earn an equal profit to offset the loss. If prices were to increase over the 90-day period the profit from the cash sale would similarly offset the loss in the futures position. The outcome of both possibilities would be a higher return for the 90-day period than if the money were invested in lower yielding 90-day spot instruments.

The same logic applies when shorter term rates are higher than longer term rates—an inverse yield curve. A corporation with 180-day money might find 90-day rates more attractive than 180-day rates. The problem with this type of yield curve is that there is no guarantee that at the end of the original 90-day investment interest rates will be equally as high for the next 90 days. However, futures could be used to "lock in" a rate for the last 90 days of a 180-day program. In this strategy the investor would maximize return by buying 90-day paper and also buying a 90-day futures contract. If the whole yield curve has shifted lower at the end of the first 90 days, the profit from futures would effectively increase the yield for the last 90 days. If rates were to go higher, the higher reinvestment rate for the last 90 days will be partially or entirely offset by the loss in the futures.

Hedging Long-Term Interest Rates

Corporations may wish to hedge the cost of long-term borrowing when the time between the decision to borrow and the actual process of borrowing is protracted. For example, corporations who have planned to borrow in the future may wish to lock in today's futures market rates. This can often be the case when corporations contract to have capital goods built. The construction process is financed by short-term borrowing, but after completion of construction long-term debt is sold to finance the asset. When the period of construction is lengthy the corporation may not want to pay both short-term borrowing and long-term borrowing costs, particularly if it does not wish to risk paying higher long-term rates at a later time.

To hedge such a risk the borrower can establish his rate today by shorting T-bond futures contracts. To accomplish this the hedger should do the following:

1. Complete a correlation study to find which futures contract provides the most constant basis relationship with the debt that will be eventually sold.
2. Study changes in the size of the basis, including those caused by credit differences. A mathematical function can be statistically derived through regression analysis of past relationships.
3. Adjust for changes in rate resulting from differences in maturity.
4. On a present value basis, using the expected coupon rate of the bond for a compounding factor, calculate the amount of money that must be made on the futures to cover increased interest costs.

Once these four steps have been taken the appropriate number of contracts should be shorted. If interest rates increase between hedge date and bond-sale date, the profits from futures would be added to the proceeds of the bond sale to reduce interest costs of the sale. In effect, the corporation would be receiving a premium for its bonds. To illustrate this process consider the following.

Hedging Corporate Bond Issuance

A company with a single A bond rating currently foresees the need to issue $50,000,000 of debt six months from now. Believing that rates will increase, the company wishes to hedge against any rate rise.

The company now can issue 20-year debt at a coupon rate of 10%. If rates were to rise 1%, the added cost over 20 years will be $50,-

000,000 $\times$ 0.01 $\times$ 20 = \$10,000,000. The present value of this potential future cash out flow is \$4,289,772, which is determined from the equation

$$PV = \sum_{i=1}^{N} \frac{PMT}{(1 + R)^i}$$

where

N = the number of semiannual payments

PMT = the amount each semiannual payment will increase per 1% rise in interest costs

R = semiannual discount factor, which is the current semiannual rate

PV = the present value of a 1% increase in rates

Once the additional cost of a 1% change in rates is known, the number of T-bond contracts needed to hedge this potential increase in costs should be determined. For now, it is assumed that when corporate bond rates increase 1%, so will T-bond rates. This assumption will be relaxed later on.

At the present time, the CBT's cheapest deliverable bond is the 11¾% of 2010 maturities cash T-bond. The futures market will trade in tandem with this issue. A 1% change in yield in the cash bond can be represented by a 8²²⁄₃₂ price movement.

The CBT's contract specifies that the futures price (for invoicing delivery purposes) be multiplied by a delivery factor. As the price of the cash bond changes, the futures price movement can be represented by

$$\text{futures price} = \frac{\text{cash price}}{\text{delivery factor}}$$

Assuming December 1980 delivery, the delivery factor is 1.3974 for 11¾. The price change in the futures market for a 1% change in yield will be

$$\text{futures price } \Delta = \frac{\text{cash price } \Delta \text{ per 1\% yield change}}{\text{current delivery factor}}$$

Plugging values into this equation, the futures price change per 1% yield change will be 6⁷⁄₃₂, or (8²²⁄₃₂) $\div$ 1.3974.

Thus for a 1% yield change, we now know that the futures price will move 6⁷⁄₃₂, with a value of $6218.75. Still assuming that a corporate yield change will be equally matched by an equivalent move in government bond yields, the $6218.75 should be divided into $4,289,772 to determine how many contracts should be used:

$$4,289,772 \div 6,218.67 = 690 \text{ contracts}$$

Historical data covering the period January 1974 to June 1980 shows that single A rated, 20-year corporate bond yields move at a rate of 1.02 to 1.00 against yields on 20-year government bonds. Because of this, when rates are rising, the company's interest rates will rise faster. Earlier it was assumed that the rates moved at an equal rate. To adjust for this differential, the corporate hedger should use (1.02 × 690 contracts =) 703 contracts to most efficiently hedge against rates rising on a 20-year $50,000,000 debt issue.

CHAPTER SEVENTEEN

Internal Record Keeping and Corporate Control Systems for the Hedge

As in many things, success in hedging depends on having good people and good records. Once the decision has been made to establish a hedging program, immediate attention should be paid to the internal record keeping, control, audit, and accounting procedures. This section will deal with the record keeping, control, and internal audit aspects.

In establishing a system of internal control, an organization must give due consideration to the risks involved and to the costs of maintaining the system. Therefore, the system will differ between hedging organizations, depending upon such things as the volume of trading and the sophistication of the system needed for covering the trading activity. Nevertheless, every system should include the following:

1. A definition of the authority and responsibility of the personnel to be involved in the hedging decisions.
2. Segregation of duties such that no one individual has simultaneous control of both the trading activity and the record-keeping activity.
3. The establishment of independent checks and balances against which transaction details can be checked.

4. The use of after-the-fact internal audit devices to check the accuracy and propriety of recorded transactions and accounting and operating data.

PROCEDURES

In most instances firms establish procedures relating to the trading and the documentation necessary for record keeping. This facilitates both internal audits and the reporting procedures for top management.

Generally the record keeping procedures include:

1. A listing of the authorized brokers with whom the firm will trade.
2. A statement of the trading limits and the description of the procedures to be followed if the limits are exceeded by any one trader.
3. A description of the accounting records to be used to control and monitor the activity.
4. A description of the documents to be received from the broker with whom the trading is being conducted.
5. A description of the various reports that are to be generated for senior management.

In establishing trading limits, the hedger should consider setting them at three levels—totals for the entire organization, for each trader individually, and for each contract maturity. These three limits should be referenced to the cash position.

As each trade is made, the trader should prepare a trade ticket that becomes the starting point for the accounting information flow. Trade tickets should contain all essential information, such as the date of the trade, whether it is a buy or a sell, contract description, quantity, price, trader's name, and the description of the cash position being hedged. The accuracy of the trade ticket is the responsibility of the trader and as a verification the trader should "balance out" nightly with the broker with whom he is dealing.

Although the form of the records varies from one hedger to another, a corporation typically develops ledgers segregated according to the various futures contract maturities that coincide with their cash market activity. Thus, an independent ledger is kept to include trade date, trader, reason for trade, whether buy or sell, quantity, price, and commission expense. Such a ledger provides detail for preparing the following:

1. A general ledger memorandum reflecting total futures positions.
2. A record reflecting commission expenses.
3. A trial "balance" of futures positions.
4. Reports to management on trading activity and positions taken by each trader.

It is also advisable that weekly margin runs be prepared by the hedger's broker and received by someone independent of the trading and the record-keeping function. This individual should verify the open positions and contract prices as well as the margin balance to assure that they are correct and to assure that the appropriate debit or credit tickets are prepared for recording losses and gains.

Keeping records in such detail as outlined above assures that the hedger will properly manage its money and the cash flow between it and its brokers.

REPORTING TO MANAGEMENT

The primary objective of the procedures mentioned above is to ensure that all trades are properly recorded in both the general ledger and the supporting subsidiary ledgers. But it also forms the basis for generating reports to senior management that provide an overall evaluation of the entire trading and hedging operation. Generally, reports should be required weekly by top management. Such reports should reflect all open positions and the related income effects of both realized and unrealized gains or losses. These reviews allow management to determine whether the policies they've established are being followed. Further, the reviews highlight the financial effect on current operations and the economic impact of the overall hedging operation.

CHAPTER EIGHTEEN
Arbitrage and Spreading Strategies

One of the most intellectually challenging and potentially rewarding trading strategies is one designed to take advantage of the temporary discrepancies that occur in price relationships between markets or between securities. These discrepancies occur frequently, arising because of temporary supply and demand imbalances or time lags in the market response for various securities.

These price discrepancies disappear rather quickly and the prices move back to their natural equilibrium because sharp traders quickly recognize the situation and immediately buy the cheap instrument or contract and sell the more expensive, causing the lower priced instrument to rise and the higher priced instrument to fall in price.

When this process of simultaneous buying and selling involves two different markets—such as the cash and futures market, or two different securities on the same yield curve such as T-bills and GNMAS's—it is referred to as arbitrage. When it is conducted within the same marketplace or between different futures months of similar securities, it is called spreading. Hence, a position of long December T-bill futures and short March T-bill futures is a spread. This chapter provides a brief explanation of the concepts of arbitrage and spreading.

ARBITRAGE

Although both the spread trade and arbitrage attempt to profit from relative price changes that might occur as market conditions are chang-

239

ing, spread trading makes a statement about the spreader's attitude on which way the market is going to move, while arbitrage does not.

To illustrate this point let's look at the hypothetical yield curve shown in Figure 18.1. The arbitrageur would study the market and note the yield difference between the various issues, A through G. He would look at the comparison between security D and security E, for example, and realize that D was cheaper than normal in comparison to the yield curve, and that E was expensive relative to the yield curve.

The arbitrageur would also consider the characteristics of the two securities in assessing their relative prices. Such characteristics would include:

1. The credit rating. Different credit ratings would cause the issues to trade at different relative values.
2. The interest rate coupon of each security. Differences in coupons would cause securities to trade differently under changing market conditions.
3. The maturities of the two securities. An arbitrageur would seldom be in risk in the transaction. A position of long security A and short security G would reflect expectations of long-term rates rising faster than short-term rates. An arbitrageur does not "ride" the yield curve or bet on yield curve changes in this fashion. He expects that securities D and E, however, since they have the same maturity, will eventually trade at even prices regardless of changes in the yield curve. He concentrates on these.
4. Liquidity. Good arbitrage opportunities require that the liquidity of the two securities be roughly comparable.

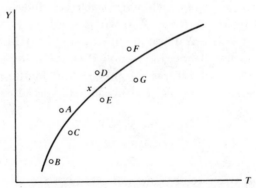

Figure 18.1   Hypothetical yield curve.

If the arbitrageur found that the characteristics of D and E were similar, he would purchase security D and sell E. His anticipated profit would be the gain on D as it moved down to the yield curve (point x), and the gain on E as it moved up to the yield curve. In this arbitrage the investor seeks to make a profit on both securities. This type of trade would not necessarily be affected by a shift in the yield curve or any changes in general market conditions.

Cash and Futures Arbitraging

Cash/futures arbitrage involves simultaneous transactions in the two markets for securities of the same credit, coupon, and maturity. Arbitrageurs are trying to profit only from price discrepancies. They are not interested in taking on the additional risks associated with different securities. Until recently, liquidity in the futures market was a problem in doing cash/futures arbitrage. But recently this has been of less concern as long as one stays in the nearest three futures contract months. Liquidity in the more distant futures is still a concern and must be carefully considered when arbitraging longer futures contracts. The lack of liquidity can cause transaction costs to rise and frequently masks dangerous trading situations as apparent arbitrage opportunities.

The Essence of Cash/Futures Arbitrage

In cash/futures arbitrage, comparisons are not of similar securities on a common yield curve, but are of similar securities on different yield curves. One, the cash market, is an existing yield curve. The other, the futures market, is an expected yield curve. The comparison is between prices for securities in the futures market and the prices for the same security in the cash market. As explained in Chapter 13, there is a natural price differential between futures and cash based upon the spot price for money, plus or minus the net cost of carry, and the effect of investors' expectations. When the price differential between cash and futures is greater or less than the aggregate cost of carry, there is an opportunity for arbitrage.

ARBITRAGE OPPORTUNITIES

When the prices for futures, after adjustment for cost of carry, are greater than cash prices, the arbitrageur purchases cash securities and sells futures contracts. This is referred to as "long arbitrage." When the prices for futures, after adjustment for cost of carry, are less than the cash prices, the arbitrageur sells the cash market and buys the futures contract. This is referred to as "short arbitrage."

The arbitrageur usually does not hold the positions for an extended period of time. The position would normally be taken off when the price relationships return to normal. Sometimes, however, the arbitrageur will continue to hold a position if the cost of carry considerations continue to remain profitable even after the differential has been dissipated.

It is important to weigh carefully all cost and revenues in an arbitrage situation. Table 18.1 shows cost and revenues for various arbitrage possibilities.

PROFITS AND RISKS OF ARBITRAGE

Arbitrage risk arises from two sources: changes in financing costs and variations in the price of the securities and/or contracts held. In actual trading, long-cash arbitrage positions would probably outnumber short-cash arbitrage positions. This is because futures pay no interest, and financing costs are considerably higher for a short position in the cash market than for either a long cash position or a short futures position. Although the general principles outlined in this section apply to both, the following discussion of strategy will be formulated in terms of a long-cash position.

Financing Costs

Let us abstract from the problem of fluctuations in the market value of arbitrage positions by assuming for the moment that cash market prices are fixed. The expected profit would then be the sum of the interest earned on the cash bill (INT), the financing cost (FIN), and the arbitrage pickup (ARB):

Table 18.1

Revenues	Costs Long cash/short futures
Interest income earned on the cash position.	Interest cost of financing the cash position, or the opportunity cost of money used to purchase the cash position.
Price appreciation of the cash position and price depreciation of the futures position.	Price appreciation of the futures contract and price depreciation of the cash security.
The value of cash that may be received from the clearinghouse if the futures position depreciates in value and cash is paid to the trader.	Cost of execution: brokerage fees and transaction costs. Transaction costs include the market movement caused by the execution of an order on the exchange. Cash market reflects the difference between the bid and ask.
	The opportunity cost of negative cash flow as a result of maintenance margin calls if the futures appreciate.
	Short Cash/Long Futures
Interest income on cash securities used to collateralize borrowing of cash positions, or interest earned on the reverse repurchase agreement entered into to obtain the cash security for delivery on the short sale.	Accrued interest paid on the cash security sold in the market.
Price appreciation of the futures position and price depreciation on the cash security.	Price depreciation of the futures contract and price appreciation of the cash contract.
Value of cash received from the clearinghouse if the futures position appreciates in value.	Any borrowing fees incurred if the cash security is borrowed to fill the short sale delivery (usually .5%).
	Transaction costs: brokerage fees. Difference between bid and ask and execution cost of the exchange.
	Opportunity cost of negative cash flow as result of maintenance margin call if the futures market depreciates.

$$\text{INT} = D \times \frac{h}{360} \times 10{,}000$$

$$\text{FIN} = -RP \times \frac{h}{360} \times 10{,}000$$

$$\text{ARB} = \Delta d \times \frac{h}{360} \times 10{,}000$$

$$\text{PROFIT} = \text{INT} + \text{FIN} + \text{ARB}$$

where D is the (constant) cash discount, h is the holding period of the arbitrage measured in days, RP is the average repo rate during the holding period, and Δd is the initial difference between the implicit and actual forward discounts that should be eliminated during the holding period. The profit formula simplifies to

$$\text{PROFIT} = \left[(D - RP)\frac{h}{360} + \frac{90\Delta d}{360} \right] \times 10{,}000$$

The first term, $(D - RP)h/360$, is the carry on the position, and the second term, $90\Delta d/360$, is the expected arbitrage pickup valued at \$25 per basis point. This equation reveals that profits are inversely related to the repo rate and directly related to the forward discount discrepancy. The earnings derived from carrying the position are proportional to the holding period, but the arbitrage pickup is fixed. As long as the position yields a positive carry, total earnings will increase with the length of the holding period.

To evaluate an arbitrage, the following four principles must be considered:

1. The spread between the bid and asked quotations in the cash market imposes an immediate turnover cost when the position is acquired.
2. The cash discount does not remain fixed, but is permitted to converge gradually to the implicit forward level during the period remaining until contract settlement. The higher the futures rate premium relative to spot rates, the smaller the earnings on the cash security.
3. The repo charge is levied against the current discounted market value of the bill, not its maturity value.
4. Brokerage and clearing fees for the futures transaction must also be deducted as an expense.

A sample run of the profit projection incorporating these four revisions into the preceding profit equation produces the characteristic

time pattern of daily profits shown in Figure 18.2. In the early days of
the arbitrage, profits are dominated by the fixed arbitrage pickup,
which in this illustration more than offsets the transaction costs. As the
holding period is lengthened, the fixed arbitrage pickup diminishes on
a daily basis and eventually becomes overshadowed by the position's
carry as a source of profit.

Market Price Fluctuations

The normal variability of interest rates presents a twofold problem.
First, a change in the cash bill discount will not necessarily be accompanied by an equivalent basis point change in the associated futures
discount. Second, a given basis point change in the cash discount may
translate into a different dollar value than an identical change in the
futures discount.

Imperfect Basis Offset. To the extent that the market correctly discounts an impending movement in interest rates, the expected change,
when it arrives, will tend to have a more pronounced impact on the spot
market than on the forward market. With efficient money market

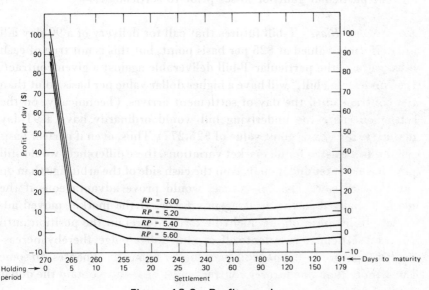

Figure 18.2   Profit per day.

pricing, one might expect this type of movement to occur more frequently than the converse possibility—a change in forward rates in excess of the movement in spot rates. Nevertheless, futures have a history of overreacting to economic events, and this nervous behavior may lead to transitory swings in the forward rate of much greater extent than the corresponding movements in spot rates.

If a long arbitrage position were held, its value would appreciate in response to a fall in the cash bill discount if not offset by an equivalent fall in the forward discount. The arbitrageur would tend, *ceteris paribus*, to shorten the holding period in order to realize the gain. On the other hand, if either the forward discount fell further than the cash discount, or the cash discount advanced more than the forward discount, the arbitrageur would suffer a loss. Supposing the dollar value of a basis point to be roughly the same in the two markets; the arbitrageur would be inclined to extend the holding period in order to allow convergence of the two markets to proceed.

Long-term arbitrage allows for convergence of the spot and forward discounts; it is only *unanticipated* interim gyrations in these markets prior to settlement that pose a market risk. While it is known that a dollar hedge would be achieved by locking in a trading profit or loss amounting to the difference between the cash price and futures prices (if the position were retained until settlement), this provides no assurance of particular gains or losses prior to settlement.

Basis Point Bias. T-bill futures that call for delivery of a 90-day bill are uniformly valued at $25 per basis point, but this is not true of cash bills. In fact, the particular T-bill deliverable against a given contract, the "underlying bill," will have a higher dollar value per basis point than the contract until the day of settlement arrives. (Technically, on the settlement date the underlying bill would ordinarily have a 91-day maturity, for a basis point value of $25.277). Thus, even if perfect basis point offset existed for all market variations, these differences would still produce a greater dollar change on the cash side of the arbitrage than on the forward side. This, of course, would prove advantageous if the market changed in the arbitrageur's favor. If the market moved adversely to his position, he might be forced to retain the position until contract settlement in order to effect a full dollar hedge, thereby increasing his exposure to the possibility of higher financing expenses. In some cases, more than one futures contract must be used to obtain the dollar equivalency.

FINANCING

In choosing between overnight and term repos, it is doubtful if any invariant rule can be specified, since each type of financing has advantages and disadvantages. Overnight financing seems preferable whenever flexibility is particularly desired—in newly acquired positions where a quick arbitrage pickup is anticipated, positions close to a contract settlement date, or positions showing a trading profit that might be realized prior to an inversion point. Term financing is the superior method when an increase in the repo rate appears imminent, or when a trading loss is to be deferred until an inversion point.

SPREADING IN FINANCIAL FUTURES

Spread trading in financial futures is a method of speculation for the trader who wishes to assume slightly less risk than occurs in owning a one-sided or "net" position. Spread trading comprises the simultaneous buying and selling of two different futures contracts. The purpose of the trade is to anticipate the potential change in the *relative* values of two different contracts. In financial futures there are two different types of speads: intracontract, and intermarket.

INTRACONTRACT SPREADS

This is the most common type of spread. It consists of buying and selling different settlement months of the same contract. The intent is to purchase the month that will increase in value and sell the month that will decrease. To be successful at this type of spreading the trader must fully understand what makes the price differentials between delivery months. This was discussed earlier. However, those same concepts can be used to explain the two basic intracontract spread trades, the bull spread and the bear spread.

The Bull Spread

The bull spread is so named because it is put on in anticipation of bullish conditions in the money markets. When short-term financing costs are decreasing and security prices are on the rise, nearby financial futures contracts tend to gain on the more distant contracts. The bull spreader therefore buys a nearby contract and simultaneously sells a distant contract against it, looking for the *relative* change in their prices to earn him spread profits. (This is also called "buying" the spread, or going "long" on the spread. Conversely, if the nearby position is the short side of the spread, the spreader is considered to have "sold" or be "short" the spread.) In a general sense spreads "bull" because the *net cost of carry* is becoming positive or more positive.

In our example the trader has bought the spread at 120 points premium to December:

	Price	Price difference
Long—June 90-day T-bills	80.00	
Short—December 90-day T-bills	81.20	120

Lets further assume the spread changes to 100 basis points:

	New price	Price difference	Profit (loss)
Long—June 90-day T-bills	80.20		+500
Short—December 90-day T-bills	81.20	100	—
			$500

In this example the trader was long the June/December T-bill spread. As the long side gained 20 points on the short side, the trader realized a $500 profit for each spread he was long, before deducting commissions.

Bull spreads can be put in any financial future by buying a nearby contract and selling a distant contract.

Assume 90-day T-bills are trading at 10%, and the price of T-bills does not change; if the cost of financing is 12%, the price curve for T-bill futures would be P_1 in the accompanying diagram. However if financing costs change to 8%, the price curve will change to P_2. If a June/Decem-

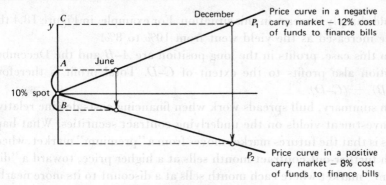

Figure 18.3 Price curves.

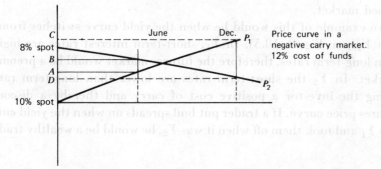

Figure 18.4 Price curve in a negative market; 12% cost of funds.

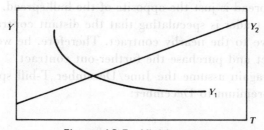

Figure 18.5 Yield curve.

ber bull spread in T-bills had been purchased prior to the change in rates, the trader would have lost money on the June bill equal to $A–B$, and his profit on the short in December T-bills would have been $C–D$. Because $C–D$ is greater than $A–B$, the bull spread would have shown a profit of $(C–D) — (A–B)$.

In the real world, what would most likely happen is that spot price would sharply increase in this situation. For example, in Figure 18.4 the price increased as the yield went from 10% to 8%.

In this case, profits in the long position are *A–B* and the December position also profits to the extent of *C–D*. Total profit is therefore *(A–B)* + *(C–D)*.

In summary, bull spreads work when financing costs decline relative to investment yields on the underlying contract securities. What happens is that the futures market moves from a "premium" market, where each further-out contract month sells at a higher price, toward a "discount" market where each month sells at a discount to its more nearby contracts. This type of price behavior usually occurs when the yield curve for cash securities moves and becomes a "normal" or positively sloped market.

An example of this would be when the yield curve switches from Y_1 to Y_2 (see Figure 18.5). In Y_1, short-term interest rates are higher than long-term rates, therefore the futures market would be a premium market. In Y_2 the short-term rates are lower than long-term rates, giving the investor a positive cost of carry and thereby a discount futures price curve. If a trader put bull spreads on when the yield curve was Y_1 and took them off when it was Y_2, he would be a wealthy trader.

The Bear Spread

The "bear" spread is just the opposite of the bull spread. In this type of spread the trader is speculating that the distant contract will gain ground relative to the nearby contract. Therefore, he would sell the closer contract and purchase the further-out contract.

Let's once again assume the June/December T-bill spread at 120 basis points premium to December:

	Price	Price difference
Short June T-bill futures	80.00	
Long December T-bill futures	81.20	120

If financing costs were to go higher, the price curve would move to a higher premium and the spread would change to reflect this:

	New price	Price difference	Profit
Short June T-bill futures	80.10		−250
Long December T-bill futures	81.40	+1.30	+500
			+250

In this case the bear spread profited $250 (gross) because the price differential moved from 120 points to 130 points (10 points × $25 = $250). What happened in this spread is the that price curve shifted upward as negative carry became greater.

In summary, spreads tend to "bear" when the cost of financing goes higher on the yield curve for cash securities become more negative. Remember the key to spread trading is the forecasting of repurchase agreements, or the cost of financing securities.

INTERMARKET SPREADS

Intermarket spreads comprise the simultaneous buying and selling of different interest rate futures contracts. An example would be to sell GNMAs futures and buy U.S. Treasury bond futures. The purpose of the spread is the same—to take advantage of relative price changes between two futures contracts. Intermarket spreads can also be either "bull" or "bear" spreads.

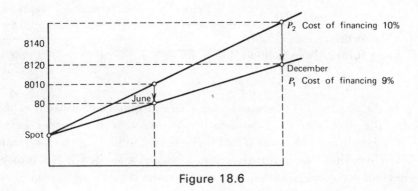

Figure 18.6

Spread Changes Due to Yield Curve Changes

This type of spread is profitable when the trading correctly forecasts changes in the yield curve for fixed income securities. To take advantage the trader would buy the portion of the yield curve that should be relatively strong and sell the weaker portion of the curve. An example of this is the GNMA/T-bond intermarket spread. Let's assume the yield curve for the cash market is shaped like Y_1 in Figure 18.7. If the spreader anticipates that the yield curve will change to Y_2, then the trader would sell the U.S. T-bond issue, which trades off the 30-year bond market, and purchase the GNMA future contract, which is based on the 12-year average life of GNMAs. If the curve does move to Y_2, then the yield on 30-year bonds will increase and the price will decline. This will cause the price of GNMA futures to decline, creating a profit in the short position in U.S. T-bond futures shorted as part of the intermarket spread. The yield and price of GNMAs would remain constant and therefore the spread would be profitable. The following GNMA/T-bond spread illustrates this:

	Price Y_1	Price differential
Long position, June GNMA	78	
Short position, June T-Bond	80	+ 2 points

The yield curve shifts to Y_2:

	Price Y_2	Price difference	Profit spread
GNMA future, June GNMA	78		—
T-bond future, June T-bond	77	− 1 pt	+ 3000
			$3000

In the jargon of the futures business this intramarket spread is called after the position in the T-bond futures contract. If the spreader is *long* the T-bonds and short the GNMAs, he is said to be *long* the intermarket. When the T-bond futures position is *short* and the GNMA futures contract is the long position, then the spreader is short the intramarket.

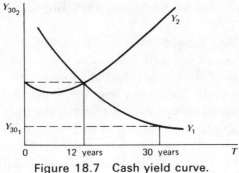

Figure 18.7   Cash yield curve.

As in intramarket spreads a trader *buys* or goes long the spread, or sells or goes short the spread.

RISK AND SPREAD TRANSACTIONS

Spreading may be touted as the most conservative form of futures trading, but as anyone who followed news reports during the latter part of 1982 is aware, some spreads can lead to very large losses. It seems that sometime during the previous year, customers of one large broker-age house were encouraged to establish a spread position in which they would be short Treasury bond futures and long Ginny Mae futures. The assumption was that with interest rates falling, both Treasury bonds and Ginny Mae futures would rise in value. Falling interest rates always make existing yield curves more attractive, just as rising yields make older and lower yielding securities less desirable. Because Ginny Mae futures were selling well below Treasury bonds, it was assumed that they would rise faster, thus generating profits.

What happened in reality, however, is that Treasury bond futures soared in price while Ginny Maes moved up only modestly. For exam-ple, between September 1 of 1982 and November 1 of 1982, the De-cember Ginny Mae futures rose from 64 to 69 and 8/32s, while the Treasury bond futures jumped from 66 to 76 and 17/32s. Each thirty-second of a point represented $31.25 on contracts with a $100,000 face value, and both with 8% coupon. The result was that during this time period the Treasury bond futures, which had been sold, lost about $10,531, while the Ginny Mae side of the spread gained only $5,250.

This meant a net loss of $5,281 on each spread, not counting the commissions.

The major error made in this transaction was that someone overlooked a fundamental fact with respect to the contract specifications and the workings of the markets in the two securities.

To put it simply, the futures contract for Ginny Maes and for Treasury bonds allows the seller to select the instrument that he wishes to deliver within the terms of the contract. In the case of both futures, at delivery the deliverable instruments are adjusted in price to equal the 8% coupon. All that matters is that the short seller delivers certificates with the face value of $100,000 at a price equivalent to an 8% coupon regardless of whether the actual instruments are selling at a premium or discount to their face value.

In the specific case at hand of the Ginny Maes, the average life of a mortgage is assumed to be 12½ years, but, because of a prolonged period of high rates, many Ginny Mae certificates had been issued with much higher coupons that 8%. When interest rates fall, Ginny Mae mortgages tend to be prepaid as homeowners refinance at lower rates. Hence, the higher premium and interest coupon, the shorter expected life there is for a Ginny Mae. Investors do not like to hold mortgages that can be prepaid because it reduces the yield or return on investment. The marketplace recognized these drawbacks to owning high coupon Ginny Maes and priced them accordingly; that is, at lower levels. The sellers of futures found that high coupon issues were the cheapest to deliver and it was exactly those issues that buyers did not want to receive. For that reason, the spread between Ginny Maes and T-bonds did not narrow, but rather widened.

Causes of Yield Curve Changes

The causes of yield curve changes are many and often misunderstood. The best explanation rests on two fundamentals.

First, changes in expectations of future yield curve shape are generally believed to be the chief mover of the yield curves. This occurs because future yield curve expectations are really the market's perception of the future supply and demand of and for debt securities. These expectations of supply and demand of debt securities are based on what investors think the general level of economic activity will be in the near future. Once the investing public guesses what the economy will be doing, they then know what type of yield curve to expect. When they expect a yield curve to be a certain way they usually force it to meet that expectation. A trader makes money in intermarket spreads by being able to understand the psychology of the market and what that psychology will do to the yield curve. If we assume the economy is in the late stages of an expansionary business cycle, the yield curve usually will be shaped similar to Y_1 in Figure 18.8. This environment usually is characterized by high interest rates, high inflation, and large demands for short-term credit. Under these conditions the Federal Reserve usually pursues a tight credit policy. These conditions and these types of yield curves existed in 1982, 1979, 1973, and 1968.

If the public assumes the expansion has come to an end and the economy is going into a downturn they can expect the yield curve to switch to Y_2. This happens because economic activity slows, demand for short-term credit declines, the Federal Reserve eases and credit becomes easier.

The spread trader would see this basic change taking place and sell the intermarket spread, selling 30-year maturities and buying futures contract in GNMAs, Treasury notes, or even Treasury bills.

To take advantage of this type of spread the correct leverage or dollar equivalency must be used.

Fluctuations in short-term supply are the second fundamental cause of changes in yield curves. For the active trader who wishes to be in the market more frequently than when fundamental economic changes are occurring, trading the intermarket on a relative supply basis may be profitable.

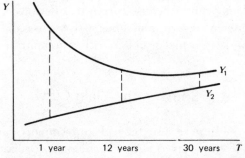

Figure 18.8 Yield curve showing late stages of expansionary economy.

Assuming no changes in basic economic conditions, intermarket spreads often react sharply to periods of heavy temporary supply in the cash market. When the supply of a specific type of cash security expands faster than other cash securities, underwriters of the cash security sell the futures to hedge their commitments and investors demand discounts for these securities. The prices of these securities then become depressed, in relative terms, until a distribution of the cash security takes place.

The following are the three most common supply induced intermarket spread opportunities:

1. Quarterly Treasury refundings occur every February, May, August, and November. During these refunding dates the Treasury almost always sells a large number of long-term Treasury bonds. This causes the long-term Treasury bond market to be temporarily more heavily supplied than the GNMA market, which has no sudden influx of supply. Therefore, it is often profitable to sell the GNMA/Treasury bond intermarket spread some weeks before the actual refunding period and unwind it a few weeks after the refunding.

2. Housing starts are a good indicator of the future supply of mortgages and eventually GNMAs. When housing starts fall or rise sharply the market frequently begins to discount the relative supply of GNMAs versus T-bonds, causing the spread to change. All other factors being constant, on low housing starts buy GNMA futures and sell Treasury bond futures.

3. Large temporary buildups in the corporate bond market's new financing calendar often puts pressure on the long Treasury bond market while having much smaller relative impact on the GNMA market. This occurs because corporate offerings usually tend to be of a long-term nature, and underwriters use the Treasury bond futures market to hedge underwriting commitments.

Shifts in the Yield Curve

Shifts in the yield curve also take place frequently and offer trading opportunities to the active market participant. Unlike the yield curve changes discussed earlier, the trader does not need to forecast fundamental changes in the yield curve shape, only shifts up or down in the curve. This can be illustrated by comparing Figure 18.9a with b. Figure 18.9a shows a change in the yield curve, and b shows a shift up in the yield curve.

To take advantage of price movements in Figure 18.9b, the trader is really taking advantage of dollar equivalency. As the yield curve shifts up and down equally, money can be made by having equal numbers of different futures contracts in spread position.

Intermarket Bull Spread. If the spreader feels the curve will not change its basic shape, but only shift lower in yield, he would want to buy the intermarket, or go long T-bond futures and short GNMA futures. As yields move proportionately lower, T-bond futures prices will rise faster than GNMA futures prices.

Intermarket Bear Spread. An equal shift upward in the yield curve causes prices to decline as yields rise. The correct strategy is to sell the spread, short T-bonds and purchase GNMAs. As yields go higher prices of GNMAs will drop less than T-bond prices because of the maturity difference.

The Combination Spread. To achieve maximum return on the bull and bear intermarket spread the spreader would not always sell the same month in T-bonds and GNMAs. As discussed earlier, in rising price markets nearby contracts usually outperform further out contracts. Therefore, when putting on a bull spread in the intermarket it often pays to go long a close T-bond contract and short a further out

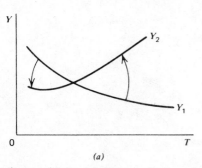
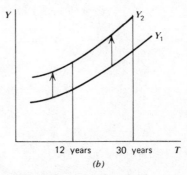

Figure 18.9 (a) Change in the yield curve; (b) shift up in the yield curve.

GNMA futures contract; for example, purchase June Treasury bonds and sell December GNMA futures. This would offer two profit possibilities:

1. The profit from the shift in the cash yield curve as shown in Figure 18.9*b*.
2. The profit from a shift in the futures price curve as shown in Figure 18.9.

When bear spreading the intermarket sell longer T-bond contracts and purchase nearby GNMA futures. However, be very careful with this combination: greater potential return also means greater risk.

CHAPTER NINETEEN
Accounting and Tax Treatment

It is fair to say that one of the most confused and confusing aspects of trading in financial futures relates to the application of accounting principles to hedge transactions and the subsequent tax treatment of the gains and losses. Much of the confusion arises because the concept of hedging interest rates is new to the regulatory authorities who have responsibility for overseeing many of the financial institutions in the United States. Further, the accounting profession contains very few experts on hedging with futures. Lastly, the regulatory authorities and the accounting profession have issued conflicting statements on proper accounting procedure.

This section will attempt to sort out some of the basic issues that must be addressed by market participants.

Most of the material in this and the next two chapters is taken directly from a publication entitled *Interest Rate Futures Contracts: Federal Income Tax Implications.* That publication was prepared by Arthur Andersen & Co. at the request of the IMM in Chicago. It is the best and most complete treatment in existence today on the subject of taxes and accounting for interest rate futures. It is reprinted here with the kind permission of both the IMM and Arthur Andersen & Co.

The reader is forewarned however, that the analysis is necessarily based on the then existing statutes, regulations, published rulings, and court cases regarding the tax implications of the activities discussed and should not be viewed as conclusive in all instances. In an area of taxation as new and volatile as interest rate futures it should be understood that complex rules are always subject to contrary interpretation. Thus, the views expressed here may ultimately differ from those expressed by other authorities. In any event a user of these instruments and contracts should not rely entirely upon the advice provided here but should obtain further explanation, updating, and advice from professional advisors on an individual case-by-case basis.

A BRIEF HISTORY

In late 1976 the Comptroller of the Currency's office, at the urging of the commodities exchanges on which financial futures were traded, issued Circular 79 which set forth the conditions under which national banks could participate in the GNMA and T-bill futures markets. Among the conditions set forth in Circular 79 were:

1. A requirement that national banks obtain prior approval from the Comptroller of the Currency's office to engage in GNMA and T-bill trading.
2. A requirement that futures contracts purchased or sold by such entities correspond to an appropriate cash transaction and be undertaken only to "substantially reduce the risk of loss resulting from interest rate fluctuations." In short, banks were not allowed to speculate; they could only hedge.
3. Some fairly extensive record-keeping requirements that would provide the Comptroller of the Currency the assurance that the second condition (above) was being honored.

The immediate result of Circular 79 was that most of the national banks who were at that time engaged in trading futures stopped trading until they had time to obtain approval to be in the market. In addition, there was a good deal of confusion over the interpretation of the record-keeping requirements needed to demonstrate that the futures contracts bought and sold reflected a corresponding and appropriate cash transaction. About a year later, during the late summer of 1977, the Comptroller issued a supplement to Circular 79. That supplement recognized the differences between the forward placement market and the futures market. Further, the approval requirement of #79 has been reduced to a simple notification filing.

The issues became clouded further as the Treasury Department, Federal Reserve, SEC, Department of Labor, IRS, Federal Home Loan Bank Board, National Credit Union Association, state bank regulators, and state insurance regulators entered the act. All of them took an active interest in the interest rate futures regulatory jungle because, like many bureaucratic organizations, they sensed an opportunity to expand the scope of their activities. They also were concerned about the potential for abuse or misuse of the futures markets by entities under their jurisdiction. Much of this concern arose because of their lack of understanding and their confusion about the differences between the forward trading market and the futures market. Some well-publicized cases involving small dealers who had sold forward contracts they were ultimately unable to fulfill also heightened the regulators' concern. Regulators had failed to note the distinction between the relatively unregulated forward market and the closely regulated futures trading system.

The forward contract is merely a cash market transaction in which two parties agree to the purchase and sale of a security at some time in the future under such terms as the two parties state. In contrast to the futures market, the terms of forward contracts are not standardized. The forward contract is usually not transferable, and it can be canceled only with the consent of the other party. Often such consent can be obtained only for further financial consideration or penalty.

A further important feature distinguishing between the futures and the forward contract is the payment and delivery process. In the forward market the purchaser or seller looks to the party with whom the commitment was made for delivery or payment. Thus, settlement or completion of the commitment is dependent directly upon the viability of the other party. In the futures market the buyer or seller looks to the clearinghouse for delivery or payment. The clearinghouse guarantees the delivery and demands receipt of the commodity at the time the contract matures. The day-to-day settlement and the margin money posted at the clearinghouse are additional safeguards to assure the financial integrity of the transaction.

In summary, Circular 79 and its supplement helped focus some of the issues, but they also left a number of unanswered questions.

CLASSIFICATION OF USERS FOR TAX PURPOSES

In general, users of financial instruments contracts fall into three broad categories for tax purposes:

1. Dealer—a seller who profits from a markup or commission on the goods sold.
2. Trader—one engaged in a trade or business but who profits from price fluctuation.
3. Speculator/Investor—one who profits solely from price fluctuation and income earned on property held.

   A transaction hedger is treated for tax purposes in one of these categories, depending on the motivation for the trade.

   A user can fall into different categories for different transactions. For example, a dealer may have investment transactions. The distinction among the categories is important since different users are subject to different tax rules: dealers generally are subject to ordinary tax treatment while traders and speculator/investors usually receive capital tax treatment. Unfortunately, the distinction among users is not always clear and the rules are at times imprecise. However, as the following discussion suggests, existing regulatory and judicial authority provides some guidance in determining the appropriate tax status.

Dealer

Dealer transactions are generally afforded ordinary income or loss treatment for tax purposes. Like a dealer in securities, a dealer in financial cash instruments is a merchant who sells to customers with a view to making profit from a markup in price and/or commission. In this, he is no different from other types of merchants who generally sell their products to customers with a markup to produce a profit. Anyone who maintains an inventory of cash instruments with the hope of making a profit by reselling to customers at a markup (principal transaction), and not intending to hold the contract for investment or speculation, is a dealer for tax purposes. A dealer can also act in an agency capacity when he earns commission income from buying and selling for customers. Transactions in financial futures contracts are performed in an agency capacity and generate commission income.

Numerous statutory and judicial authorities indicate when a party is a dealer. Treasury Regulation Section 1.471–5 describes a securities dealer in these words:

"... a dealer in securities is a merchant of securities, whether an individual, partnership or corporation, with an established place of business, regularly engaged in the purchase of securities and their resale to customers; that is, one who as a merchant buys securities and sells them to customers with a view to the gains and profits that may be derived therefrom. If such business is simply a branch of the activities carried on by such person, the securities inventoried as provided in this section may include only those held for purposes of resale and not for investment. Taxpayers who buy and sell or hold securities for investment or speculation, irrespective of whether such buying or selling constitutes the carrying on of a trade or business, and officers of corporations and members of partnerships who in their individual capacities buy and sell securities, are not dealers in securities within the meaning of this section."

The taxpayer bears the burden of establishing dealer status. Court cases have held that no single factor is controlling; the determination of dealer status is always a question of fact, and depends on the specific circumstances of each case. In general, the following characteristics will be weighed to determine if the taxpayer qualifies as a dealer:

1. Maintains an inventory of the physical commodity.
2. Maintains a customer list.
3. Profits by a markup in his inventory or earns a commission on a purchase or sale rather than making a profit from mere market changes.
4. Maintains at least one regular place of business.
5. Is licensed as a dealer.
6. Advertises to the public as a dealer.
7. Subscribes to various services commonly used by dealers.
8. Executes a large number of transactions.
9. Maintains salesmen and customer accounts.

When the courts speak of transactions with the "public," that "public" need not be the general public but can be a more specific public, such as financial institutions, other broker-dealers, etc. Early cases suggest that a commodities merchant cannot be a dealer unless he deals with the general public. More recent judicial decisions, however, have emasculated the conclusions of these older cases. The critical factor is the manner of dealing with the "public." None of the authorities suggest that all the previously listed factors must be present for the taxpayer to be a dealer. On the other hand, the fewer characteristics exhibited by the taxpayer, the more the taxpayer approaches trader or speculator/investor status, with consequent capital gain/loss tax treatment.

In general, a dealer in commodities or financial instruments reports gains and losses generated from his business as ordinary income, as any other merchant does on the sale of his wares. Consequently, dealer income generally does not qualify for favorable capital gains treatment. However, it is possible for dealers to maintain a separate investment account and derive capital gains tax treatment from those investment account transactions. Internal Revenue Code Section 1236 provides for these tax consequences to dealers in *securities.* There is no similar provision for dealers in commodities. Section 1236 can, however, be used for guidance.

Section 1236(a) provides that gains by dealers on the sale or exchange of securities not be considered capital in nature unless the security was clearly identified as a security held for investment within 30 days of its acquisition and the security was not held thereafter primarily for sale to customers in the ordinary course of the taxpayer's trade or business. Under Section 1236(b), a loss by a dealer on securities transactions is not an ordinary loss if the security at any time was clearly identified in the dealer's records as a security held for investment.

Certain government instruments, such as Treasury notes or bonds, may possibly be classified as securities for tax purposes and therefore fall within these statutory rules. However, many other government instruments, precious metals, currencies and agricultural commodities would not be considered "securities." Common law definitions of what constitutes a dealer, therefore, could be determinative. Case law suggests that if a commodities dealer adequately identifies, segregates and consistently treats certain commodities and commodity contracts as investments rather than inventory, such classification will be recognized for tax purposes. However, this classification should be made immediately upon purchase since the 30-day "look-back" provision only applies to securities. Due to the lack of clear statutory authority, the classification of certain commodity contracts as investments by a dealer should be approached with caution.

The situation can also arise where the dealer maintains a trading account in commodities that have not been identified to an investment account. Such commodities, not having been identified as investments by the dealer, are not accorded capital tax treatment. Since they are not included in the dealer's investment account, the question arises whether they should be treated as inventory for tax purposes. Dealers typically treat such goods as inventory and the normal year-end inventory valuation rules (cost, market or lower of cost or market) would thus be applicable. Theories may be advanced in support of this treatment. However, there is no clear statutory or case law authority.

Trader

A trader's transactions are generally afforded capital gain or loss treatment for income tax purposes. The U.S. Tax Court has defined a trader as a seller of securities who performs no merchandising function and whose status as to the source of supply of the securities is not significantly different from that of those to whom he sells. A trader performs no services that need be compensated for by a price markup on the securities he sells. His access to securities is no greater than that of anyone else. The trader intends to make a profit through a rise in value or an advantageous purchase and resale.

Numerous judicial decisions have held that a trader in securities or commodity futures does not hold them for sale to customers and, therefore, receives capital gain or loss treatment. Thus, trader gains are capital gains and qualify for beneficial tax treatment if long-term; trader losses are treated as capital losses subject to the capital loss limitations.

Tax advantages that are not available to a speculator/investor may flow to a trader. For example, the individual trader may be entitled to deduct against adjusted gross income certain business expenses, such as interest paid, that a speculator/investor may claim only as itemized deductions. However, the distinction between a trader and a speculator/investor is not well defined. It ultimately may be determined by the volume of activity and the ability of the trader to establish that his activities constitute the active conduct of a trade or business, as opposed to mere investment activities engaged in for profit.

Speculator/Investor

A speculator/investor's trading activities are generally afforded capital gain or loss treatment for income tax purposes. A speculator/investor trades for his own account and performs no services or merchandising functions compensated for by a price markup. Instead, he intends to profit solely from a market increase in the value of the assets purchased and from any income earned thereon (e.g., interest). His motive is purely speculative. Therefore, any user engaging in purely speculative transactions will be treated as a speculator/investor with respect to those transactions. The tax implications of maintaining this status are discussed in detail in the next chapter.

CHAPTER TWENTY

Tax Rules Pertaining to Financial Instruments Futures

Critical to an understanding of the tax rules applicable to futures trading is the concept that, for tax purposes, transactions in futures contracts are not viewed as dealings in the underlying commodity (or financial instrument) itself. Instead, they are viewed as transactions in the rights to the specific commodity. A commodity future is a mere executory contract and, therefore, the holder has no tax basis until the contract is executed or sold.

Whereas the underlying commodity may be tangible property, the future rights to the commodity are clearly intangible property. Transactions in intangibles generally give rise to capital gain or loss treatment unless the transaction, viewed as a whole, constitutes a hedge. Therefore, futures contracts will generally be viewed as capital assets unless the specifics of the transaction bring into play one of the doctrines requiring ordinary income treatment (for example, dealer or hedging activities).

TAX TREATMENT

In recent years some taxpayers engaged in commodity and commodity-related transactions not only for speculative purposes and to guard

267

against the risk of economic loss, but also to create tax benefits to shelter other income, which was technically permissible under the tax laws. Congress, reacting to perceived abuses, opted to change these laws and establish a new set of specific tax rules for these types of transactions.

The Economic Recovery Tax Act of 1981 (ERTA '81) identifies four basic types of commodities transactions and prescribes the tax treatment for each type. They are:

- Transactions in regulated futures contracts.
- Straddle transactions in other than regulated future contracts.
- Identified straddles.
- Hedging transactions.

Regulated Futures Contracts (RFCs)

RFCs are contracts for the delivery of actively traded personal property that are traded on or subject to the rules of a commodity exchange or board of trade designated as such by the Commodity Futures Trading Commission and which are subject to the mark-to-market method for determining margin deposit requirements. In addition, the IRS may designate other exchanges as having adequate rules so that these provisions will also apply to transactions on these exchanges. A taxpayer must "mark-to-market" (i.e., determine the fair market value of) all RFCs held at yearend and include the unrealized gains or losses in income for the year.

Contracts terminated during the year (through offsetting positions or by making or taking delivery) must also be marked to market by determining their fair market value immediately before termination. All RFCs must be marked to market whether or not balanced, offset or part of a straddle.

RFC gains and losses, whether realized or unrealized, are netted for the year. The net RFC gain or loss is, by statute, deemed to be a 40% short-term and 60% long-term capital gain or loss. This results in a net maximum effective tax rate for individuals of 32% for 1982 and thereafter.

A taxpayer (other than a corporation) may carry back a net RFC loss (retaining its current year's short- or long-term character) for three years to offset net commodities futures gain, but may not carry it back to a year before 1981.

These rules do not apply to qualified hedging transactions.

APPLICABILITY OF THE WASH SALE RULE

The wash sale provisions of the Internal Revenue Code provide that no deduction for a loss on the sale of stock or securities will be allowed if substantially identical property is acquired (directly or by option or contract to purchase) within 30 days prior to or 30 days subsequent to the initial sale or exchange. The tax benefit of the loss is not lost forever but merely deferred by becoming an adjustment to the basis of the property acquired. Some older case law to the contrary, the IRS has since ruled that commodity futures contracts are not stock or securities for this purpose and the wash sale rule does not apply to transactions solely in futures contracts. However, care should be taken that there is a business purpose, apart from tax considerations, for effecting such a transaction.

Certain cash financial instruments may be considered securities for this purpose. Therefore, when the cash instrument is sold at a loss and, within 30 days before or after such sale, a long futures position in such financial instrument is acquired, the wash sale rule could apply to disallow the realized loss.

For RFC transactions, the abuses contemplated by the wash sale rule are avoided through application of the "mark-to-market" concept. In addition, for solely non-RFC market or RFC/non-RFC market trades, the IRS is empowered to issue regulations that will produce the same result as the statutory wash sale rule through introduction of a "balanced and offsetting position" theory in addition to the existing "substantially identical" rule.

APPLICABILITY OF THE SHORT SALE RULE

A short sale is a contract for the sale and delivery in the future of property that may, or may not, currently be owned. The sale can be completed by a purchase in the marketplace of the underlying property or by delivery of property already owned but not delivered to the buyer at the time of the sale. The taxable event does not occur until the short sale is completed (covered or closed) by delivery.

The statutory short sale rule is relevant in determining the holding period for long-term capital treatment. The holding period of the property delivered to close the short sale determines whether a short- or long-term capital gain or loss results. These rules can be summarized as follows:

1. If on the date of a short sale of a futures contract, substantially identical property has not been held for the requisite long-term holding period or is acquired after the short sale but before the closing date, then *gain* on the closing of the short sale will be short-term regardless of the holding period of the property actually used to close the short sale. The holding period of the substantially identical property acquired begins on the date of closing the short sale.

2. If substantially identical property has been held for more than the requisite long-term holding period at the time of the short sale, any *loss* on closing the short sale will be a long-term loss even if the property actually used to close the short sale was not held for more than the requisite long-term holding period.

The short sale rule will apply only if *substantially identical* property was held or is acquired. In the case of commodity futures contracts traded subject to the rules of a commodity exchange or board of trade, the Internal Revenue Code provides that "a commodity future requiring delivery in one calendar month shall not be considered as property substantially identical to another commodity future requiring delivery in a different calendar month." The practical effect of this definition is that a futures contract would be substantially identical only to another contract for the same commodity requiring delivery in the same month.

The short sale rule applies to commodity futures contracts but not to cash commodities, other than those considered a security. Therefore, the purchase of a cash commodity and the sale of a commodity futures contract are not generally covered by this rule. Certain financial instruments may be considered securities for purposes of the short sale rule. Arguably, if a financial instrument future is sold short at a time when an underlying deliverable financial instrument has not been held for more than 12 months, the short sale rule could operate to cut off the holding period of the underlying instrument. Long-term capital gain treatment may not then be obtained unless the underlying financial instrument was sold more than 12 months after the close of the short sale of the future. There is no statutory or case law guidance in this area.

The IRS has authority to issue regulations expanding the scope of the statutory short sale rule to cover balanced and offsetting positions, even if not substantially identical. However, the statutory provisions of the short-sale rule specifically do not apply to qualified hedging transactions.

REVENUE RULING 77-185

Before ERTA '81, the timing and characterization of gain or loss generated from transactions in different commodity futures contracts were not affected by the short sale and wash sale statutory provisions. The IRS attempted to accomplish results similar to those statutory provisions through administrative means by the issuance of published revenue rulings. In 1977, the IRS issued a ruling concerning silver futures contracts. The taxpayer in this situation sought to convert a short-term capital gain to long-term capital gain and to defer the recognition of the gain for one year. This was accomplished by a series of silver futures spreads carried over the two-year period. This ruling held that because of the balanced positions (equal numbers, although of different months, of long and short futures contracts in the same underlying commodity) maintained by the taxpayer, no tax recognition would be given to the loss realized in the earlier year. Further, the ruling infers that balanced position trading has no economic substance. The net result of such trading, at least if a loss results, will not be recognized for tax purposes at any time. The IRS reiterated this position in a 1978 ruling, stating that it also applied to U.S. Treasury bill futures contracts.

On March 5, 1982, the U.S. Tax Court rendered its opinion in *Smith, et. al. v. Commissioner* (78 T.C. No. 26). This case litigated the actual facts that were the basis for the 1977 ruling. The court held in favor of the IRS, finding that the taxpayers lacked an economic (nontax) profit motive in entering into the transactions. *However,* the Tax Court opinion disavowed all of the other theories the IRS raised in the case.

HEDGE TRANSACTIONS

Economically, an interest rate hedge is a transaction that a lender, investor or borrower of funds uses to protect against the effects of interest rate changes by taking a position in the futures market opposite to a position taken in the cash market. For example, a corporation with borrowings tied to the prime rate could attempt to hedge its interest cost by short selling U.S. Treasury bill or certificate of deposit futures contracts. If short-term interest rates increase, then presumably the price of the futures contracts should fall and *vice versa*. The hedger anticipates that the gain or loss on the short futures position will offset the increased or decreased borrowing costs as interest rates fluctuate.

A hedge is designed to mitigate the effect of future changes in interest rates. In the above example, the corporation with annual interest costs may not be interested in speculating on whether interest rates will rise or fall and, therefore, may sell interest rate futures contracts currently to control the ultimate cost. The hedger is perfectly willing to let someone else—perhaps a speculator/investor—take the risk of fluctuating interest rates.

The nature of the commodity underlying the futures contract used in a hedge transaction is critical in determining the tax treatment. Four different situations commonly occur.

Often the underlying commodity is a product sold or inventoried by the taxpayer. Income/loss from the sale of a related commodity futures contract is treated as ordinary income. The reasoning behind this is simple: the merchant is merely using the hedging technique as a tool to help market his wares. He holds neither the underlying inventory nor the futures contract with any speculative intent, and therefore he should not be accorded capital treatment on his profits or losses.

The second situation in which the hedge transaction is commonly used is when a taxpayer uses a raw material or cash market financial instrument in his trade or business. For example, a taxpayer may be a government bond dealer and maintain long and short positions in various instruments and may also enter into forward delivery purchase and sale contracts. To seek to protect against loss on these transactions due to fluctuations in the market interest rate, the dealer will enter into futures contract positions.

In this situation, the futures contracts should be treated as noncapital property, and any income or loss generated from the futures transactions should be treated as ordinary income or loss. Again, the reasoning behind this conclusion appears sound, since the futures contracts as well as the underlying financial instrument are used by the taxpayer in the production of his income and there is clearly no speculative motive.

The third situation in which a hedge is often utilized is when, for whatever reason, the taxpayer is obligated to buy or sell a commodity. This could occur in a variety of contractual and noncontractual situations whenever a taxpayer faces a future delivery or acceptance date. In this situation, a futures contract will allow the taxpayer to lock in the purchase or sale price of the commodity he is required to either buy or sell and to avoid bearing the risk of price fluctuations. The tax consequences of such a transaction vary, depending upon the nature of the underlying contractual obligation that is being hedged.

The fourth situation that commonly occurs is when the speculator/investor or trader uses a hedge to protect an unrealized gain in his investment portfolio. For example, if a financial instrument is held in an investment portfolio, the taxpayer may sell a futures contract on the same instrument to lock in his unrealized profit. The gain generated in settlement of the futures contract by delivery of the cash instrument or by other means will generally be accorded capital tax treatment. This tax consequence follows since the commodity being hedged is a capital asset in the hands of the taxpayer. This is not, however, the type of transaction normally considered a "hedge" with resultant ordinary treatment.

HEDGES FOR TAX PURPOSES

The earliest pronouncements of the Internal Revenue Service, supported by numerous court decisions, established that, where futures contracts were entered into only to insure against fluctuations in the price of inventory to be sold or purchased at a later date, a tax hedge existed. Under this concept of hedging, the commodity future did not have to be in the same commodity utilized in the taxpayer's business, but there had to be a showing of both a relationship in the price of the two and of a balanced position between the quantity of the product being hedged and that represented by the futures contracts.

This limited concept of hedging was expanded by the Supreme Court in the Corn Products case. This case gave rise to the so-called "Corn Products Doctrine," which results in a finding of a hedge where the transactions constitute an integral part of the taxpayer's business. Therefore, the background of the transaction, needs of the business and motivation of the taxpayer become relevant considerations.

Court decisions subsequent to the Corn Products case have not consistently applied this doctrine. However, some general rules can be enumerated. A hedge for tax purposes will clearly exist when there is a *direct* relationship between the commodity futures transaction and the risk of exposure endemic to the taxpayer's everyday trade or business, and the price of the commodity moves in some discernible relationship with the price of the product of the business.

The following factors will tend to indicate that a hedge for tax purposes does *not* exist. Courts do not consistently apply these factors and, therefore, no one of them will necessarily be determinative:

1. The commodity is not used in the taxpayer's business.
2. The value of the futures position does not move in the same direction as the price of the commodity being protected.
3. The expected profit from the hedge exceeds the potential loss.
4. The quantity of hedging contracts exceeds the quantity of goods protected. However, quantity should not be a factor if the relative values of the two result in a balanced position.
5. Futures trading is done at a time when the taxpayer is not exposed to the risk of loss or continues after the risk ends.
6. Rapid activity in the futures market is not directly related to changes in the underlying business risk.
7. There is the presence of *any* speculative motive. In this regard, some courts have held that substituting one contract for another is proof of speculative intent.

ERTA '81 provided, for the first time, a statutory definition of hedging. To qualify for tax purposes, a hedging transaction must be identified as such and entered into by the taxpayer in the normal course of his trade or business primarily (1) to reduce either the risk of price change or currency fluctuations on ordinary assets held or to be held by the taxpayer or (2) to reduce the risk of interest rate changes or currency fluctuations on borrowings made (or to be made) or obligations incurred (or to be incurred) by the taxpayer. A special rule for banks requires the transactions only to be entered into in the normal course of the taxpayer's trade or business. However, the previously enumerated case law doctrine may still be considered to verify whether or not the definition has been met.

Once an asset has been identified for tax purposes as part of a qualifying hedging transaction, its disposition can never be treated as capital. Qualifying hedging transactions are exempted from the mark-to-market, straddle loss deferral, cash-and-carry capitalization, wash sale and short sale rules. However, if a taxpayer hedges in a tax sense, but fails to comply with the identification criteria, the transaction still generates ordinary income, but it would be subject to the mark-to-market rules.

STRADDLE TRANSACTIONS
IN OTHER THAN RFCs

A straddle is defined as the holding of offsetting positions—including a futures, forward or option contract—in any type of personal property (excluding corporate stock) that is actively traded. Personal property also includes actively traded stock options that are part of a straddle unless they are traded on a U.S. exchange and expire in less than one year.

An offsetting position is deemed to exist when there is a "substantial diminution" of risk of loss in holding one position by virtue of holding one or more other positions in personal property. The following five rebuttable presumptions are used for determining when offsetting positions exist:

- The positions are in the same personal property.

- The positions are in the same property even though in substantially altered form.

- The positions are in debt instruments of a similar maturity or other debt instruments prescribed in regulations to be issued by the IRS.

- The positions are sold or marketed as offsetting positions.
- The aggregate margin requirements are lower than the sum of the margin requirements of the two positions.

Offsetting positions that exist between holdings of defined related parties or between a taxpayer and flow-through entities (such as partnerships or trusts) also are subject to these rules.

Recognized losses from straddle positions in other than RFCs (non-RFC straddles) are deductible only to the extent they exceed unrealized gains from offsetting positions acquired before the recognition of the loss. Any loss that is not allowed by reason of this rule is carried forward to the succeeding year when it is again subject to this limitation. The unrealized gain is determined in the same fashion as under the mark-to-market rule for RFCs and must be reported in the investor's tax return for information purposes. Reporting is not required if there are no losses realized in any position (including RFCs) during the year.

A taxpayer may have a mixed straddle, i.e., a straddle consisting of an RFC in at least one position of the straddle, with the defined personal property in the other. In this situation, the taxpayer may irrevocably elect to have the entire straddle taxed under the non-RFC straddle rules discussed above. However, the RFC must be identified as part of the mixed straddle by the close of the day on which it was acquired. If no election is made, the components are treated under the applicable general rules for RFCs and non-RFCs.

Finally, as previously discussed, non-RFC straddle transactions will be subject to the concepts similar to the wash sale and short sale rules under regulations to be issued by the IRS. It is anticipated that this will be accomplished by treating components of balanced and offsetting positions as if they are "substantially identical."

Interest expense and carrying charges allocable to personal property that is part of a straddle must be capitalized. This regulates the so-called "cash-and-carry" transactions. In this type of transaction, for example, a taxpayer would purchase a physical commodity to be held as a capital asset and then sell the same commodity for delivery one year later. The taxpayer borrows to make the purchase and currently deducts the interest, storage charges and insurance. The price differential between the current price and the future price is usually a function of these carrying costs. Under prior law, the taxpayer had an ordinary deduction in one year and could realize gain in the next year by closing out the short sale position.

Identified Straddles

The tax rules applicable to RFCs and non-RFC straddles do not apply to identified straddles. If a taxpayer has an identified straddle, no loss may be recognized before the day on which all the positions of the straddle are disposed of. An identified straddle must be recorded as such by the taxpayer by the close of the day on which it was acquired. To qualify, all of the original positions must be acquired on the same day and all positions disposed of on the same day. None of the positions of the straddle may be a part of a larger straddle.

SPECIFIC TAX RULES—TREASURY BILLS

As with all types of futures contracts, the cash (or spot) market in U.S. Treasury bills is an integral part of the workings of the futures market. Short-term government obligations—those issued at a discount with a maturity of one year or less (generally, U.S. Treasury bills)—are treated as capital assets. Upon disposition at a gain, the part of the gain representing the ratable (straight-line amortization) share of "acquisition discount" (difference between purchase price and face value) is ordinary interest income, and the excess gain over that amount, if any, is short-term capital gain. Losses are wholly capital in nature. Thus, if a $1 million, 90-day U.S. Treasury bill is purchased at issuance for $962,500 and sold 30 days later for $980,000, the seller would recognize $12,500 of ordinary income and $5,000 of short-term capital gain.

Futures Contracts

U.S. Treasury bill futures contracts represent contractual rights to the underlying instruments. The IRS has ruled that these contractual rights are distinct from the underlying bills and represent a separate asset that is capital in nature.

TRADING STRATEGIES AND TAX IMPLICATIONS

The tax implications of trading strategies may vary for nonspeculative and speculative, or investment, transactions.

Nonspeculative Transactions

Generally, dealers and commercial or institutional users report gains or losses generated by futures transactions as ordinary gain or loss when they are engaged in normal dealer or hedging transactions. But these users may also engage in transactions that are investment/speculative in nature. Such transactions should be subject to the tax considerations discussed in the following section.

It is important to note that few special rules relate to traders, since most statutory authority refers only to dealers or investors. If a user is classified as a trader for tax purposes, his gains and losses will generally be treated in the same manner as those of a speculator-/investor.

Speculative/Investment Transactions

The tax consequences of the various profit-motivated strategies discussed below arise if the taxpayer's transactions are investment or speculative in nature. These strategies are available to any user who anticipates investment activity, including users generally classified as dealers or commercial users, but who, for a specific transaction or group of transactions, invest with a speculative motive.

This discussion deals only with the probable income tax consequences of the trading strategies and is not an evaluation of potential profitability or economic soundness. Accordingly, each user should consult his own investment advisor before engaging in any of these transactions. A transaction should have economic substance resulting from genuine risk and appropriate profit potential. Without this, it is likely that the IRS would challenge the transaction and disallow any losses generated and any expenses incurred in the transaction.

The following trading strategies are frequently used and could result in income tax benefits.

Futures Strategies

A spread position in financial instruments creates an opportunity for economic profit. In a typical spread position, the user will be long and short in substantially the same number of futures contracts but in different delivery months. Therefore, one position may result in the realization of a loss while the other may result in gain. If the price relationships of the long and short futures positions to the cash market and to each other remain constant, there would be no net gain or loss on the two positions. However, if the price relationships of the positions do not remain constant over the life of the contracts and the spread relationships change, and the user has correctly assessed the economics of the marketplace, the gain realized on the profitable position will be greater than the loss realized on the unprofitable position. The user has, in effect, protected his assessment of the way the market will move by covering part of his downside risk—which, of course, will also limit the amount of his upside profit potential. At the same time, the potential return on invested capital over a very short period of time can be very attractive.

Before ERTA '81, the closing of trading positions could have been timed to provide beneficial tax consequences. As stated above, if the user is long and short in approximately the same number of contracts in different months, the movement of market prices will generate a loss in one of the positions and a gain in the other. It is possible to close the loss position in one taxable year and the gain position in another. Once one position is closed, the user can limit further economic exposure to his open profit or loss position by reestablishing the spread relationships with additional futures contracts. Under prior law, if the gain was realized in the long position and that position was held for more than six months, long-term capital gains treatment would have been achieved. If, however, the profit was realized on the short position, a short-term capital gain would have been realized no matter how long the short position was held.

Taxpayers who wanted to achieve certain tax benefits could have used this basic trading strategy framework and other opportunities existing in the old tax law, such as:

- The disparity in tax treatment between cash U.S. Treasury bills and U.S. Treasury bill futures.

- The disparity in long-term capital holding periods between futures contracts and cash commodities.

- The tax benefits of financing the acquisition of cash commodities.

- Issues regarding the recognition of gain or loss upon making or taking delivery.

By properly timing the closing of such spread positions, a taxpayer was able to achieve the following tax benefits.

- Defer taxable capital gain income from one tax period to the next by recognizing the loss position in one tax period and the gain position in the next.
- Convert a short-term capital gain into a long-term capital gain by realizing the gain position in the contracts purchased (long) after a six-month-plus holding period.
- "Freshen" the carryover period of a net operating loss about to expire by realizing the gain position in the first tax period and the loss in the next. The latter loss may, however, have been a capital rather than an ordinary loss.

Because of the new rules for the taxation of commodity transactions, these benefits are generally no longer available. The mark-to-market concept eliminates the ability to defer recognition of gain on open futures positions. U.S. Treasury bills are now capital assets.

Financing costs incurred as part of a spread are required to be capitalized for tax purposes. The new law did, however, give the investor the benefit of making 60% of the capital gain from short futures positions long term rather than wholly short term.

Repurchase (Repo) and Reverse Repurchase (Reverse Repo) Agreements

Acquisition or disposition of a cash financial instrument, typically a T-bill, is often accomplished through financing arrangements known as repos and reverse repos. An investor seeking to acquire a long position in a financial instrument would finance the acquisition by selling a financial instrument to a creditor and simultaneously agreeing to buy back the financial instrument (repo) at a later date at the same price plus interest. A reverse repo is the opposite situation: the investor would become the creditor by advancing funds for another party's acquisition of a financial instrument in return for an interest payment.

These repo and reverse repo agreements are normally treated as mere financing transactions for tax purposes and a sale or exchange is normally deemed *not* to have occurred. If these agreements are construed to be mere financing arrangements, interest income will be generated on the reverse repo and interest expense on the repo agreement. This interest expense will be subject to the investment interest limitation rules. The previously discussed rules governing the capitalization of interest and carrying charges allocable to personal property that is part of a straddle may also impact the treatment of this interest expense.

It is arguable that these financing arrangements represent sales or exchanges of the underlying financial instrument, with consequent gain or loss treatment. It is also arguable that the repo and reverse repo agreements represent separate contract rights and when such rights are settled gain or loss results that is capital and not ordinary. Under either of these two positions, any interest income or expense would not be considered as resulting from transactions in federal or municipal investments. Although these two positions are arguable, it has historically been the ruling posture of the IRS and of the courts that such transactions are financing arrangements.

PROBLEMS OF ALIEN USERS

Futures trading by aliens (non-U.S. citizens) raises a number of special problems. If an alien is a U.S. resident for tax purposes, he will be taxed as a U.S. citizen subject to the rules discussed previously. If, however, the alien is a nonresident, the tax treatment is more difficult to predict.

The Internal Revenue Code provides that nonresident aliens (individuals, corporations, partnerships, etc.) will be taxed at a flat rate of 30% on income (such as interest and dividends) not connected with a trade or business in the United States. However, if an alien individual has activity in the United States that constitutes carrying on a trade or business, as could be the case if he is a "trader," the nonresident alien will be taxed on the activities the same as a U.S. citizen. Such problems may also arise if the alien user is a member of a broker/dealer or investment partnership carrying on a U.S. trade or business.

In general, a nonresident alien is taxed on capital gains generated from assets in the United States only if he is present in the United States for 183 days or more during the tax year in which he generates these gains.

The 30% rate is often reduced by tax treaties that exist with numerous foreign nations. Therefore, due to the wide variance in treaty requirements and to the numerous exceptions and complexities in the Internal Revenue Code and Regulations, an alien user should consult his own tax advisor to determine his specific tax results.

In addition, it may be necessary for the payor of certain types of income or distributions to aliens to withhold federal income tax from the amount they remit to aliens. Since the payor is generally liable for the proper amount of withholding, it is advisable to determine the exact amount to be withheld prior to making payment to an alien.

CHAPTER TWENTY-ONE

Financial Accounting Treatment of Financial Instruments Futures and How It Differs from Tax Rules

Tax accounting treatment for various financial futures instruments depends on a number of factors and differs, sometimes significantly, from financial accounting treatment.

TAX ACCOUNTING TREATMENT

Dealer

A dealer in commodities, like any other merchant, is required to maintain and value inventory in accordance with the guidelines set forth by the Internal Revenue Code, Treasury Regulations and published Revenue Rulings. While the following discussion is based on these published IRS positions, alternative positions may be sustainable.

In valuing an ending inventory of cash commodities, a dealer may utilize the normal inventory valuation methods of cost or lower-of-cost-or-market. However, since an industry practice will be recognized for tax purposes if the resulting answer clearly reflects taxable income, a dealer can also value his ending inventory at market value even when this exceeds cost.

A more difficult problem is to value the dealer's futures contracts positions that constitute hedges (as previously discussed) against his underlying inventory. As a general rule, the value of long or short positions in futures contracts cannot be included as part of the ending inventory, since title to the goods has not yet passed. The potential gain or loss not yet realized on futures transactions cannot be included in the cost of the ending inventory, since they represent unclosed transactions.

An exception concerns the treatment of unrealized gain or loss of open futures contracts. A taxpayer is allowed to include in taxable income the unrealized gain or loss on open futures trades that represent hedges, when this is a common industry practice that results in the clearest method of identifying operating cost or profit for the period and is consistently applied. However, this income or loss is treated as a period cost and not as part of ending inventory.

Trader or Speculator/Investor

The trader or speculator/investor is not required or entitled to maintain an inventory for tax purposes. Unrealized gain or loss is not recognized on open regulated futures contracts positions in conformity with the new mark-to-market rule. This rule also applies to the dealer who maintains investment or speculative futures contracts, but only to those contracts.

FINANCIAL ACCOUNTING TREATMENT

Until recently, there has been little guidance in accounting literature on the proper financial accounting for transactions in financial instrument futures contracts. In September 1978, Arthur Andersen & Co. released a report entitled *Interest Rate Futures Contracts—Account-*

ing and Control Techniques for Banks. While this report was directed primarily toward banks, the principles and techniques recommended in that booklet apply to other financial institutions as well. The Arthur Andersen & Co. report was followed in early 1979 by a revision to the American Institute of Certified Public Accountants' (AICPA) *Audit and Accounting Guide for Savings and Loan Associations.* The accounting treatment recommended by the AICPA guide is consistent with the accounting treatment suggested in the Arthur Andersen & Co. report.

As the financial instrument futures market continues to grow and new users enter the market, the related accounting issues have been addressed by other committees of the American Institute of Certified Public Accountants and the Financial Accounting Standards Board though not all issues have been resolved. Readers are cautioned to review with their auditors and accountants the current rules and practices. They may vary from those described below.

Overall Basis of Accounting

Transactions in futures contracts involve a deposit of funds or the pledging of an acceptable security, representing a margin deposit. Funds deposited as margin should simply be recorded as a "deposit." Consistent with the accounting treatment for other future or forward type activities (e.g., foreign exchange forward contracts), the gross amount of securities deliverable on futures contracts should not be reported in the balance sheet.

Generally, unrealized gains and losses resulting from the change in quoted market values of futures contracts, as well as realized gains and losses, should be recognized currently in the income statement. This basis of accounting (commonly referred to as "mark-to-market") should be followed when (a) the futures contracts are entered into for speculative purposes, (b) the futures contracts represent hedges of existing asset positions, contemplated asset purchases or short positions, all of which are carried at or will be carried at market value, or (c) the criteria for "hedge accounting" for specific hedging transactions, discussed later, are not met. However, the lower-of-cost-or-market valuation method for valuing futures contracts may be followed rather than the "mark-to-market" method when an entity's accounting policy for similar types of short-term or trading assets or short positions is lower-of-cost-or-market.

A minor problem relating to the amount of gain or loss recognized on a closed futures market transaction involves the determination of the price for the particular position closed. Most brokerage firms confirm and calculate their P&Ss on transactions on a first-in, first-out basis (FIFO). Most hedgers will probably find a combination LIFO-FIFO to be the most convenient method for them to calculate their cash market transactions as well.

In accounting for commissions and other transaction costs, one should expense them as they are incurred. They should be calculated as part of the gain or loss on futures market activities. Generally, commissions for transactions on financial futures are very small relative to the typical hedging gains and losses.

HEDGE ACCOUNTING FOR SPECIFIC HEDGES

Exceptions to the general mark-to-market approach are acceptable when specific hedges are entered into. In general, a specific hedge exists when the futures contract can be identified with a specific asset, liability, or commitment at the date of execution of the futures contract, and the financial instrument futures contract utilized has a high positive correlation (prices tend to move in the same direction with similar magnitude) with the specific asset or commitment identified.

ACCOUNTING AND THE INCOME STATEMENT

In those situations where futures contracts are entered into as specific hedges, there should be an attempt to achieve symmetry in the accounting treatments used for the related asset or liability being hedged. This means that the hedger must specifically identify when a futures contract is entered into as a hedge versus one entered into for speculative purposes. Generally, the following guidelines are the criteria that must be met:

1. At the time the futures contract is entered into, its purpose should be specifically identified. That is, the dollar amount and the asset

or liability being hedged should be described in specific terms and a written record maintained. There should be a reasonable and consistent relationship between the net dollar amount at risk in the cash market and the net dollar amount of futures contracts outstanding.

2. The futures contracts utilized should have a high positive price correlation with the asset or liability being hedged. That is, the prices of the two should move in the same direction with similar magnitude. The two positions, being one long and one short, will therefore create gains in one market that will tend to offset the losses in the other. The relationships should also be such that the price risk (variance of return) of the combined positions is significantly less than that of the individual commitments alone. Totally hedged positions should never increase the price risk.

3. In the case of a hedge against an anticipated cash transaction, the transaction must reasonably be expected to be fulfilled in the ordinary course of business. Thus, a "commitment" is described in terms of a "high probability of occurrence" for the transaction.

It's important to note that the first two conditions recognize that it is frequently impossible to achieve exact one-to-one matching of a futures contract with the cash position. These conditions deal with the "dollar equivalency" concept of hedging and the concept of cross hedging. (A cross hedge, to refresh your memory, refers to a situation where the instruments in the two markets are not exactly identical: for example, a 90-day CD and a 90-day T-bill cross hedge can often be used to reduce price risks substantially).

In general, the accounting described in the following text is based on a concept of "symmetry" between the accounting for the futures contract and for the asset or liability being hedged. Examples of specific hedge situations follow.

LONG HEDGE FOR INVESTMENT SECURITIES

This refers to the purchase of futures contracts to hedge against falling interest rates on expected investment purchases to be *carried at cost*. Unrealized gains and losses on futures contracts may be deferred when (a) upon execution, the futures contract is specifically identified with a commitment to purchase that can reasonably be expected to be fulfilled in the ordinary course of business, and (b) the futures contract has a high positive correlation (see definition above) with the specific commitment identified. Deferred gains or losses from a long hedge should be included in the measurement of the dollar basis of the investment for which the hedge was intended and should be amortized over the investment's holding period as an adjustment to the interest income (yield) on the investment. If the expected asset purchase does not occur at the time the futures contract is closed out, or the commitment can no longer be expected to be fulfilled, the gain or loss on the futures contract should be recognized currently in income.

SHORT HEDGE FOR INVESTMENT SECURITIES

The sale of futures contracts to hedge against a market decline in existing investment positions *carried at cost* is called a short hedge. Unrealized gains and losses on the futures contracts may be deferred when (a) upon execution, the futures contract is specifically identified with an existing asset position, and (b) the futures contract has a high positive correlation with the specific asset identified. Deferred gains or losses from short hedges should be recognized in income when the contract is closed out or the hedge position is sold (at which time the "offsetting" loss or gain on the hedged asset is recognized), whichever occurs first. If the identified hedge position is sold without the futures position being closed out, the short futures contract should thereafter be accounted for under the mark-to-market method.

HEDGING FUTURE DEBT ISSUE

This method involves the sale of futures contracts to hedge against rising interest rates on the issuance of debt. The unrealized gain or loss on the futures contract may be deferred when (a) upon execution, the futures contract is specifically identified with a commitment or intention to issue debt that can reasonably be expected to be fulfilled in the ordinary course of business, and (b) the futures contract has a high positive correlation with the specific commitment identified. Deferred gains or losses from hedges meeting these criteria should be included in the measurement of the dollar basis of the issued debt for which the hedge was intended and should be amortized over the term of the debt as an adjustment to the interest cost of the debt.

The application of these criteria for deferral should generally lead to deferral only for specific forthcoming major debt issues. Futures contracts entered into as hedges of normal, day-to-day funding activities should be construed as general hedges and the mark-to-market method of accounting should be followed as discussed below.

When gains or losses are deferred on futures contracts in contemplation of a specific debt issuance and the debt offering is delayed beyond the maturity of the futures contract, recognition of the deferred gain or loss on income may need to be considered.

HEDGING ASSETS AND LIABILITIES CARRIED AT LOWER OF COST OR MARKET

This involves the purchase or sale of futures contracts to hedge against (a) market declines in an existing asset position *carried at the lower of cost or market,* or (b) short positions carried at the higher of cost or market. Unrealized gains and losses on the futures contracts may be deferred when (a) upon execution, the futures contract is specifically identified with a commitment or an existing asset or liability position, and (b) the futures contract has a high positive correlation with the specific asset, liability or commitment identified. In determining the lower of cost or market value at the end of each reporting period, deferred unrealized gains and losses on open futures contract hedges of existing assets, liabilities or commitments should be included in the amount of any writedown (i.e., it is appropriate to value the asset, liability or the commitment and the related futures contract as a unit).

Deferred gains or losses from these hedges should be recognized in income when the contract is closed or the hedged commitment or position is honored or sold, whichever occurs first. When an asset being hedged continues to be held after the maturity of the futures contract, it is also acceptable to include the deferred gain or loss on the matured futures contracts in the cost basis of the asset being hedged, which asset (at its adjusted cost) is subject to the lower-of-cost-or-market test at each subsequent accounting or reporting date.

In order to utilize hedge accounting as set forth above, it is assumed that the intended hedge transaction will occur in the cash market and conform to the timing originally contemplated. Instances of asymmetry between the futures contract and the cash market transaction (for example, the related asset is not purchased under a "long hedge") would be an indication that the transactions represent a "trading" activity. In this situation, the mark-to-market method of accounting for futures contracts should be followed.

GENERAL HEDGES

Financial instrument futures contracts may be used as an integral part of an entity's overall asset-liability management, which involves a number of considerations, including an attempt to match, on an overall basis, interest-sensitive assets with interest-sensitive liabilities or conversely to match fixed-rate assets with fixed-rate liabilities. An entity may find it advantageous to use futures contracts as a hedge against the interest rate exposure associated with potential mismatches in interest-sensitive assets and liabilities. For example, in the case of a commercial enterprise, futures contracts may be used as part of the normal day-to-day treasury function—cash management, short-term borrowings and investing in money market instruments. An enterprise may desire to hedge on an overall basis against interest rate fluctuations.

Because of the general nature of asset-liability management and the overall treasury function, the specific identification of futures contracts with individual transactions or positions is not practical, as contrasted with the specific hedging situations described above. Thus, when interest rate futures are used in overall asset-liability management or the treasury function, the futures contracts should be characterized as a general hedge rather than a specific hedge. General hedges should be accounted for under the mark-to-market method.

PART FIVE

Foreign Exchange Futures; Stock Index Futures; Options

CHAPTER TWENTY-TWO
The Foreign Currency Futures Market*

As noted in one of the opening chapters in this book, the first financial futures contracts developed were those for foreign currencies on the IMM. At the same time plans were laid for trading interest rates; and with very good reason, as there is a very close relationship between fluctuations in interest rates and fluctuations in the value of currencies. Thus, if you have a good understanding of interest rate futures, you will find ready application of the same concepts to foreign exchange futures. This chapter introduces the reader to some of the basics of trading in foreign exchange futures contracts offered on the IMM and the NYFE.

THE PRICE OF MONEY

The price of a currency is determined in the same way as the price for any other commodity—by the forces of supply and demand. If the people in the U.S. begin to demand more English-made products, the demand for pounds sterling goes up; as the demand for pounds sterling increases, Americans will have to pay higher prices in order to induce holders of sterling to sell. Conversely, if the British devel-

*Most of the material in this and the next chapter has previously appeared in "Getting Started in Commodity Futures Trading" by Mark Powers, published by Investor Publications 219 Parkade, Ceder Falls, Iowa.

oped an overwhelming taste for U.S. goods, they would have to sell more and more pounds sterling for the U.S. dollars to pay for the products they bought. This increase in the supply of sterling being offered for sale would cause the price to drop relative to dollars assuming stable demand for sterling.

RECENT HISTORY OF INTERNATIONAL
MONETARY SYSTEM

Cash or spot foreign exchange transactions are usually done through a foreign exchange trader located at a bank, and it has been so down through history. Foreign exchange dealings became relatively common with the development in 11th-century Europe of the Champaigne fairs where merchants bought and sold goods in their counterparts' currencies. Bankers attended the fairs to act as money changers, the modern-day equivalent of the foreign exchange trader. But even before then foreign exchange was traded—and not always on "free market" principles. The Persians in the sixth century attempted to thwart the basic forces of supply and demand by fixing an immutable gold/silver ratio. They failed.

A more recent attempt to fix prices was made in 1944 when a group of economic and finance experts from 47 Western nations met in a New Hampshire resort town called Bretton Woods. Their purpose in meeting was to develop a post-war plan for reconstruction of world trade and national economies. Out of that meeting came a plan for an international monetary system. It had four key points:

1. The establishment of a super-national agency called the International Monetary Fund whose purpose was to oversee the international monetary system and to assure its smooth functioning.
2. The establishment of par values or fixed exchange rates for currencies and an agreement among the countries that they would manipulate the supply and demand for their currencies in such a way as to maintain that rate. They did this by entering the market to buy their currency when its price fell 1% (in practice, ¾ of 1%) below the declared par and by selling their currency when the price rose 1% (in practice, ¾ of 1%) above the par value.
3. Agreement that the U.S. dollar would be the kingpin of the system

and other countries would accept and hold it for payment of international debts.

4. Agreement that the U.S. dollar was as good as gold and that any time a foreign government wanted to exchange its dollars for gold it could do so at the U.S. Treasury at the rate of $35 an ounce.

This system was in effect from 1944 to 1971, and world trade did indeed expand during those years. It expanded largely because the U.S. was willing to run its international business affairs at a loss. The U.S. continually imported more than it exported. It paid for its imports by running the printing presses and printing dollars. As long as others were willing to accept paper dollars, the U.S. received fine wines, nice automobiles, radios, televisions, and so on, in return.

Ultimately, however, there were a lot more dollars held by foreigners than the U.S. held gold. Foreigners had from time to time turned in their dollars for gold and gradually the U.S. gold supply had disappeared until clearly the dollar was overvalued in terms of gold.

On August 15, 1971, President Nixon declared that the U.S. would no longer abide by the Bretton Woods agreement of 1944. Accordingly, he said that the dollar was no longer convertible into gold; that is, that foreigners would no longer be able to turn their dollars in to the U.S. Treasury and obtain gold. Further, he said that the exchange rate for the dollar would no longer be fixed, instead it would be allowed to "float"; that is, it would be determined by free market forces.

The dollar floated just like a rock—straight down. It was devalued. Since that time, except for a brief period in 1972 when fixed rates were again reinstated, the value of the dollar has been determined more or less by free market forces with some governmental intervention.

The result of the devaluation of the dollar was that the relative purchasing power of the U.S. dollar was changed dramatically. Imports into the U.S. suddenly cost more (it took more dollars to buy the same amount of deutsche marks), and exports from the U.S. were lower priced (fewer deutsche marks would equal the dollar price). For example, between 1972 and 1973 the value of a bushel of wheat at Rotterdam increased by 122% in U.S. dollars, 117% in yen, 185% in deutsche marks, and 129% in sterling. Thus, it took about one-third fewer deutsche marks to buy the same bushel of U.S. wheat in 1973 than it took in 1972. Put another way, the same number of deutsche marks would buy one-third more U.S. wheat in 1973 than in 1972.

THE SPOT MARKET

The buying and selling of spot currencies (for immediate delivery or use) is accomplished through banks. Banks all over the world have accounts with each other in order to serve their customers, many of whom are multinational companies that deal in many different currencies. Every day these banks make deposits and withdrawals for their customers. These deposits or withdrawals result in transfers of funds from one country to another and, therefore, the conversion of one currency into another. Hence, banks worldwide are constantly buying and selling currencies and providing a ready spot market.

This buying and selling is done by telephone and teletype. If a dealer in Frankfurt, Germany, wants to buy dollars and sell deutsche marks, he will probably call several New York banks and ask each for its rate. When he finds a bank with a rate that suits him, they agree to the trade and exchange specially coded telegrams confirming the transaction. The bank in Frankfurt will then credit the account of the New York bank with the proper amount of deutsche marks.

If a businessman desires to convert dollars into deutsche marks to pay a bill, he can simply notify his banker and, after receiving proper information, the banker will see that the proper German bank account is credited. For example, if a businessman imports German bicycles and needs deutsche marks to pay for them, he simply notifies his banker who, in turn, contacts other bankers in Germany or elsewhere in the world to buy the deutsche marks for the importer and have them deposited in the German bank account of the bicycle manufacturer. The U.S. bank will then deduct the dollar cost of the deutsche marks from the U.S. account of the importer. The importer will never see the deutsche marks; the bankers will simply debit and credit the appropriate accounts.

EVALUATING FOREIGN EXCHANGE RATES

What makes foreign exchange rates fluctuate from day to day? Why does the U.S. dollar buy less in Germany in 1976 than it did in 1966? Would an increase in the general level of interest rates in England be bullish or bearish? For whom?

These questions and many more are of great importance to anyone dealing in foreign exchange. And, as you may have guessed, the answers are not easily determined. Fundamental analysis of the money markets is more difficult than fundamental analysis in other commodities. There is a definite lack of good data, and the markets are highly sensitive to political elements. Yet, over the long run, fundamental economic factors will be the dominant considerations in determining the value of currency.

It is not possible to cover all of the factors in detail here; however, we will touch on some of the highlights of each of them.

INTERNATIONAL TRADE AND CAPITAL BALANCES

The single most important long-run indicator of impending exchange rate changes today is the country's trade balance, also called the balance of goods and services. It reflects the relative value of merchandise imports and exports.

If exports are greater than imports, there is a trade surplus. This is a sign of currency strength. A shift in the trade balance to a deficit (imports greater than exports), on the other hand, is an indication of currency weakness.

A second important indicator is the official monetary reserves of a country, including gold, special drawing rights (SDRs) on account at the International Monetary Fund and foreign currency holdings. These reserves indicate the ability of the country to meet its international obligations—for example, its ability to repay loans, to finance imports and to intervene in the foreign exchange market to support (manipulate the value of) its currency. Official reserves should be building up when there is a trade surplus. Official reserves may, but not necessarily will, be falling when there is a trade deficit.

A third important international economic indicator is the capital balances of a country, including the direct foreign investment and the short-term speculative funds that flow to or from a country. Capital movements are very sensitive to short-term interest rates.

With the almost instantaneous speed of the world's financial system, funds may be transferred nearly anywhere in the world. These funds move in response to changes in the interest rates. Capital flows can have tremendous impact on short-term exchange rates. If three-month interest rates in Canada increase to 1% over U.S. rates, people will send their money to Canada. As they do so, they must sell U.S. dollars and buy Canadian dollars. An increase in a country's capital account reflects an increase in demand for assets denominated in that currency, such as time deposits or T-bills. This increased demand indicates fundamental strength in the currency. Conversely, a deficit in capital accounts indicates a weakening in the demand and an expectation that the price of the currency will fall.

DOMESTIC ECONOMIC FACTORS

The underlying influences of the balance of trade, official reserves, and capital flows are the domestic interrelationships among income, prices, and interest rates.

Among the factors to consider in evaluating the domestic health of a country are:

1. The rate of real (after adjustment for inflation) growth in gross national product. Steady growth is an overall indicator of good economic health for an economy.
2. The rate of growth in money supply and interest rate levels. These are important indicators of future economic conditions. The short-term interest rate differential is important in short-term capital flows. Such flows directly affect the demand for a currency.
3. The rate of inflation relative to the index of industrial capacity utilization. Differing rates of inflation in different countries are another very important factor affecting the price of a particular currency. The end result of inflation is an erosion of purchasing power, which ultimately means a weakening of the currency if other countries are not experiencing the same amount of inflation. High inflation with high utilization suggests that inflation is likely to stay high because "the machine" is already working at capacity, yet the people are demanding more goods. This would suggest a weak currency.

The general price level of a country affects the exports of that country. The U.S. is a good example. It has nearly priced itself out of the international market in some goods while Japan, on the other hand, making many similar goods, is able to sell them at lower prices. This reduces the exports of the United States and increases the imports to the U.S. from Japan, creating an outflow of dollars and what economists call an "unfavorable" balance of trade.

Each country should be studied individually and then one country compared against another. Since the futures contracts reflect other currencies relative to the U.S. dollar, other countries' expected and actual economic conditions should be compared to the U.S. If the conditions seem more favorable to other countries relative to the U.S., buy the futures. If the conditions favor the U.S., sell the contract.

POLITICAL AND GOVERNMENTAL INFLUENCES

Political and governmental activities affect exchange rates by helping or hindering the international trade of a country and thus its balance of trade. Study carefully such things as import taxes, negative interest rates (a favorite of the Swiss, this means you pay them interest on savings accounts instead of the other way around), interest equalization taxes, embargoes, and so on.

The internal political stability of a country also bears on the issue. Even in the more well-established industrial nations of the world, the unsettling influence of political elections is reflected in the foreign exchange market. Major economic policy changes, as well as revaluations or devaluations, are often made with an eye to the next election. A change in the political party in power very often brings a change in economic policy. Even the anticipation of a new party being elected to power can affect exchange rates, which leads us to the significance of what people think is going to happen.

EXPECTATIONS

Timing is all important. Expectations about changes in price level and the timing of such changes can have a great impact on the market. Many observers, for example, expected the British pound to be devalued toward the end of 1972, just before Britain entered the Common Market. Early in the year numerous money interests began to act in anticipation of the event and the British government was forced to float the pound in early summer, probably months before they would have liked to. Similarly, many people expected the Mexican peso to be devalued during the latter part of 1976 because a change of political administration would make it a convenient time to do so. The market anticipated the event, although not the exact magnitude, long in advance. The peso was devalued by about 40% on September 1, 1976.

CHAPTER TWENTY-THREE

Expected Interest Rates and Foreign Exchange Spreads

Money moves almost instantaneously from one part of the world to another, continuously seeking the highest return available. Thus, if interest rates change in one country relative to another, capital flows from the country of lower interest rates to the country with the higher interest rates.

In the years ahead, investment managers and advisers will need to be skillful at moving funds around the world to various security markets and financial centers. That sort of operation will require an understanding of foreign exchange markets and the concept of interest arbitrage.

Interest arbitrage refers to the purchase and sale of spot and futures in money in order to take advantage of differences in interest rates between the two countries. This illustrates a very important principle in using the foreign exchange markets: There's a very strong relationship between exchange rate movements and interest rate changes in different countries. The basic rule of thumb is: at equilibrium, the currency of the higher (lower) interest rate country should be selling at a forward rate discount (premium) in terms of the lower (higher) interest rate country's currency.

Thus, if interest rates in Canada tend to be 3% below U.S. interest rates, one would expect a forward U.S./Canadian exchange rate to reflect a 3% discount for U.S. dollars. Market forces will assure this result (assuming certain other factors to be discussed below) because if the exchange rates don't reflect interest rate differentials (plus transactions costs) exactly, arbitrageurs can make money by borrowing funds in the high interest rate country, transferring them to the low interest rate country, and hedging them with a transaction in the forward exchange market. If enough money moves from one country to another in this manner, the spot prices of the two currencies will change relative to the forward price until the spread between spot and futures exactly reflects the differences in interest rates between the two countries. At that point, the arbitrageur's profit opportunities in transferring funds from one country to another will have disappeared and the exchange rate between the two countries will be at what is called "interest rate parity."

The explanation for this relationship is most easily understood through an example. Suppose 90-day interest rates were 11% in Canada and only 9% in the United States. Investors would send money to Canada in order to obtain the 2% greater yield. As they did so they would need to sell U.S. dollars and buy Canadian Dollars. Assuming the supply of Canadian dollars remains constant, the increase in demand for them would cause their price to rise slightly.

Now most investors who would move their dollars to Canada in order to gain the 2% greater interest rates will not leave their exchange risk uncovered, since only a small change in the exchange rate will cause the 2% advantage in interest rates to disappear. To hedge they will, at the same time they buy the spot, sell the forwards contract until it precisely mirrors the 2% difference in interest rates between the U.S. and Canada.

Some important assumptions have been made in order to show how interest rate arbitrage is conducted. It works only under certain conditions:

1. Free flows of funds between the two countries concerned must be possible. In recent years, more and more countries have been instituting certain barriers and controls on the movement of capital into or out of their country. Obviously, if the controls are effective, great disparities between interest rate differentials and exchange rates may exist for long periods of time and interest arbitrage will not be possible nor will exchange rates reflect interest rate differentials.

2. Expectations of a devaluation, revaluation, or imposition of capital controls on the currencies must be such that they do not outweigh the interest rate differential factor. Sometimes, people hold such strong expectations of changes in the exchange rate due to factors other than interest differentials that interest rate parity considerations are simply overwhelmed.

Hedged interest arbitrage transactions, like those described above, are virtually risk free. The only major risk you take in those transactions is that a country will introduce strong capital controls that could prevent the fulfillment of the futures contract or the repatriation of the funds.

The theory of interest rate parity suggests a strategy for trading spreads based on expected changes in interest rate differentials. Spreads between futures contract months for a currency reflect expectations about interest rate differentials at a future point in time. Therefore, if interest rates today on three-month paper in Germany are at 4% and in the U.S. are at 10%, the differential is 6% under interest rate parity and one should expect the forward discount on U.S. dollars to be about 6% (i.e., if the spot rate of exchange is 50¢ per deutsche mark, then the 90-day forward rate should be about 50.75). If tomorrow 90-day interest rates in Germany rise to 5% with no change in U.S. interest rates, then the 90-day forward exchange rate will change to about 50.625¢ for each deutsche mark. The difference between the December deutsche mark futures and the March deutsche mark futures reflects *expectations* about what this three-month interest rate differential between the U.S. and Germany will be in December.

The correct guidelines to follow in implementing the spread strategy are:

1. If the forward prices are at a premium and you expect interest rate differentials to decline, then you should buy the nearby futures, and sell the distant futures.
2. If the forwards are at a discount and you expect the interest rate differentials to increase, then buy the nearby futures, and sell the distant futures.
3. If the forwards are at a premium and you expect interest rate differentials to increase, then buy the distant futures, and sell the nearby futures.
4. If the forwards are at a discount and you expect interest rate

differentials to decrease, then buy the distant futures, and sell the nearby futures.

How would this strategy have worked in practice?

Consider the following. On February 16, 1979, the interest rate differential between the United States and Germany was 6.5%. The forward discount for the U.S. dollar reflected in the June/September futures was 6.2% annualized.

On May 18, 1979—about three months later—the interest rate differential between Germany and the United States was 5.5% annualized. The forward discount for the U.S. dollar reflected in the June/September spread was 4.3% annualized.

Had you followed the above-suggested trading strategy and correctly anticipated a narrowing of the interest rate differentials, you would have gained 27 points on the spread and at $12.50 per point the profit would have been $337.50. The margin requirement for such a spread was at $500 on February 16, 1979.

In summary, paying attention to the interest rate differentials between countries is important to successful foreign exchange trading. During recent years these differentials have been the single most important influence in affecting short-run exchange rate trends.

HEDGING IN FOREIGN CURRENCY

In earlier chapters we discussed the concept of hedging and demonstrated its application to interest rate sensitive assets and liabilities. These same concepts apply to foreign currency hedging.

The following examples illustrate some potential hedging situations available to different sectors of the economy.

The Buy Hedge

Assume a Chicago tractor maker has a Canadian plant that is doing very well and has a certain amount of cash on hand in the form of Canadian dollars. It has no need for those funds until Canadian taxes are due in six months. Assume also that the same Chicago tractor maker has an engine plant in Milwaukee that has need of a short-term loan to meet operating expenses. The best move for the tractor maker may be to transfer those funds from the Canadian plant to the Milwaukee plant for six months. In the interim, he would sell the spot Canadian Dollars for U.S. dollars and buy Canadian Dollars for future delivery, thus establishing a buy hedge. The summary of the transaction would look like this:

Cash market	Basis	Futures market
March 1 Sell 500,000 Canadian dollars for $0.84600 = $423,000	100	Buy 5 September Canadian dollar futures, 100,000 CD each at $0.84500 = $422,500
September 1 Buy 500,000 Canadian dollars at $0.84900 = $424,500	10	Sell 5 Canadian dollars futures contracts, 100,000 CD each at $0.84890 = $424,450
Loss = 300 points ($1500)	90	Gain = 390 points ($1950)

In this example the hedger had a $1500 loss in the cash market that was more than offset by a $1950 gain in the futures market. His basis declined from 100 points to 10 points for a net decline of 90 points. Each point is worth $1.00 or $90 for each contract for a total of $450.

The Sell Hedge

Suppose a Chicago bank has excess funds to invest in the short term, and the highest short-term interest rate currently being paid is in Canada. Let's say 91-day Canadian T-bills are yielding 10%, and U.S. T-bills are yielding only 9%. The Chicago banker will buy Canadian dollars in the spot market, transfer them to his Canadian banking correspondent with instructions to purchase 91-day Candian T-bills. At the same time he will sell Canadian dollars in the futures market for delivery three months hence. The amount of the Canadian dollars he sells in the futures market will include the original number plus enough to cover the interest that will accrue.

The advantage of this hedge is that the banker will have fixed his selling price for the Canadian dollars 91 days from now, so he can be assured that the interest in T-bills will not be lost in the conversion back to dollars if the price of Canadian dollars goes down during the period.

TO HEDGE OR NOT TO HEDGE

In any hedging decision the manager must answer the same type of questions we covered earlier on interest rate hedging.

1. What is the net risk exposure?
2. What is the probability of a loss as a result of this risk exposure?
3. Which of the alternative methods available for managing this risk will provide the optimum coverage?

WHAT IS THE NET RISK EXPOSURE?

Net risk exposure refers to the amount of money that would be lost if the exchange rate for a currency changes. It is an objective measure of the impact a devaluation or revaluation will have on the value of a firm's assets and liabilities. If a currency is devalued, any liability (such as loans) a foreign firm owes in that currency can be paid back with cheaper money. Conversely, if it has been revalued, the currency needed to pay back that loan will cost more.

There are a variety of ways by which the net risk exposure can be calculated. Current assets minus current liabilities is one very simple but probably incomplete way. Most firms today use a more sophisticated procedure that takes account of such things as receivables booked, liabilities incurred, and the method by which the balance sheet values are converted from one currency to another. This is a very complex topic on which whole books can be and have been written. Suffice it to say, before you venture into this area, get your accountant's advice. A thorough understanding of accounting rules and tax laws is of key importance here.

WHAT IS THE PROBABILITY OF LOSS ON NET EXPOSURE?

This is a subjective evaluation that should be based on an analysis of the economic and political information available about a country. The same sort of information was covered in the preceding chapters. In making this determination, the manager should first estimate the probability that there will be a change in the exchange rate. Is there a 50% chance that the peso will be devalued this month? this year? An 80% chance? And, second, estimate the probability of the size of change in the exchange rate. Will it be 10%, 20%, 30%, or even 40%?

HEDGE YES, HEDGE NO

Armed with these three pieces of information—net exposure, probability of loss and probability of size of loss—you can then calculate the expected value of a loss to the firm by multiplying the probability of a loss times the probability of the size of the loss. (See Steps a, b, c, and d in Table 23.1.) Once you have that answer, you are then in a position to compare the expected value of the loss (this is calculated by multiplying the probability of a loss by the probable size of the loss) to your cost of hedging.

To estimate the cost, a manager needs to ask: which of the alternative methods available, singly or in concert with another alternative, will provide the most complete coverage of the risk at the least cost? Generally, he has a number of alternatives available to him. He can self-protect through various management techniques; he can hedge by going to his bank and obtaining a forward contract; or he can hedge on a futures contract on the IMM or the NYFE. In making this determination, he must examine the cost of each alternative.

To the foreign exchange trader, the cost of the hedge includes not just the commission cost, the interest on the margin for the futures contract, and the bid-ask spread but also any premium or discount that is reflected between the futures contract and the expected spot price. For example, if your expected spot price is 3% under the six-month forward price, the "cost of the buy hedge" includes that 3% premium. If the cost of the hedge is less than the expected loss, hedge. If that cost is greater, do not hedge.

Table 23.1   A Hedging Model

a. Net exposure	$10,000,000
b. Probability of loss	50%
c. Probable size of loss	10%
d. Mathematical expectation of loss (b × c)	5%
e. Cost of hedge	3%
f. Decision—compare d to e. If d is greater than e, hedge. If d is less than e, do not hedge.	

A caveat—one should not enter into a hedging transaction without considering the tax implications and the effects on cash flows. Any business firm that is engaged in foreign exchange transactions would do well to integrate its hedging transactions and its accounting decisions in order to assure it gets the maximum *net* benefit of its risk management efforts.

DELIVERY POINTS FOR THE FUTURES CONTRACTS

Delivery of a currency contract can be made to any bank selected by the buyer located in the country that issued that currency. The seller of the futures contract instructs its bank to contact and follow the instructions of the buyer's clearing member at the exchange regarding the bank and the name of the account to which the delivery is to be made. Choice of the delivery point, specific bank, and account is the responsibility of the buyer.

TO SUM UP

In summary, the world monetary system is in a continual state of transition. As a result, the risk of doing business internationally is increasing right along with the increased demands for international trade. As more and more businesses and banks seek means of protecting themselves from currency losses due to exchange fluctuations, the role of the foreign currency futures will undoubtedly grow in importance.

The currency futures markets can be used by a wide variety of commercial interests. The following are just a few categories in which futures hedging could be helpful:

1. Companies building plants abroad.
2. Companies financing subsidiaries.
3. Manufacturers importing raw materials and exporting finished products.
4. Exporters taking payment in foreign currency.
5. Companies dealing in goods bought and sold into foreign countries.
6. Companies abroad financing operations in Euro-currencies.
7. Stock purchases or sales in foreign countries.
8. Purchases or sales of foreign securities.

The possibilities are virtually limitless. Everyone who deals in or with foreign countries has a need for a hedging mechanism to avoid major losses due to exchange rate fluctuations.

Additionally, through the open, competitive futures market, the general public has an opportunity to make known its hopes, fears, and beliefs about the value of a currency. And with daily reports from a futures exchange of trading volume and price fluctuations, there is a public weathervane providing daily signals of the true value of a currency—giving the public a clearer insight into the effect that political actions, monetary policies, balance of trade, and other factors have on the economics of world commerce. All of this, of course, provides for differences of opinion and trading opportunities.

CHAPTER TWENTY-FOUR
Stock Index Futures

The old Wall Street saying that you can't buy the market averages isn't true any more. Now if you have an opinion on the market as opposed to an individual stock, you can buy or sell the whole market —if you buy and the market goes up, the index will go up and you will make money. Stock index futures eliminate the need to make an individual decision on each stock. In other words, the index futures now allow you to get in on the price action of broad groups of stocks by buying or selling the futures contracts, or the options, on those indices.

Trading in stock index futures, specifically the Value Line Averages, began in February, 1982. For several years prior to that time, the Kansas City Board of Trade had been working actively on the concept of trading futures on stock indices, but due to regulatory problems, had been unable to make it a reality.

The last major regulatory hurdle was crossed in mid-1981 when the Commodity Futures Trading Commission finally granted approval for the concept of cash settlement of futures contracts. Cash settlement means exactly what it suggests; that is, at delivery time, the buyer and the seller exchange cash equal to the difference between the actual price of the product on that day and the price at which they had originally made their contract. Thus, in the case of the stock indices, there is no need for the seller to scurry around at delivery time collecting, in the correct proportion, the various shares of the various companies that make up the index.

Since Kansas City inaugurated the trading, other exchanges have also listed stock index futures. The Chicago Mercantile Exchange offers futures on the S&P 500, and the New York Futures Exchange lists futures on the New York Stock Exchange Composite Index. The quick success of stock index futures has prompted the development of a variety of new indices (both cash and futures) on other stock groupings, including some highly specialized selections in utility indices, financial indices, consumer staples indices, and oil and gas indices, et al.

Not all of the indices are derived the same way. The Value Line index futures (VLA), which was the first futures traded, is an index reflecting all of the stocks included in the Value Line Average of 1700 stocks. In the VLA, each company is weighted equally. Thus, the VLA represents one share of each of the 1700 companies.

The S&P 500 Stock Index, a widely recognized representation of the stock market as a whole, is based on the equity prices of 500 different companies—400 industrials, 40 utilities, 20 transportation companies, and 40 financial institutions. The market value of the 500 firms is equal to approximately 80% of the value of all stocks listed on the New York Stock Exchange.

The S&P 500 is a weighted index of the prices of the 500 firms. Each stock in the index is weighted so that changes in the stock's price will influence the index in proportion to the stock's respective market value. To determine the weight for the stock of any particular firm, the number of its shares outstanding is multiplied by its market price per share; thus a stock's market value determines the relative importance of the particular stock in the index. For example, General Motors accounts for approximately 1.35% of the S&P 500, while Rexnord accounts for .01%.

The New York Stock Exchange Composite Index (NYSE) is an index reflecting the value of the shares of all companies listed for trading on the New York Stock Exchange. Similar to the S&P, the company shares are not weighted equally, but rather are included in the index according to the formula reflecting the stock's respective market value. The formula takes account of the number of shares outstanding and the market price.

So, both the S&P and NYSE attempt to measure the total value of the stocks included in their indices, while the VLA attempts to measure average value. The NYSE measures every common stock on the NYSE. The S&P and VLA measure a designed market sample.

The contracts also differ in size (see Table 24.1 for further differences in contract specifications). The VLA was valued on opening day at about $65,000—the S&P at about $70,000, and the NYSE at about $35,000. Recently the contract sizes have been reduced. The size differences are also reflected in the margin requirements; since the NYSE contract is approximately one-half the size of the S&P, margin requirements are likewise about half.

COMPUTING A STOCK INDEX

The best way to demonstrate the computation of an index is to actually show the computation. To illustrate, consider the S&P 500. That index is calculated using the base years 1941 to 1943 equal to 10. The price of each stock is multiplied by the number of shares outstanding for that company. In the case of the S&P 500, the value for each of the 500 shares is totalled giving a total dollar value. To create the index, the total dollar value is then compared to the base value and the index is set according to the base index of 10. As a simple example, suppose the index was composed of only 5 issues:

	Outstanding Shares	Price	Value
Company A	100	30	3,000
Company B	500	10	5,000
Company C	200	50	10,000
Company D	400	4	1,600
Company E	300	20	6,000

Current Market Value = 25,600

If the 1941–43 market value was $2,500, then 25,600 is to 2,500 what X is to 10.

$$\text{Current Market Value} \; \frac{25,600}{2,500} = \frac{X}{10}$$

1941–43 Market Value $256,000 = \$2,500X$

$$X = 102.40$$

Table 24.1   Stock Indices—Futures[1] and Options[2]

Exchange	Contract traded	Contract value
Chicago Mercantile	S&P 500 futures	$500 x index
	S&P 100 futures	$200 x index
	S&P 500 options (futures)	1 S&P 500 futures
Chicago Board Options	S&P 100 options (actuals)	$100 x index
American Stock (Amex)	Major Market options (actuals)	$100 x index
New York Futures	NYSE composite futures	$500 x index
	NYSE composite options	1 NYSE future
Kansas City Board of Trade	Value Line future	$500 x index
	Mini-V. L. futures	$100 x index

[1]Stock index futures: Obligation to buy or sell an index at a stated price before a stated date.

[2]Stock index options: Right to buy or sell an index at a stated price by a stated date. Calls give the options buyer the right to buy an index. Puts give the options buyer the right to sell an index.

CORRELATIONS BETWEEN INDICES

To some extent the indices are substitutes for each other; that is, they measure the same thing. The correlation coefficients shown below in Table 24.2 demonstrate that the S&P and the NYSE are almost perfectly correlated (a perfect correlation equals 1.000); hence, they measure nearly the same thing and will be almost equally useful in hedging a portfolio. The Value Line, however, and the DJIA are not so highly correlated with the other two; hence, they would be less widely applicable as hedging devices.

Table 24.2   Correlation Among Four Major Indices 2/1/71 to 4/1/82

	S&P	VLA	NYSE	DJIA
S&P	1.000	—	—	—
VLA	.882	1.000	—	—
NYSE	.989	.928	1.000	—
DJIA	.729	.507	.644	1.00

VOLATILITY OF INDICES

Like other futures contracts, index futures offer a way to play price movements with a lot of leverage. Leverage allows one to get more bang for your buck. Substantial movements in the value of your account will occur with small investments in the index. All three of the exchanges have structured their contracts so that a 1.00 move in the relevant index represents a gain or loss of $500. The stock market, as represented by the various indices, is highly variable when measured over long periods of time; for example, a study done by the Index and Options Market (IOM), which is a subsidiary of the Chicago Mercantile Exchange, shows that the average daily change in the S&P 500 was 2.58 between February 2, 1981, and March 12, 1982. In terms of *futures* contract value, that is equal to $1290 per day (258 × 50). Further, during that time period, on at least one day, it changed by 526 points or $2630 (see graphs for charts showing the relative movement in the various indices).

Although the futures prices move in the same direction as the underlying indices do, the futures tend to be more volatile than the underlying indices. Prices frequently drop below, and fall faster than, the relevant index when investors are bearish. Further, they tend to push above it, and rise faster, when investors are bullish. This volatility tends to get accentuated in some of the more thinly traded months and the more thinly traded futures. As with most elements of volatility, these swings offer opportunity for making money and losing money.

In general, stock index futures have not been trading long enough to provide sufficient data for economists and market researchers to do effective research. However, Gregory Kipnis and Steve Tsang of ACLI/DLJ did study the activity in the various indices during the last half of 1982. Here is what they found.

1. All daily futures price changes were more strongly correlated with each other than they were with their respective market index and all of the futures price changes were about equally correlated with the popular Dow Jones industrial average.
2. The Value Line futures have the greatest volatility relative to their underlying index—S&P futures, the least.
3. The least volatile, measured in absolute terms, is the Value Line index. That result could be expected because the geometric averag-

ing technique used to calculate the index tends to dampen the effect of large changes.

4. Daily futures price moves frequently were inconsistent with the movement of the underlying index, and there was some evidence that the indexes tend to lead the stock market. That information, obviously, could be helpful to stock traders in timing their purchases and sales. However, one wants to keep in mind that futures prices are more volatile than the stock market, which means that one could also be vulnerable to many false moves which cannot be distinguished easily from real turns in the market.

In the long run, the stock index futures will trade like all other futures. The prices for them will stay in close relationship to the current cash price, plus carrying costs. Generally speaking, when prices of futures stray away from their theoretical values, arbitragers push them back into line by buying when the price seems low and selling when the price seems high relative to its cash market value.

TRADING THE STOCK INDICES

There are a number of reasons why investors or money managers may be interested in participating in stock index futures. For example, one might have an overall opinion on the market direction and would buy or sell the market outright—thereby taking a position on market direction.

One might want to sell the stock index futures to protect an existing investment, or in anticipation of a sale of all or part of a portfolio.

Traders may take both a long and short position in the market, but in different delivery months. That technique of spreading one month against another works in stock indices just like it works in other commodities. One can buy the near-term futures and sell the distant futures or vice versa, hoping to gain as the price differences between the two months change. One should be aware that such spreading techniques are not always low risk—particularly in stock indices where there is not yet a good understanding of how to price these differences. One may also be interested in integrating the stock indices into the overall management of the stock market portfolio. For example, one could take 10% of his capital and place it in stock index futures, putting the remainder in money market funds at a high yield. If, in late 1982, one had $75,000 in money market funds and felt that the stock market was going up but did not have the time or resources to make the difficult decisions on individual stocks, one could have bought two NYSE contracts which would have been worth approximately $75,000. Approximately 20% of the capital would be necessary to margin those futures positions. The remainder of the money, $69,000, would stay invested in the money market fund at a higher rate of return than the dividend yield on the portfolio. This strategy would allow you to participate in the stock market while still maintaining a high yield on your funds.

HEDGING ILLUSTRATED

As noted earlier in this book, a major use of futures markets is for hedging. In this instance, you may want to use the market to hedge your current market holdings or a portfolio of individual stocks. You may hold the stock investments and sell the stock index. If the market goes lower and the value of your individual investments declines with it, you will have a gain on the futures which can offset the loss on the value of the individual shares.

Suppose you owned a 10-stock diversified portfolio with a current market value of $35,000. Suppose, also, it generally reflected the value movements in the NYSE Index. If the stock market generally declines as reflected in the NYSE Index by 10%, your market loss would be about $3,500. You could protect against this loss by selling 1 NYSE Index Futures. Suppose at the time of the sale, it had an approximate value of $33,000. If you buy it back after the market has fallen, and if the index has in turn fallen by 10%, you will have made $3,300 on your hedge. That hedge will reduce your net market loss from $3,500 to $200.

While this may not work as an exact hedge, ways can be found to efficiently tailor (see the next section) a futures position to a particular portfolio to give you the most efficient hedge possible. Generally, one would not be well advised to use the futures market to hedge a portfolio, unless it could be statistically demonstrated that the stocks which make up the portfolio do move in concert with the index used. If that can't be demonstrated in advance, the hedger might find himself in the unfortunate position of losing on both the stocks and the futures. If the portfolio is composed of small, little-known firms which are not included in the underlying index, or if included are a very small proportion of the index, then it is unlikely that one will find efficient hedges. If, on the other hand, you have a portfolio that is composed of a small, but diversified group of stocks that include such big names as IBM, you may indeed find the futures a reasonable hedge.

THE PORTFOLIO MANAGER AND HEDGING

A portfolio manager is one who takes responsibility for managing money invested in a group of assets usually including a range of securities. His objective is usually capital appreciation and income. In making investments, the manager must consider the risk or safety of the investment, while attempting to achieve a reasonable return. Usually the higher the risk, the higher the potential for return.

When a portfolio manager considers hedging, his objective with the hedge is akin to doing a balancing act with a scale. On one side of the scales, he has a group of investments with a particular risk associated with them. He attempts to construct a futures position on the other side of the scale which will maintain a dollar balance with changes in the value of the portfolio. The success of his hedge will depend upon his success in constructing the proper futures position so that a dollar lost on one side of the scale will be offset by a dollar gain on the other side. He can construct that by selecting those futures contracts which are most closely correlated (as determined by statistical analysis) with the individual or groups of stocks in his portfolio.

Once he has identified the appropriate futures to use, he then must determine the number of futures contracts necessary to balance the scales. Normally, that calculation is accomplished through a statistical technique called regression analysis. Regression analysis is used to measure past price relationships for individual issues, or groups of related issues, relative to the underlying index chosen for the hedge. That volatility relationship will be expressed as a "beta" and is a statistical measurement reflecting the average relationship. Although this "beta" is based on past history, it is probably, in the long run, the best measure of future price relationships.

To determine the correct number of futures contracts to sell in order to balance the scale, the hedger should calculate a weighted beta for his portfolio. If the overall portfolio beta is 1 as measured against any of the indices, it indicates that virtually all of the risk contained in the portfolio is accounted for, or eliminated, if an equal dollar amount of futures contracts are sold. If the portfolio beta is different than 1, the number of contracts sold must be adjusted accordingly.

For example, if a portfolio manager found an average weighted beta coefficient of 1.20 for his portfolio, he would determine the appropriate number of contracts to sell by dividing the value of the portfolio by the value of the futures contract and multiplying by 1.20. To illustrate, assume the manager's portfolio value is $20,000,000, and the manager intends on using the NYSE Composite Index Futures, which we will assume is valued at $35,000:

$$\$20,000,000 \div \$35,000 \times 1.2 = 685.7 \text{ contracts}$$

The manager would round that number up and would sell 686 contracts as the appropriate number of contracts for his short hedge.

Now, if past relationships hold, and the market changes by 10%, the value of the portfolio should change by $2,000,000 and the dollar value of the change reflected in the index futures should be $2,000,000 as well.

It will be unusual if the hedge works out as perfectly as just illustrated. Even with all of the statistical techniques mentioned above, it is likely that there will be some variation in the total amount of gain or loss on the futures side compared to the total amount of the gain or loss in the portfolio. This variation will be due in part to the fact that the futures market may move more, or less, than individual stocks in the portfolio. Further, the timing of the two moves may not coincide exactly. One may move today and the other may move tomorrow or next week. This is referred to as basis risk. It must be noted that betas and other statistical calculations are based upon historical data, and the future seldom reflects past history exactly.

Before leaving this example, it would be reasonable to ask why a manager of a large portfolio would take a short futures position rather than simply sell the stock. One of the reasons may be liquidity. A highly liquid futures contract can absorb a hedge without affecting the futures market price significantly, while sales in the stock market of the same magnitude could pull the price of those individual stocks down to a much greater extent. Further, many portfolio managers do not find liquidation a feasible alternative because they are restricted to stocks of a particular kind. The cash generated from the sale of those stocks could not be immediately reinvested in other alternative areas. The futures market gives a manager the opportunity and the flexibility to make potential adjustments in his portfolio without going through complete liquidations.

THE LONG HEDGE

Stock index futures can also be applied by the portfolio manager as a means of pricing future acquisitions of stock for his portfolio. Most managers receive periodic inflows of capital, resulting from contributions to pension funds, dividends received, etc. If in the portfolio manager's estimation the market is cheaper now than it will be at the expected time of the inflow, then he may wish to use the index futures to price the cost of his purchases now. Later, when he actually receives the funds and makes the purchase of the securities, he will offset his futures. In doing so, he protects himself from a rise in the market before he receives his funds for investment. Of course, should the market fall during that time period, he will have losses on his futures which will offset the opportunity gains he had from purchasing stock at a lower level. As with all properly constructed hedges, he gives up the opportunity to make windfall profits in order to protect himself against substantial losses.

OPTIONS ON STOCK INDICES

Not only are there futures on stock indices, but there are also options on stock index futures and options on the underlying stock indices. The options on both of these have the same underlying characteristics as options on other instruments. The trading techniques, strategies, language, and examples discussed in Chapter 25 apply to options on stock indices and options on stock index futures.

CHAPTER TWENTY-FIVE

Commodity Options

Commodity options trading has been conducted in this country on an intermittent basis since the early 1860s. History shows that whenever prices have entered a period of great volatility, shrewd operators emerge who sell people options on commodities or on futures. An option is a unilateral contract that provides the buyer the right, but not the obligation, to complete a transaction with the seller at a predetermined price, usually within a specified period of time.

Sometimes, in the past, the seller of these options has been a legitimate operator. In many instances, though, the commodity options arena was a favorite playground for scam operators.

In 1936, it was charged that options played a role in a particularly blatant—and successful—attempt to manipulate the grain markets on the CBT. Congress held hearings on the matter and subsequently passed the Commodity Exchange Act, which barred all trading in options on commodities under the regulation of the Commodity Exchange Authority.

In 1974, and again in 1982, during hearings to revise the Commodity Exchange Act, Congress once again addressed the question of allowing options to be traded on regulated exchanges. After a good deal of testimony extolling the economic virtues of commodity options, Congress decided to leave the decision up to the discretion of the Commodity Futures Trading Commission.

That Commission, after a good deal of study and debate, has decided to allow commodity options on futures to be traded on organized exchanges in the U.S. for an initial three-year test period. This pilot program is to provide a means by which the commercial usefulness of options and their impact on the underlying futures and cash prices can be studied. No matter which form (futures or physicals) the options trading takes, the basic principles outlined in this chapter are applicable.

In general, the trading of options is a complex topic. Whole books have been written on the subject. All that can be done here is to introduce you to the topic and language to make you aware of some of the rich variety of ways in which options can be a part of your investment strategy.

THE LANGUAGE

Under current regulations options may be written on actual commodities or on futures contracts. Trading strategies and concepts are basically the same, however.

Options trading has its own terminology, which is considerably different from that of futures trading. For example, a "call option" is an obligation of the grantor (seller) to provide a long futures position to the grantee (buyer) at a predetermined price on or before the exercise date of the option contract, if and when the buyer chooses to exercise his right. Thus, a call option is a right to buy. It establishes a buying price for the buyer of the call.

A "put" option is an obligation of the grantor (seller) to provide a short futures position to the grantee (buyer) at a predetermined price on or before the exercise date of the option contract, if and when the grantee chooses to exercise his right. Thus, a put option is a right to sell. It establishes a selling price for the buyer of the put.

A "double" option allows the purchaser the right to acquire either (not both) a long or short futures position at a specified price on or before a specified date if and when he chooses to exercise his right.

The "striking price" is the predetermined price at which the futures position is transferred from the seller to the buyer if the option is exercised.

The term "exercise" refers to the buyer's decision to require the seller to fulfill the terms of the contract. If a call option is exercised, the option seller must provide to the buyer a long underlying futures position at the striking price specified. When a put option on a futures contract is exercised, the seller of the option must provide a short futures position at the striking price specified.

The "premium" is the amount of money paid by the buyer of an option to the seller for the right to exercise the option at the striking price. The seller receives the premium regardless of whether or not the option is actually exercised. That is a one-time payment to the seller. Irrespective of what happens to price, there are no further payments by the buyer unless he exercises.

The "exercise date" or "expiration date" is the last day on which the buyer of an option must decide whether to exercise or to abandon his right to exercise the option.

An option is said to be "at-the-money" if its strike price is equal—or approximately equal—to the current market price of the underlying futures contract.

A call is said to be "in-the-money" if its strike price is below the current price of the underlying futures contract (i.e., if the option has intrinsic value). A put is "in-the-money" if its strike price is above the current price of the underlying futures contract (i.e., if the option has intrinsic value).

An "out-of-the-money" option is a put or call option which currently has no intrinsic value—that is, a call whose strike price is above the current futures price or a put whose strike price is below the current futures price.

The "intrinsic value" of an option is that part of its premium which represents the difference between its exercise price and the current price of the underlying figures contract. See the explanation of "in-the-money."

An option "margin" is the sum of money which must be deposited —and maintained—in order to provide protection to both parties to a trade. The Exchange establishes minimum margin amounts. Brokerage firms often require margin deposits that exceed Exchange minimums. In turn, they post and maintain customer margin with the Clearing Corporation. Buyers of options do not have to post margin since their risk is limited to the option premium.

"Margin calls" are additional funds which a person with a futures position or the writer of an option may be called upon to deposit if there is an adverse price change or if margin requirements are increased. Buyers of options are not subject to margin calls.

"Naked writing" of an option refers to writing a call or a put on a futures contract in which the writer has no opposite cash or futures market position. This is also known as uncovered writing.

An option "series" refers to all options of the same class having the same strike price and expiration date.

An option "spread" refers to a position consisting of both long and short options of the same class—such as having a long position in a call with one strike price and expiration and a short position in another call with a different strike price and/or expiration.

An option "straddle" is a combination in which the put and the call have the same strike price and the same expiration.

The "time value" of an option is the amount by which an option premium exceeds the option's intrinsic value. If an option has no intrinsic value, its premium is entirely time value.

The "writing" of an option refers to the sale of an option in an opening transaction.

OPTIONS VS. FUTURES

There are some important differences between an options contract and a futures contract. A futures contract is a bilateral contract requiring action by both parties and obligating both the buyer and the seller to fulfill the conditions by delivery and payment. An option contract, on the other hand, is a unilateral contract. Unlike a futures contract, the buyer and the seller of the option do not have an equivalent obligation to perform. The purchaser of an option has the right but not the obligation to require the seller to perform under the contract, and the seller is obligated to do so only if the buyer exercises his right. The converse, however, is not true. The seller of an option cannot require the purchaser to exercise. Only the buyer has the right to require fulfillment of the contract terms.

Perhaps the most distinguishing feature of an option contract is the limited liability of the purchaser. The potential loss to an option purchaser is limited to the "premium" which he pays to the seller at the time of the purchase of the option. His potential for gain, theoretically, is limited only by the extent of the price movement of the underlying contract. In contrast, on the futures contract the holder of either a long or a short futures position remains liable to margin calls as long as his position remains open.

In short, therefore, the purchaser of an option contract can lose at a maximum only the amount he pays for the option. This is so because, if the price does not move in his favor, he fails to "exercise" his option. Instead, he simply abandons it. An analogy can be drawn with an insurance contract. The writer of the insurance policy receives the premium for undertaking the risk but has to stand ready in the future to make any payments due the person who bought the insurance if that person submits a valid claim. If he does not submit the claim, the insurance company still keeps the premium.

One major advantage of options over futures markets for the business person is that, when prices are extremely volatile, options can reduce the demands on cash flow. For example, if you have purchased a futures contract and it declines, you will have to pay in more margin, which, of course, must be paid in cash. If, on the other hand, you have purchased a call option, you will have a one-time payment; no matter how far price falls, you will not be asked to post more money. The converse of this is, of course, also true. If prices go up, the futures position will yield cash to you while no such thing will happen with the option. Options thus provide more certainty in planning cash flow exposure.

Options permit a range of investment and resource management strategies not available from futures. Options used in conjunction with futures and actual inventories of a product afford a wide range of strategies for a merchandiser, producer, or processor in managing inventories. They can provide greater control with lower capital requirements than do futures alone.

To a large extent, options are substitutes for stop orders on futures. You can attempt to limit your risk on a futures position by placing a stop loss order at whatever level you choose. Then, if the market touches that level, your broker would automatically offset the futures contract at the price stipulated or at the next best possible price.

In essence, the purchase of an option serves the same purpose as the stop loss order serves in the futures contract. They are both there to limit losses. The difference between the two, however, is:

1. A stop loss order may not always be exercised at the price stipulated, so the loss cannot be absolutely fixed in advance. The size of the option premium, however, is fixed in advance, and the loss cannot exceed the size of the premium.
2. A poorly disciplined trader may decide not to use stop loss orders and to meet margin calls when he should not, thus sticking with a losing position in the hope that the market will reverse. This can lead to very large losses. An option, on the other hand, does not give that discretion to the holder. Once he buys the option, the

marketplace decides whether it will be profitable to exercise it. The holder has no more decisions to make if the market moves against him.

3. One can get whipsawed in a market using stop loss orders. The market can set off a stop order, causing the offset of the futures contract, and then the market could turn around and go the opposite direction. Due to the offset, you would be without a position in the market and unable to take advantage of the price move.

In sum, the option is a more certain way of limiting losses. The value of this certainly has to be weighed against the size of the premium paid. It may be a very high price to pay for the luxury of not having to exercise the self-discipline in using stop loss orders or for the potential that you will get whipsawed.

Other differences between options and futures will become apparent as you read some of the strategies for trading options discussed in the next chapter.

STRATEGIES FOR TRADING OPTIONS

The trading applications of options are numerous, and motives for buying and selling options are as varied as they are for trading commodity futures contracts. However, in addition to the limited risk advantages options offer to speculators, they also perform certain economic functions and can be used for hedging purposes.

The potential for commodity options contracts to serve as a risk-shifting medium for individuals and firms dealing in a cash commodity is somewhat analogous to hedging in futures markets. A call option, by providing its buyer the right to acquire a commodity or futures contract at a fixed price, can provide price protection to a person who has a short position in the cash market; for example, a signed contract to deliver a T-bond. Buying a put option can also provide the same manner of price protection to its purchaser as can a short futures position. Both of them establish a sale price. In contrast to futures, however, options contracts provide price protection only to purchasers because only purchasers have the right to exercise an option. Sellers of options have a firm price for their product only if the buyer exercises, but they cannot require a buyer to exercise. Thus, the risk transfer is not as complete or as symmetrical in options as it is in futures.

Using Options in Business

Following are some examples of how the options market might be used for hedging. Although the mathematics will be different, the basic concepts apply equally well to options on "actuals" or options on futures. Suppose a producer of mortgages wishes to secure a selling margin by selling his mortgages forward but wants the right to cancel the deal should prices rise. He can achieve this by purchasing a put option on GNMA mortgages for a forward delivery date. In the event that prices fall, he would exercise his option and, thus, have a secured sales contract. (If it is an option on a futures contract, he will have a short futures position which he can deliver upon or offset as a normal hedge. If it is an option on the actual mortgages, he will deliver the mortgages to the seller of the option.) But if prices rise, he could abandon the option and sell his mortgages at the higher level ruling in the market. The cost of the ability to make this choice would be the option premium.

Exactly the reverse of this example would apply to someone who invests in mortgages and wants to buy mortgages forward for delivery at a future date. The use of a call option to secure the purchases allows him the choice of abandoning the option if prices decline or of exercising his option if prices rise.

A holder of an inventory, such as a mortgage banker or government securities dealer, may use the options market to generate income on inventory by selling a call option on that inventory, thus giving the buyer the option to purchase the inventory. If the option is abandoned by the buyer because the price falls, the seller will still carry the inventory but his net cost of carry and cost of ownership will be reduced because he has received the option premium and interest on it. This is a form of price speculation, and any businessperson undertaking it should so realize. If prices rise and the option is exercised, then the seller must deliver the physical goods against the contract. This, of course, is an attractive procedure only if, at the time the option is sold, the striking price of the option is higher than the spot price, since the option seller obtains this differential together with the option premium and interest.

In short, options provide a businessperson:

1. More flexibility in strategy than do futures contracts alone.
2. More certainty in planning cash exposure than do futures.

3. More control over the decision-making environment. This is partic-
    ularly true when buying options because only the buyer may deter-
    mine when and whether to exercise. Options allow the buyer to buy
    time during which he can wait for the future to be revealed. If the
    future turns out to his advantage, he exercises the option. If not,
    he abandons it, suffers the loss of at least part of his premium and
    makes his transaction through another channel.

Buying a Call to Insure Investment Yield

Suppose you are a government bond portfolio manager expecting to
have a certain sum of money available for investment at a later date.
Assume also that you expect interest rates to decline (prices to rise)
before your capital becomes available for investment. You can buy a
call to protect your ultimate purchase price.

A call gives the purchaser the right to obtain a long position in the
underlying futures contract. Hence, if you expect prices to rise, you
would purchase a call, giving you the right to buy a futures contract
at the strike price stated at any time before the call expires. The net
result of your option and futures transaction will be applied to the price
of the government bonds you ultimately buy.

Suppose on September 1 that December T-bond futures are trading
at 74–00 and that, after careful analysis of the market, you come to
expect December T-bonds to trade above the 78–00 level. There are
two ways to take advantage of this expectation: (1) you can buy a
futures contract for delivery in December. That will cost you approximately $2,000 in margin plus, say, a $45 commission. If the price falls
to 72–00, you will have lost your entire $2,000 margin plus your $45
commission. If, on the other hand, the price does rise to the 78–00 level,
you will have made $4,000 minus commission.

(2) An alternative to buying the December futures contract would
have been to buy a call option on the December futures. Suppose you
could purchase, for 2–00 ($2000), a call option with a strike price of
74–00. You would then be potentially long one December futures
contract at 74–00 with a breakeven point of 76–00 (2–00 +74–00).
Now if the price rises to the 78–00 level, the option will be worth $4000.
You can sell (offset) the option to obtain the $2000 profit. Or you can
"exercise" (notify the seller of the call that you wish to buy the Decem-

ber futures at 74–00. You can sell the futures acquired by exercise and accept your profit of $2000 on the transaction. If the price fails to rise to the 78–00 level, you will simply be out the amount of your premium, $2000, plus commissions. If it rises to 75–00, the intrinsic value of the option will fall to $1000 and you will suffer a net $1000 loss.

The maximum loss to the call buyer can never exceed the premium cost—in this instance, $2000. That maximum loss will occur only if the option is not exercised, which would happen if the market does not move above the 74–00 level. If the market does move above the 74–00 strike price but does not reach the 76–00 level before the expiration date, it is best to offset or exercise because the size of the loss decreases as the price rises to the break-even point. As the price rises above the break-even point, the option becomes profitable, and the profit increases as the price continues to advance.

Selling a Call Option Against a Bond That You Already Own

Your investment portfolio may include a U.S. Treasury bond that you do not wish to sell, but that you fear will decrease in value because of rising rates. Writing call options can provide a way to increase investment return while protecting against an interest rate decline in the near term.

EXAMPLE: You own a $100,000 face value U.S. Treasury bond with an 8% coupon. Your current monthly interest accrual is $667. Let's say that in June, the September futures price for such a bond is 66–00 and an out-of-the-money September/68 call can be sold for a premium of $1,000. You decide to sell this call.

If the futures prices are below 68–00 at the end of September, the option will expire worthless and you will still own the bond. In addition to about $2,000 worth of interest accrued during the three months, you will have earned $1,000 from the option premium, increasing your return by 50%. Your costs on this transaction will include the initial margin and variation margin which must be deposited by option sellers.

Calculating Return on Investment

In comparing transactions in the futures market with transactions in the options market, you should compare them on the basis of return on investment (ROI) which is calculated by dividing the dollar investment into net profit before taxes. Thus,

$$\text{ROI} = \frac{\text{Net income before taxes}}{\text{Total dollar investment}}$$

In the two examples above, the ROI would have been 100% for the options transaction and 200% for the futures transaction, assuming T-bond contract reached 78–00. An important reason for this is that the break-even point on the futures is close to the purchase price. The futures market price needs to move only a small amount (commission plus interest on margin) to reach the break-even point. On an option it has to move at least the amount of the premium and, if the strike price is above the current level, then it must move the amount of the premium plus the difference between the strike price and the current market level before the break-even price is reached. For example, in the above cases you would begin making money on your futures position as soon as it rose above the 74–03 level (the $45 commission and interest on the margin at 10% for three months would equal approximately 3/32). The market would need to rise only to 74–19 to provide you a $500 profit, and if you were brave and fortunate enough to hold your position all the way up to 78–00, you would have realized a profit of $4000 minus the commissions.

In the case of the option, the market has to move up enough to reach the strike price and then rise another 0–16 to yield the $500 profit. Of course, the maximum loss on the down side was the 2–00 premium or $2000. The maximum loss potential on the downside with the futures was the entire value of the futures contract unless you entered a stop order and it was executed. At 74–00 the value of the futures contract was $74,000. For this loss to occur, the price of T-bonds would need to fall to zero, an unlikely possibility.

Determining the Option Premium

In exchange for the rights granted by the option, the buyer pays the seller a premium. This is the price of the option.

The premium amount is credited to the seller's account, whether or not the option is later exercised.

$$\text{Premium} = \text{Intrinsic Value} + \text{Time Value}$$

The premium for options is made up of two components:

Intrinsic value—the amount (if any) by which the current market price of the futures is above the strike price for calls and below the strike price for puts.

Time value premium—the amount by which the premium exceeds its intrinsic value.

For example, when the price of futures is either sharply under the strike price for puts or over the strike price for calls, the premium is almost totally composed of its intrinsic value; the time value premium is greatest when futures are trading at the strike price. See Figures 25.1 and 25.2 below for a graphic illustration of the relationships between strike prices and option premiums.

The factors that affect the intrinsic and time value of the option premium include:

1. The current price level of the underlying commodity relative to the strike price of the option.
2. The length of time the option has left before it expires. The longer the life of the option, the more time you are buying and the greater time there is for the market to reach the strike price.
3. The volatility of the price for the underlying commodity. The more volatile the price, the greater chance that the market will reach the strike price within a given time period.
4. The expectation that the commodity price will change. This is related to each of the three preceding elements.
5. Interest rates—higher interest rates generally mean higher premiums.

When trading options, it is wise to keep in mind some fundamental principles with respect to price behavior.

1. The value of the option is directly related to the expected volatility of the market and the probability that a particular price level will be reached during a given time period.
2. When trading options on futures, examine closely the price structure (relationships) between futures months. If the more distant months are at a higher price than the nearby months, a buyer of a put has, everything else remaining equal, a better probability of a profitable trade. But, of course, everything else is not always

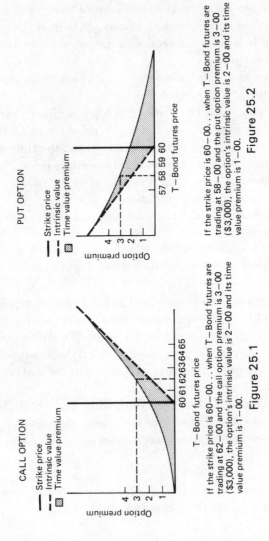

CALL OPTION

— Strike price
‑ ‑ Intrinsic value
▓ Time value premium

If the strike price is 60—00. . . when T—Bond futures are trading at 62—00 and the call option premium is 3—00 ($3,000), the option's intrinsic value is 2—00 and its time value premium is 1—00.

Figure 25.1

PUT OPTION

— Strike price
‑ ‑ Intrinsic value
▓ Time value premium

If the strike price is 60—00. . . when T—Bond futures are trading at 58—00 and the put option premium is 3—00 ($3,000), the option's intrinsic value is 2—00 and its time value premium is 1—00.

Figure 25.2

equal. Price relationships may remain the same, but price levels which are the important element may change. The question is: Will they change during the life of the option? Further, and just as importantly, has the size of the premium already accounted for any reasonable probability that they will not change?

Time Value: Rate of Decay

The passage of time affects an option differently at different points in its life cycle. The rate of time value decay increases as an option approaches expiration. Figure 25.3 depicts graphically the relationship between time value and remaining life of an option.

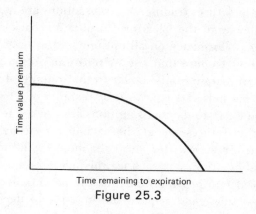

Figure 25.3

What Option to Trade?

An important decision for an investor selecting among option strike prices and maturity dates is the determination of which option to select. Should one select an option with a short period of time until expiration or an option with a long period of time until expiration? An in-the-money option or an out-of-the-money option?

Generally, the premium costs will be higher the longer the time remaining until expiration. Such an option provides the buyer more time for his price expectations to be realized and, thus, a greater likelihood of his actually earning a profit. Generally, the longer time remaining until expiration, the lower the cost of each additional time unit; that is, a six-month option may not cost twice as much as a three-month option.

The decision of purchasing an at-the-money or an out-of-the-money option is equally important. The option premium is usually higher for an at-the-money option than for an out-of-the-money option. An at-the-money option stands a greater chance of yielding a profit. However, an out-of-the-money option usually costs less and involves a smaller potential loss; but, also, a smaller potential profit.

Margins, Futures Clearing Corporation, and Exercise Rights

The Clearing Corporation plays a major role in options transactions, just as it does in futures trading. All transactions are handled through clearing members and the Clearing Corporation backs all open positions, assuring performance on all options sold.

It is important to note that the writer of an option must make an initial deposit of margin funds similar to that required for participants in the futures markets. To assure the availability of adequate funds to cover losses on a day-to-day basis, options are marked to market in the same manner as futures are at the exchange clearinghouse. So, for example, if an investor writes an at-the-money call, and the futures price moves above the exercise price, his margin requirement will be increased in order to provide funds for the potentially increased loss. In some cases, this could require the investor to deposit additional funds. Conversely, a price movement in favor of the option writer could offer an opportunity to withdraw excess funds.

Since both options on futures and the futures themselves are processed through the same clearing system, exercise can be accomplished automatically.

Whenever an option is exercised, opposite futures positions are established for the buyer and the seller by the Clearing Corporation. If a call is exercised, a long futures position is recorded in the buyer's account and a short futures position in the seller's. The reverse is true if a put is exercised. A short futures position is entered in the buyer's account and an opposite long futures position in the seller's.

AFTER EXERCISE

	Put	Call
A buyer assumes	a short futures position	a long futures position
A seller assumes	a long futures position	a short futures position

Both positions are entered at the strike price and both accounts are immediately marked-to-market. Then, following normal variation margin procedures, the Clearing Corporation collects any losses and pays any profits.

After exercise, the trader can liquidate the futures position immediately . . . maintain the position and liquidate it at a future date . . . or hold the contract until it expires and make or take delivery.

In practice, most option traders offset positions before the options expire. The profit or loss is the difference between the premium (the price) when the option was bought and the premium amount when it was sold.

Taxes and Options

Before you get too deeply involved in establishing an options trading strategy, you should evaluate carefully the impact of the tax laws on options transactions. That topic is too complex to study here, but it may be well worth your while to check with your tax advisor prior to entering into options transactions.

Using Options in a Futures Hedging Program

Options can become a most valuable tool in managing a hedge. For example, suppose that a short hedger has just gone through a period of protracted interest rate rise and had experienced a substantial positive cash flow on his futures position. Assume also that he feels the futures have moved further than he expects the cash market to move (i.e., the basis has moved strongly in his favor) and he wishes to temporarily remove his hedge. If he removes the hedge he will be exposed to interest rate risk, which means that if he is wrong and interest rates continue to rise, he will be unhedged and worse off. If, on the other hand, rates fall, he will be wise to have removed the futures hedge. To protect against this type of risk, he may want to consider purchasing put options when he removes his futures hedge. The put option will, for a known cost, provide the same protection against rising rates that the futures did and will at the same time expire worthless providing no hedge if rates fall. This is an example of having your cake and eating it too.

TO SUM UP

To summarize, when considering options relative to futures, remember:

1. Options provide you known and limited risk. Futures do not unless you use stop orders and then they do only if the stops actually are executed at or close to the stated level. This is sometimes hard to do if a market is fluctuating wildly and is locked in to limit moves.
2. To obtain this known and limited risk, you pay a premium. Weigh the size of the premium against the confidence of using stops and your desire to avoid being whipsawed. The size of this premium will be related to a lot of factors, the most important of which are price volatility, the remaining life of the option, and the probability that the price will reach the strike price before expiration date.
3. The break-even point on a futures transaction may be reached with a much smaller price move than in the case of an option.
4. Trading futures against an option provides flexibility to an investment strategy and allows the holder of the option to make full use of all the "time" he paid for when he bought the option.
5. There are advantages to using a put option instead of futures to hedge a profitable call option and vice versa.
6. There are a number of business uses for options. Many of them duplicate the advantages offered by futures contracts. Some of

them, however, reflect advantages not available from ordinary futures hedges.

7. Before you open an account and make a trade in options, shop around and ask a lot of questions of your broker about the particular option deal being offered. There is no substitute for self-protection.

CHAPTER TWENTY-SIX

Options Strategies— Illustrated

This section illustrates the rich variety of strategies available for foreign currency traders, stock index traders or interest rate futures traders. The strategies illustrated apply equally well in all areas and to both options on futures and options on actuals.

1. Buy Put Options

Assume you are anticipating an increase in long-term interest rates and a corresponding decrease in futures prices. To take advantage of your expectations, assume you buy a Treasury bond March 76 Put at a premium cost of $2000, reflecting an interest rate on long-term bonds of about 11%. If, by expiration in March, the interest rate has increased to 12%, the futures price will have decreased to 70–00 and you should be able to sell the option at a difference in value of $6000. Your profit on this transaction will be $4000 ($6000 less your $2000 premium) minus transactions costs.

If by the time March rolled around, interest rates had decreased to approximately 10.5%, the futures would be selling for about 79–00 and your put option with a strike price of 76–00 would expire worthless. You would have lost the entire $2000 paid for the option.

In many cases, you might decide not to wait until expiration to close out your position. If, in the above example, interest rates started falling

339

with expiration a month or so away, you might have decided to sell the option before it reached a value of zero. By selling the option at say $500, you would reduce your loss to only $1500 ($2000 premium minus $500), plus the transaction costs.

2.   Buy Call Options

If you anticipate an increase in prices, your strategy should be to purchase call options. A call option, as noted above, gives you, the buyer, the right to buy the underlying futures contract at the specified strike price. You will realize a profit if the intrinsic value of the option at expiration is greater than the premium you paid for the option. For example, assume it is June and you expect the S&P 500 Stock Index to be higher in September. Assume you pay a $2000 premium to buy a September 140 call option. If, when September rolls around, the S&P Index has risen to 150, the futures price should have increased to 150 also. You should then be able to sell the call option at its intrinsic value of 10 ($5000). Your net profit would be $3000 less the transaction costs.

Suppose, however, that when September rolled around, the futures price was 130 or below. In that case your call would expire worthless and you would lose the entire $2000. If, on the other hand, the futures price is at 140, your call would be worth the same price you paid for it. If the futures price has increased to 160, your call should be valued at 20, to yield an $8000 net profit.

3.   Sell (Write) Call Option in Anticipation of Lower Prices

Writing (selling) options involves risks and rewards that are the exact opposite of the risk and rewards involved in buying options. The option writer assumes unlimited risk with the prospect of limited reward, while the option buyer assumes limited risk, with the prospect of potentially unlimited reward; hence, one who enters into the writing of options wants to do so with great caution.

He must be ready to respond promptly to any adverse change in the futures price. The prudent option writer will decide in advance the futures price at which he will "buy back" the option in order to avoid or limit a loss if his expectations on price turn out to be wrong.

When writing uncovered or naked call options, the investor needs to take account of his price expectations and his tolerance for risk at the time the call is written. The investor has several alternative strategies to follow with regard to his tolerance for risk. He can write at-the-money calls, in-the-money calls, or out-of-the-money calls.

Writing an at-the-money call is probably most appropriate for an investor who feels strongly that prices are likely to remain flat during the life of the option, or, if any change occurs, that it will be in the direction of a slightly upward-trending price. If the investor is right in this expectation, his call option will expire without being exercised and he will retain the premium received from writing it. For example, assume that in June, an investor sells a September 70 call option on Treasury bonds at a premium of $2000. If, when September comes, the futures price is 70–00 or below, the option will not be exercised and the investor will retain his $2000 premium. As an option seller, he had to post margin at the clearinghouse. Had his required margin deposit on the call been $2000, the $2000 premium would amount to a 100% return on his original investment. The risk, however, is that the investor will incur a net loss. For example, if the futures price in September when the option expires is above 72–00, the loss will exceed the $2000 he earned from writing the option.

If our investor however, decided to write an out-of-the-money call, the premium which can be earned by writing such an option will be smaller, thus providing a greater margin for error in anticipating correctly the direction of prices. Let us assume that at a time when the futures price is 70–00, the investor earns a premium of only $1000 by writing a call option with a strike price of 74–00 for the Treasury bond futures. Unless the futures price at expiration is above 74–00, the option will not be exercised and the investor, as the writer of the call, will retain the full $1000 premium, a 50% profit on his original $2000 margin deposit. His break-even point with this transaction is 75–00. If the futures price is above 75–00, the loss when the option is exercised will exceed the $1000 premium he earned.

If our investor decided to write an in-the-money call, he will undoubtedly receive a correspondingly higher premium because the premium will reflect the combination of the intrinsic value and the time value of the option. Let us assume in this case that the call writer receives a premium of $3000 on an in-the-money call with a strike price of 68–00 at a time when the futures are at 70–00. If the futures price is 68–00 or lower when the option expires, the investor will retain the

full $3000 premium. However, should the futures price decline only to
69–00, the call with a 68–00 price will be exercised at a $1000 loss, and
the investor will have a net profit of $2000. He will have an unlimited
potential loss, however, if the futures price when the option expires is
above 71–00, because the loss on the option will then exceed the $3000
premium he received.

4. Writing Put Options in Anticipation of Higher Prices

Writing put options is the opposite strategy to writing call options. It
is the strategy to follow when an investor has at least a mildly bullish
outlook on prices. If the futures price stays above the exercise price of
the put that has been written, the option is unlikely to be exercised and
the writer will retain the full amount of the option premium. A note
of warning, however; just as with writing calls, the profit and risk
considerations in writing puts for investment income are identical.
There is great profit potential and unlimited risk.

Let us assume an investor expects stock prices to be either flat or
slightly upward-trending over a coming period of time. Let us also
assume that on the basis of his expectations, he decides to write puts
on the NYSE Stock Index Futures. Assume he writes an at-the-money
put at a premium of, say, $2000, and deposits his initial margin of
$3500 with his broker. In this case, if the option expires without being
exercised, he will retain his $2000 premium, and reap a net return on
his investment of about 57.1%.

Just as with the writing of call options, the writer of put options can
adjust his potential risk/reward ratios by writing at-the-money puts,
in-the-money puts, or out-of-the-money puts, and by judicious selection
of the maturity of the option. For example, an option with only three
months until expiration is less likely to be exercised than an otherwise
identical option with six months until expiration. That lower risk will
be reflected in a lower premium. An out-of-the-money option will also
have lower risk and is likely to carry a smaller premium.

5. Sell Futures and Buy Call Options

The purchase of a call option in conjunction with a short futures
position effectively creates a put, thereby making it possible to limit the

otherwise unlimited risk involved in selling futures contracts. In effect, the call option provides insurance against major loss.

For example, suppose you were expecting higher interest rates and you sold a September U.S. Treasury bond futures contract at the price of 70–00. At the same time, to protect yourself against major losses which could result if futures prices rise, you might decide to pay a $2000 premium for the purchase of a September 70 call option. The most that you could lose if futures prices rise instead of falling is the $2000 cost of the call option. Shown below is a summary of how this transaction could turn out under various scenarios.

Scenario Summary of
Sell Futures–Buy Call Option

Sell Sept. T-bond futures @	70–00
Buy Sept. 70 T-bond futures call @	$2000

P or L at Expiration

Futures rise to 76–00	
Buy futures @ 76–00	$6000 Loss
Sell call @ 76–00	$4000 Gain
	$2000 Net Loss
Futures do not change	
Buy futures @ 70–00	No Gain–No Loss
Sell call @ 0	$2000 Loss
	$2000 Net Loss
Futures fall to 68–00	
Buy futures @ 68–00	$2000 Gain
Sell call @ 0	$2000 Loss
	0 Net
Futures fall to 62–00	
Buy futures @ 62–00	$8000 Gain
Sell call @ 0	$2000 Loss
	$6000 Net Gain

A major advantage of this strategy is the "staying power" it can provide—that is, these two transactions provide the ability to maintain a futures position despite adverse short-term price movements. The idea is to survive in order to maintain the potential for the position to eventually become profitable.

In the absence of the protection provided by the call, you might be faced with a large margin call on your futures position. If such a margin requirement can't be met, you would be forced to liquidate the futures position at a loss. The call protects against that because, as the futures position loses value, the call increases in value. The call acts as a hedge against major losses.

6. Buy Futures and Buy Put Options (A Guaranteed Stop Order)

Options can work as guaranteed stop orders in the futures markets; except compared with placing a stop order at a particular price, the purchase of the put option offers the advantage of staying power. For example, assume the purchaser of a NYSE Index Futures Contract has a position in which there has been a substantial gain. He may anticipate a continuing rise in stock prices but be reluctant to risk losing the existing profit should the market suddenly turn down. Among his alternatives would be to place a stop order to liquidate his futures position if the price drops to a particular level. An alternative and potentially more attractive strategy could be to purchase a put option. In that case, if an unexpected or temporary price decline should occur, he would be protected by the put but still have the staying power to remain in the market and profit if and when the market resumes its upward course. Had he placed a stop order, on the other hand, and the futures position been liquidated, he would no longer have had an opportunity to benefit from the subsequent price increase.

To illustrate: assume an NYSE Stock Index Futures Contract was purchased at a price of 70.00, and the price has since risen to 82.00; thus the investor has a profit of $6000. By paying, say, $600 for an out-of-the-money put with an exercise price of 80, and three months to expiration, the investor can achieve protection against any decline below 80.00. At the same time, he retains the opportunity to realize additional futures profits should the stock price continue to climb. This is a most useful technique to use in a futures hedging program.

7. Buy Futures and Write Call Options to Increase Return

Let us suppose that you were mildly bullish on prices. You expect prices to be at least flat and probably slightly upward-trending. One trading strategy to consider would involve taking a long position in the futures and simultaneously writing a call option. The objective is to earn a potentially high rate of return on a relatively small investment (the amount of the margin deposit required to buy the futures contract). Investors following such a strategy should recognize that the potential loss, however, is unlimited. The greater the decline in the futures price, the greater the loss; hence, any investor employing a Buy/Write Strategy should consider also placing stop loss orders to liquidate the long futures position if the price drops beyond a certain level.

To illustrate this strategy, assume an investor buys an NYSE Stock Index Futures Contract and posts a margin of $3500, and earns a $1750 premium by writing an at-the-money call option with an exercise price of 76.

If the futures price climbs above 76.00, the call will be exercised, meaning the writer of the call will now have a short futures position at a price of 76.00. That new futures position will offset his previously purchased long futures position purchased at 76.00. The investor's gain will be the option premium of $1750, a 50% return on his original margin deposit.

If the futures price remains at exactly 76.00, however, the option will expire worthless and, again, the investor will have a 50% gain equal to his $1750 premium.

If on the other hand, the futures price falls below 76.00, the option will expire worthless and, depending upon the extent of the price decline, the loss on the futures position will reduce or exceed the option premium he received when he wrote the call.

8. Sell Futures and Write a Put

This strategy is exactly the reverse of the one just described; instead of going long with futures and writing a call option, it involves going short with the futures and writing a put option. This strategy, instead of being most appropriate when the investor's market outlook is bullish, is most appropriate when its outlook is bearish. The objective, however, is the same—a potential high rate of return from the option premium on a relatively small investment reflected in the margin deposit on the futures. The risk is also the same—a potentially unlimited loss on the short futures position if there is an unexpected increase in futures prices. If the futures price increases, the option will not be exercised, but the loss on the short futures position will reduce or could exceed the option premium received. Note that the potential loss is unlimited.

PRICES STABLE—USING OPTION SPREADS AND STRADDLES

With the introduction of options on futures, traders now have a strategy to take advantage of stable prices—selling option straddles. An option straddle involves being long *or* short *both* a put and a call at the same strike price for the same expiration date. This strategy effectively locks in a trading range equal to the strike price, plus and minus the option premiums paid or received before commissions; thus, a trader anticipating stable prices would sell both the put and the call, hoping to pocket both premiums at expiration. On the other hand, a trader anticipating a dramatic price movement, but not sure of which direction, would buy the straddle, that is, buy the put and the call, hoping for futures prices to move in one direction or another—but in excess of the two premiums paid.

1. Buying Put/Call Straddles

An investor anticipating a sharp movement in the level of stock prices during the months ahead, but uncertain of what the direction of movement will be, would buy a put option and a call option. This strategy will produce a net profit if either of the options can ultimately be sold at a price higher than the total premium cost. There is a known and limited risk whichever way stock prices move. If stock prices drop, the put option will be profitable to exercise. To whatever extent the gain in the option that's exercised exceeds the total premium cost of the straddle, the investor will realize a net profit. On the other hand, the investor's maximum loss is the cost of the straddle; that is, the total of the premiums paid.

Assume NYSE Index Futures are trading at 76.00 and an investor expects stock prices to move sharply higher or sharply lower over the next six months; assume he pays a $2000 premium to buy an at-the-money call and a $2000 premium to buy an at-the-money put. Each

$1.00 change in the NYSE Index equals $500. For the investor to recover the $4000 total premium cost and to realize a profit, the NYSE Index at expiration must be either below 68.00 or above 84.00. It must move more than 8 points below or above the exercise price of 76.00.

If the futures climb to 86.00, the call option will have an intrinsic value of $5000, yielding the investor a $1000 profit on his investment. Similarly, if the futures decline to 66.00, he will have a $1000 net profit on the put option to be sold or exercised. Unless the futures price at expiration is exactly equal to the options' exercise price of 76.00, one or the other of the options will be worthwhile to exercise and the investor will recover at least a portion of his investment.

In the example above, the buyer of the put/call straddle expected prices to change in one direction or the other, but had no opinion as to the most probable direction. An investor who considered a change in one direction somewhat more likely than a change in the other direction, may wish to purchase a put/call combination in which the put and the call have different strike prices. The lower premium cost will increase his net profit if he is right about the most probable direction. A combination such as this enables an investor to adjust the break-even parameters of his transactions as well as to reduce the maximum potential loss.

2. Writing Put/Call Combinations

Another straddle technique would involve writing both a put and a call. An investor who employed this technique would be one who does not expect any substantial change in the level of prices during the coming months. As long as the futures price remains within a range, the investor will normally realize a profit because the total option premiums received will exceed the loss incurred on whichever option is exercised; hence, this strategy is employed when one expects relatively flat prices.

To illustrate, assume the NYSE Index Futures Contract is at 76.00 and assume also the investor earns a $2000 premium by writing an at-the-money call and an additional $2000 premium by writing an at-the-money put; therefore, his total premium income is $4000.

If the futures price remains at exactly 76.00, neither option will be exercised and the investor will retain the full $4000. As long as the futures price remains above 68.00 and below 84.00, the investor will retain at least a part of the $4000 premium. If the index futures at expiration were at 70.00, the put would be exercised at a loss of $3000 and the investor's profit would be reduced to $1000.

If the futures contract at expiration has risen to 86.00, the call option with the 76 exercise price will be exercised at a $5000 loss. Since this is greater than the $4000 premium received the investor will incur a $1000 net loss.

From the foregoing, it should be evident that the break-even parameters of a straddle can be readily calculated. Specifically, the writer of a straddle will not incur a loss unless the futures price at expiration is outside the range of the strike prices by more than the amount of the premium received when the straddle was written. One who engages in this type of trading must pay close and continual attention to futures prices and be prepared to act promptly to liquidate one or both of the options. Otherwise substantial losses could be obtained if prices change dramatically. The risk of loss from price changes with this strategy is unlimited.

3.   A Neutral Calendar Spread

Suppose you expect that prices will remain relatively flat over the next few months. One potentially profitable trading strategy with such expectations involves writing a call option with a near-term expiration and buying a call option with the same strike price but a longer period of time until expiration. This strategy capitalizes on the fact that the time value for a near-term option erodes more rapidly than the time value for a more distant option.

For example, assume in June that an investor anticipates that long-term interest rates during the summer months will remain essentially unchanged. Assume also that he pays a premium of $2700 to buy a December 76 T-bond call and receives a premium of $1900 by writing a September 76 call. The net difference between these two premiums is $800. If, when the September option expires, the futures price is at 76.00, the September call will expire unexercised and the December call can be sold for its remaining time value. Suppose it can be sold for $2000; in such instance, the investor's net profit will be the $2000 proceeds received from the sale, less the initial $800 cost of the spread —a net of $1200. In no case, even if interest rates were to sharply increase or decrease, can the investor lose more than the $800 net cost of the spread.

Even if interest rates should happen to increase or decrease slightly, this strategy will still yield some net profit, provided that, at the time the September call expires, the premium difference between the September and December options is greater than the initial net cost of the spread. The maximum net loss will occur only if the December call no longer has time value when the September call expires.

This will happen only if it is so far out of the money that no market exists for it, or so far in the money that its premium is totally a reflection of its intrinsic value.

It should be noted that while the maximum possible loss can be determined exactly, and is equal to the net cost of the spread, the maximum potential profit can only be approximated—it depends on the time value differential between the two options at the time the near-term option expires.

4. A Bear Call Spread

During a period of declining prices, you may find a strategy known as a "bear call spread," or a vertical bear spread, attractive. It offers clearly defined and potentially attractive risk/reward (because the investor can know in advance and to the dollar the maximum net profit possible and the maximum net loss possible). A bear call spread, meaning the investor is bearish on prices, involves buying a call option with a high strike price and writing or selling a call with a lower strike price. The maximum net profit possible in this transaction is the net premium received on the sale of the call option. The maximum net loss is the difference between the strike prices of the two options less the net premium received.

For example, assume an investor is expecting higher interest rates and lower bond prices at a time when the December futures price is at 66–00. To profit from this scenario, assume he buys a December 66 call at a premium of $1900 and sells a December 60 call at a premium of $6200. His maximum net potential profit is the net premium received of $4300 ($6200 minus $1900). His maximum potential loss is $1700 (the strike price difference of $6000 less the net premium received of $4300).

In order to realize the maximum profit the futures price at expiration must be below or equal to the strike price of the option sold. If it isn't, the option should be exercised and the investor's resulting profit or loss will depend on whether the value of the option at expiration is smaller or greater than the net premium received. For example, had the futures price in this illustration above declined to 65–00, the $5000 loss when the September 60 call is exercised will exceed the $4300 net premium and the investor will have lost $700. However, if the futures price declined to 62–00, the investor would have a $2300 profit—the difference between the $4300 net premium received and the $2000 loss when the Sept. 60 call is exercised.

An investor interested in modifying the risk/reward arithmetic of a bear call spread can do so by careful selection of the options bought or written. For example, if the investor in the above illustration had bought a December 60 call at a premium of $6400 and written a September 58 call at a premium of $8100, the maximum profit would have been $1700—the difference in the premiums. His maximum loss, however, would be only $300 (the $2000 strike price difference less the $1700 net premium received).

5.   A Bear Put Spread

If you expect declining prices for stocks, you could profit by purchasing a put option with a high strike price and selling or writing a put option with a low strike price. The maximum net profit is the difference in the strike prices less the net cost of the two options. The maximum loss is the net cost of the two options.

For example, suppose in June you expect that the NYSE Composite Stock Index will rise in price through the month of September. Assume the September futures price is at 88.00. To profit from your expectations, let us say you buy a September 88 put for a premium of $2000 and you sell a September 82 put and collect a premium of $1000. Your net cost is $1000.

If the future's price in September turns out to be 82.00 or lower, your profit will be $2000, the difference between the strike price of the options ($3000 less the net premium cost of the two options: $1000).

If, on the other hand, futures prices at expiration are at 88.00 or above, both options will expire worthless and you will suffer your maximum loss of $1,000.

6. Bull Put Spreads for Rising Prices

This strategy is designed for the investor who believes prices will be rising during a coming time period. The strategy consists of purchasing a put option with a low strike price and selling or writing a put option with a high strike price. The maximum profit possible is the premium difference between the two options. The maximum loss possible with this strategy is difference in strike prices minus the net premium received.

For example, let us suppose that in June, the September Treasury bond futures price is 66–00. To profit from an expected decline in interest rates and, therefore, an increase in the futures price, assume an investor pays a premium of $2000 to buy a September 66 put, and collects a premium of $6300 by writing a September 72 put. The net premium received is $4300. If the futures price at expiration is 72–00 or above, neither put will be exercised and the investor's net profit will be the $4300 net premium received. A maximum loss of $1600 will occur if the futures price at expiration is 66–00 or below.

7. A Bull Call Spread

Perhaps a more conservative approach to a situation where you expect interest rates to decline and bond prices to rise would be one known as a vertical bull spread. With such a strategy, you would know in advance the exact maximum net profit you could possibly make, and the exact maximum net loss possible on the transaction.

Like all spreads, bull call spreads (meaning the investor is bullish on bond prices) involves buying one option and writing or selling another option. In this case, you would buy a call option with a low strike price and sell a call option with a high strike price.

Your maximum net loss potential is the net premium cost, or the difference between the premium you pay for the call you buy and the premium you receive for the call you sell.

The maximum net profit you can make in this transaction is the difference between the strike prices of the two options less the net premium cost.

For example, suppose in March you expect lower interest rates and higher bond prices and you find that the June futures price is trading at 66–00. Suppose, further, you buy a June 66 call at a premium of $2000 and sell a June 72 call at a premium of $500. The maximum net profit would be $4500, the strike price difference of $6000 less the net premium cost of $1500, and your maximum net loss would be $1500, the net premium cost. In order to realize maximum profit, the futures price at expiration must be equal to or above the strike price of the option written, in this case 72.00. If it isn't, the investor's resulting profit or loss will depend on whether the value of the purchase option at expiration is more or less than the premium cost.

Scenario Summary
Bull Spread—Call Options

	Paid	Received
Buy June 66–00 call	$2000	
Sell June 72–00 call		$500
Net premium	$1500	

P or L Summary

Futures at 72–00		
Sell June 66 call		+$6000 Gain
Buy June 72 call		0
Net premium cost		−$1500
		$4500 Net Gain
Futures at 66–00		
Sell June 66 call		0
Buy June 72 call		0
Net premium cost		$1500
		$1500 Net Loss
Futures at 69–00		
Sell June 66 call		$3000
Buy June 72 call		0
Net premium cost		$1500
		$1500 Net Gain

OPTION STRATEGIES UNDER VARIOUS PRICE SCENARIOS

As is obvious from the foregoing, the number and variety of trading strategies that can be employed using options and futures, singly or in combination, is large. In general, one can now tailor a limited risk trading, or hedging, strategy to almost any price trend (or non-trend) scenario that could occur. Table 26.1 has been compiled to help the reader better understand the variety of strategies available and the situation in which they should be used.

Table 26.1   Summary of Option Strategies Under Various Price Scenarios*

Price expectation	Possible strategy	Price expectation	Possible strategy
Declining prices	Buy put options	Rising prices	Buy call options
Declining prices	Sell futures and buy call options	Rising prices	Buy futures and buy put options
Declining prices	A "bear" call spread	Rising prices	A "bull" call spread
Declining prices	A "bear" put spread	Rising prices	A "bull" put spread
Steady to slightly lower prices	Sell futures and write put options	Steady to slightly higher prices	Buy futures and write call options
Steady to slightly lower prices	Write call options	Steady to slightly higher prices	Write put options
Relatively flat prices	A "neutral" calendar spread	Prices will be highly volatile, could change in either direction	Buy a put-call straddle
Relatively flat prices	Write a put-call straddle		

Source: Chicago Board of Trade

*Interest rates and bonds, T-bills, GNMAs, etc., move in opposite directions. So the above strategies for rising prices (falling prices) should be considered when interest rates are expected to fall (to rise).

APPENDIX

Cash Instrument	Exchange	Minimum Price Movement	Maximum Daily Price Movement	Contract Months Traded	Trading Hours (EST)	First Notice Day	Delivery Information — Last Trading Day
US Treasury Bills, 90–92 days maturity, $1 million face value	IMM	.01 points, 1 basis point, or $25	60 basis points[1] ($1500)	March, June, September, December, October, January, April, August	9:00–2:40	Last trading day	Wednesday following the third Monday in the delivery month
US Treasury Bills, 90–92 days maturity, $1 million face value	Comex	.01 points, 1 basis point, or $25	60 basis points[6] ($1500)	February, May, August, November	9:05–3:30	Last trading day	Wednesday following third Monday of the delivery month
US Treasury Bills, 90–92 days maturity, $1 million face value	NYFE	.01 points, 1 basis point or $25	100 basis points ($2500)	January, April, July, October	9:00–3:00	First business day prior to delivery day.	First Thursday of the delivery month on which one-year bills are deliverable
US Treasury Bills, one-year maturity, $250,000 face value	IMM	.01 points, 1 basis point, or $25	50 basis points[1] ($1250)	March, June, September, December	9:15–2:35	Last trading day	Monday following first one-year T-bill auction of delivery month

Contract	Exchange	Minimum price fluctuation	Daily price limit	Delivery months	Trading hours		Last trading day
US Treasury Notes,[2] four-year maturity, $100,000 face value, 7% coupon rate	IMM	1/64 points $15.62 1/2	48/64 pts ($750)	February, May, August, November	9:20–2:55	None	Fifteenth calendar day, or the last prior business day
US Treasury Notes, 4–6-year maturity, $100,000 face value, 8% coupon rate	CBT	1/32 points or $31.25	2 points[5] ($2000)	March, June, September, December	9:00–3:00	Last business day of month prior to delivery month	Eighth business day prior to end of delivery month
US Treasury Bonds,[3] 20-year maturity, $100,000 face value 8% coupon	CBT	1/32 points or $31.25	2 points[5] ($2000)	March, June, September, December, February, May, August, November	9:00–3:00	Last business day of month prior to delivery month	Eighth business day prior to the delivery month

355

Cash Instrument	Exchange	Minimum Price Movement	Maximum Daily Price Movement	Contract Months Traded	Trading Hours (EST)	Delivery Information	
						First Notice Day	Last Trading Day
US Treasury Bonds,[3] 20-years maturity, $100,000 face value 9% coupon	NYFE	1/32 points or $31.25	3 points ($3000)	February, May, August, November	9:00–3:00	Fifteenth day of delivery month if it is a business day otherwise, the first business day after the fifteenth day	Two business days after the first notice day
GNMA (CDR) Collateralized Depository Receipt, $100,000 face value, 8% interest rate	CBT	1/32 pts or $31.25	2 points[5] ($2000)	March, June, September, December	9:00–3:00	Last business day of preceding month	Eighth business day prior to end of delivery month

GNMA (CD) Certificate Delivery, $100,000 face value, 8% interest rate	Comex	1/64 pts or $15.62 1/2	1 point[6] ($1000)	January, April, July, October[7]	9:00–3:20	First business day after last trading day	Seventh business day prior to end of delivery month
Commercial Paper,[4] 30-day maturity, $3 million face value, sold at a discount	CBT	.01 points, 1 basis point, or $25	50 basis[5] points ($1,250)	March, June, September, December	9:30–2:30	Last business day of month prior to delivery month	Eighth business day prior to end of delivery month
Commercial Paper,[4] 90-day maturity, $1 million face value, sold at a discount	CBT	.01 points, 1 basis point, or $25	50 basis[5] points ($1250)	March, June, September, December	9:30–2:35	Last business day of month prior to delivery month	Eighth business day prior to end of delivery month

1 Following two consecutive limit price moves in the same direction, the limit on the third day will be 150% of the normal limit. If there is a limit move (in the same direction) on the third and subsequent days, the limit on the fourth and subsequent days will be 200% of the original limit.

2 Maturity is actually 3 1/2 years to 4 1/2 years although the futures trade as if the cash instrument is a 4-year note.

3 Maturity must be minimum of 15 years (to call date if a bond has a call feature).

4 Commercial paper must be rated A-1 by Standard & Poors, P-1 by Moodys, and must be approved by the CBT.

5 If, after three days of consecutive limit moves in the same direction, limit moves per day for the next three days will be increased to 150% of the previous limit.

6 The current near contract month has no price movement limits.

7 In addition, contracts are traded for the each of the next three months from the current date.

358

Index